KU-229-411

THIS I BELIEVE

THIS I BELIEVE

Documents of American Jewish Life

Jacob Rader Marcus

JASON ARONSON INC.
Northvale, New Jersey
London

10 9 8 7 6 5 4 3 2 1

Library of Congress Cataloging-in-Publication Data

This I believe: documents of American Jewish life/
Jacob Rader Marcus [compiler].
p. cm.
Includes bibliographical references.
ISBN 0-87668-782-6
1. Ethics, Jewish. 2. Wills, Ethical. 3. Jews—United States—
Biography—Sources. I. Marcus. Jacob Rader. 1896–
BJ1279.D63 1990
296.3'85—dc20

90-33814
CIP

Manufactured in the United States of America. Jason Aronson Inc. offers books and cassettes. For information and catalog write to Jason Aronson Inc., 230 Livingston Street, Northvale, New Jersey 07647.

To

Nettie and Merle

Contents

PREFACE

The ninety-one documents that compose the heart of this book have been chosen to illustrate, in a uniquely personal way, the nature of American Jewish ethics as it has evolved throughout the last three centuries. I have not set out to write a book on Jewish ethics, nor have I attempted to formulate or reconstruct systems of Jewish ethics that may have been employed by American Jews. Rather, I have attempted, through a study of these documents, to understand American Jews as they really are and as they have been, to bare their psyches, to crawl into their very innards. My hope is to portray their approach to life, to people, and especially to their fellow Jews. I have no desire to praise or to condemn; I wish to describe, to analyze, and to understand. However, no formal study of published Jewish sermons, catechisms, textbooks, and treatises on ethics is in prospect here. Such works are in essence apologetics; they are not sufficiently personal or revelatory.

The present study is based primarily on the documents that appear in this volume—ethical wills, statements of a moral nature, selected bar mitzvah and confirmation addresses, personal letters, "This I Believe" affirmations of notables—a broad variety of documents in which men and women express their deepest and most cherished aspirations as well as their hopes and fears. Each letter, will, statement, and avowal in this work is preceded by a brief introductory paragraph or two to help set the scene for the document that follows.

In the first section of this volume I intend to summarize my findings. The documents that are analyzed in Part I include not only those reprinted in this book, but also the American data that have appeared in the book *Ethical*

Wills by Jack Riemer and Nathaniel Stampfer, published in 1983.* These authors included in their work more than twenty significant American ethical wills and statements that had previously escaped my notice. I am happy to have them; the Riemer–Stampfer collection is an excellent one. However, I have not reprinted any of their texts here, with the exception of those I had already assembled during the years in which I was developing my own collection. There are, of course, many other ethical wills and similar documents still in private hands or buried in public archives. Indeed, I have not included all the documents of this nature that I have personally collected over the years. Many of them tend to be stereotypical; they offer little that is new.

As a historian of American Jewry I have limited myself primarily to documents that illuminate the lives and thinking of Jews living in the United States; two Canadian "wills," however, have been included. The original source of each document is indicated in the list at the end of this book; biographical data on the writers are included wherever possible. No attempt has been made to alter original spellings, although punctuation and paragraphing have often been modernized. Citations by number in the Introduction refer to the chapter numbers given to the documents, as listed—each with a representative quotation—in the Table of Contents.

It is now my privilege to thank all those who have helped me prepare this work. No volume in its final form, however modest, is entirely the work of one person; every academic production is a cooperative enterprise. At best, I can claim to be only the captain of the ship.

Professor Herbert Zafren, the librarian at the Hebrew Union College here in Cincinnati, was unfailingly helpful in supplying me with many of the works I needed to consult. I am truly grateful to him and to his staff. My colleague at the American Jewish Archives, Administrative Director Abraham J. Peck, and the rest of the staff were also most helpful, far beyond the call of duty; I am grateful to all of them. Mr. James Neiger, a former executive of the Cincinnati Hebrew Union College Library, aided me in the transliterations and translations of German documents; Ann Millin, a graduate student here at the school, assisted me in organizing my data. Leonard N. R. Simons, a well-known Detroit communal worker, and President Alfred Gottschalk of the Hebrew Union College have always evinced a deep personal interest in my studies and writings. Professor Herbert Paper of the college's Graduate School helped me in transliterating difficult Yiddish holographs. Aaron Levine of Cincinnati, a former Federated Department Stores executive, was most generous in preparing English translations of German language documents.

Judith M. Daniels, Adjunct Instructor in History at the University of Cincinnati, has carefully read my entire manuscript and made many helpful

*New York: Schocken Books

corrections and suggestions. Dr. Stanley F. Chyet, Professor of American Jewish History at the Los Angeles branch of the Hebrew Union College–Jewish Institute of Religion, graciously spent hours reading the final draft of this manuscript. His counsel has been invaluable. To all of these and a host of others who have never failed me, I wish to express my gratitude for their constant support.

Finally, there is my personal secretary, Etheljane Callner—and her forty years of service, experience, *and* tolerance! An author would do well to admit that his finished product often owes much to the efforts of a devoted secretary. Thank you, thank you, Etheljane Callner.

Jacob R. Marcus

I

The Total Jewish Ethical Literature

Chapter One

The Ethical Stance in Works Produced Throughout the Ages

Introduction

The writings that are included and discussed in this work are but an infinitesimal part of the Hebrew, Aramaic, Arabic, Yiddish, and other vernacular ethical writings that reflect the social conduct, moral principles, and ethnic characteristics of the ancient Israelites and the later Jewish people. One published bibliography on Jewish ethics alone includes over 500 entries.[1] The Jewish literature that has concerned itself with questions of good and evil began with the Hebrew Bible and then moved on to include the Apocrypha, the pseudepigrapha, talmudic and rabbinic tomes, medieval philosophic, legal, and ethical works, and a host of modern writings.

To this very day, all Jewish literature that touches on social conduct has been influenced by the teachings of the Hebrew Bible, the Old Testament. Proverbs, Ecclesiastes, the major and minor prophets—all of these may well be looked upon as ethical works. Many of the biblical narratives have been reworked by editors who genuflected in the direction of the prophets. It is equally true that the didactic method employed in these ancient Hebrew writings has molded the format of later Jewish ethical works, even to the present day. The "ethical will" approach is biblical in origin: Abraham was told by God to instruct his children to keep the way of the Lord (Genesis 18:19); Jacob in his last days addressed his sons: Listen to your father (Genesis 49:1ff.); Moses enjoined: Observe and hear all these words which I command

1. B. Friedberg, *Bet Eked Sepharim* (Antwerp, 1931).

thee (Deuteronomy 12:28). Especially notable is the conference between the dying King David and his son Solomon. In a curious mixture of morality and brutality, the King instructed his successor to observe the divine commandments, to help those who were loyal to the dynasty, and to kill off his enemies (1 Kings 2:1ff).

Apocrypha and Pseudepigrapha

The Holy Scriptures are an authoritative collection of books. Some pre-Christian Jewish works were not included in the canon, even though they were probably as old as some of the biblical books. These excluded religious writings are known as the "hidden" books, the Apocrypha, and as the pseudepigrapha, the pseudonymous works. The stream of Jewish ethics, beliefs, and practices during those early centuries runs deep and strong in these valuable collections. In the *Testaments of the Twelve Patriarchs* —the sons of the biblical Jacob—the tribal leader Dan (5:3) speaks to his sons in these words:

> Love the Lord through all your life,
> And one another with a true heart.

This typical ethical classic is matched by another in the apocryphal book of Tobit (Chapter 4). Before his death, Tobit turns to one of his sons and instructs him: Honor your mother, avoid sin and prostitutes, deal uprightly, shun intermarriage, give charity, treat laborers fairly, and always remember that if you fear God you will certainly prosper.

The Talmud

The ethics—the Jewish moral stance of the Sacred Scriptures, the Apocrypha, and the pseudepigrapha—were cherished and reaffirmed in the Hebrew–Aramaic body of rabbinic literature known as the Babylonian Talmud (The Learning), a vast collection of Jewish legal, ethical, and customary lore. The nonlegal portion, the aggada, constitutes a substantial part of the total. The thousands of pages of talmudic literature cover the period from the pre-Christian centuries to approximately the year 700 C.E. Nearly every page contains material that enlightens us about the way of life of the Jews who lived in the Mesopotamian villages. These folio tomes are important, for their legal enactments constitute the core of present-day Judaism. Judaism as a religious system stems from this body of literature, not from the Hebrew Bible. There are sixty-three tractates in the Babylonian Talmud. One of them deals chiefly with ethics; it is called *Avot*, the Fathers. The Jews deemed it so important that it was incorporated into their book of common prayer, the siddur, and a different chapter of this tractate is still read every Sabbath after Passover until the Sabbath before the Jewish New Year. The second ethical pronouncement in *Avot*, ascribed to a high priest who lived in the fourth or third pre-Christian century, is particularly significant; it described the essential activities, the ethos, of the Jewish community down to the present day:

> The world is based on three things: on learning, on the worship service, and on deeds of loving kindness.

There is no Jewish way of life without schools, synagogues, and charities.

Ethical Writings in the Middle Ages

For well over 1,000 years, rabbis, the Jewish academicians of their times, busied themselves with the study of the legal aspects of the Talmud and its literature. That was the Law for Jews; it was imperative that they adapt it to communal and individual needs if they were to survive. As Jewry grew older and wiser during the medieval centuries, scholars began to fashion ethical works. Some Jewish philosophers wrote—in Arabic, their native tongue—chapters or even whole volumes emphasizing ethics, piety, asceticism, and mysticism. Why this interest in ethics? The reasons are not completely clear. These philosophers may have been influenced by the ethical writings of Christians and Moslems; possibly, too, this resorting to story, morals, legends, the good life, provided them with a welcome release from the rigid demands of talmudic ratiocination. Numerous legal codes—shortcuts—were common, but the people, the *populus*, wanted to be edified and entertained; they enjoyed pleasurable reading, chapbooks of a sort. And, as time passed, the frequent comments on conduct and character that dot the pages of the Talmud were expanded into formal and relatively numerous works on ethics.

Moral works began to appear in the South, in Spain, the Provence, and in the Rhenish North as early as the eleventh century. A common literary genre was the ethical will. (Israel Abrahams, an English scholar, edited a two-volume work in 1926 entitled *Hebrew Ethical Wills*.[2]) Those wills, which seem to have first begun to appear in Central Europe, were not fictitious literary devices; each was an actual epistle directed to the testator's immediate family. The authors were not necessarily old men. A will-writer might well have been a younger person about to undertake a journey, and, fearing that he or she might never return, intent on leaving formal instructions for a beloved child

2. Philadelphia: The Jewish Publication Society of America.

or for the entire family. Such writings appeal to the historian who is interested in human beings rather than in world-shaking events. They reflect the ideals of the individual author. In simple, terse language, often Hebrew, they tell us about the writer's religious beliefs and ethical concepts. They reveal his hopes and aspirations: they touch on the prosaic and mundane and they strive for the heights of sublimity. Nothing was foreign to the thoughts of these writers; they wrote of the love of God and of the importance of taking a bath. Many impart advice of a very practical nature. For the most part, they extol the virtues of truth and humility, of piety and modesty. They dwell on the importance of labor and write fervently of both the love of family and the welfare of the community.

This ethical literature was most widely cultivated not in the Iberian peninsula, whose Jewish community died in the fifteenth century, but in Central and Eastern Europe, where it has continued into the present century. The medieval Ashkenazim, the Jews of these more northerly regions, evinced very little interest in philosophical speculation but they delighted in writing ethical works. Here, too, it is not easy to explain their preoccupation with morals and right conduct. They may have been influenced by the German medieval church, which produced many fine moral and devotional works. It is not improbable that their suffering prompted them, as it did the Spanish Jews, to elevate themselves spiritually when they were belittled by their Gentile neighbors. A fascinating aspect of the ethical Jewish literature of those centuries is the reaction to what was almost continuous persecution. Indeed, the cry for vengeance is not unknown, but there is also a constant emphasis on kindness and affection for Gentiles. The Jews of those centuries may have realized that hatred was self-destructive. In his *Sefer Maalot ha-Middot*, 12a,[3] Jehiel ben Jekutiel wrote the following paragraph:

> Love your children, your brothers, relatives, friends, and good neighbors. Love all mankind; be courteous to all in word and deed that they may love you and not hate you. . . . If you wish to revenge yourself on your enemies, then do so by being better.

This was written during the very years in which the Germans seized 180 Jewish men, women, and children in Munich and burned them alive in the synagogue.

Jewish Ethical Writings in the Modern Centuries

The new world of modernism that began in the sixteenth and seventeenth centuries reshaped Jewish life. Even in the Middle Ages, however, Jewry was

3. As cited in Fritz Bamberger (ed.), *Die Lehren des Judentums nach den Quellen* (Leipzig: Gustav Engel Verlag, 1928), vol. I, p. 354.

never culturally isolated. Christianity and Islam exerted a profound influence on the thinking of medieval Jewish scholars; a substantial number of academicians were never "ghettoized," either spiritually or intellectually. Later, the Renaissance did not leave the Jews of Europe untouched; the Enlightenment and the French Revolution hastened their cultural development. But the instrument that gave them new life was the "iron pen," printing. The cult of personality moved them to express themselves. Jews now began to write extensively; they wrote of religion, ethics, and morals. They published homilies, guides to daily conduct, works on philosophy, commentaries on the wisdom literature of the Bible and on the talmudic tractate *Avot*. Many, mindful of the traditional ethical wills, employed that device to instruct their children and to gain immortality through the written word. Honorable men and women, many of whom were truly great, have enriched Jewry with their moral testaments. They wrote in Hebrew, Yiddish, English, and German. So much for the form. In content there was nothing in the world of ethics, theology, religion, theosophy, mysticism, or cabbalah that escaped their notice and devotion. They described their love and fear of God; they dwelt on sin, on Satan (a very real one), on the future life, on the good and the bad, on the sufferings of the righteous and the fleshpots of the evil, on free will and morality; and they wrote of tolerance, if not love, of one's neighbor.

In the early eighteenth century, an Italian, Moses Hayyim Luzzatto (d. 1747), wrote his Hebrew guide to saintliness, *The Path of the Upright*.[4] This ascetic pietist was reaching for perfection. But as a mystic, enthralled by the thirteenth-century cabbalistic Zohar (The Radiance), he was deeply involved in the hope of redemption and the speedy coming of the Messiah. (Gershom Seixas, an American clergyman during the Revolutionary War, had a document in his possession indicating that the Messiah would come in 1783. And the Messiah *did* come, but not as a Jew; he came in the guise of the newborn American republic, which drove the British out that year and prepared the way for the emancipatory Federal Constitution.)

Ever since the 1200s, the German Jews, carrying with them their German dialect (Yiddish!), had been moving eastward into the Slavic lands. By the sixteenth and seventeenth centuries they were the largest Jewish group in the world. (They are the grandparents and ancestors of most of the Jews living in North America today.) The medieval Jewish emigrants from Central Europe brought with them to Poland their interest in ethical writings; and after the invention of printing, older Jewish ethical classics as well as more recent compositions began rolling off the presses for the edification of both Polish and German Jewry. Distinguished East European rabbis wrote many significant religioethical works until the threshold of the twentieth century.

4. In Mordecai M. Kaplan (ed.), *Mesillat Yesharim: The Path of the Upright* (Philadelphia: The Jewish Publication Society of America, 1936).

During the middle 1600s, the Jewish masses in Poland experienced almost continuous persecution; this persecution continued intermittently into the twentieth century, when they were exterminated by the Germans. The frantic reaching out for physical relief gave birth to desperate messianic expectations and soul-searching reflections on right conduct. Close upon the heels of the pseudo-Messiahs, who had betrayed the hopes reposed in them, came the rise of vigorous pietistic movements.

For the benefit of those German and Polish Jews who could not read or speak Hebrew, particularly the women, an adult education literature began appearing in the Yiddish vernacular no later than the seventeenth century. This interest in moral instruction went so far that, as early as the 1590s, enterprising publishers printed ethical broadsides—in Hebrew or in Yiddish—that were tacked onto the walls of rooms so that even he who ran could read. These were ethical "mirrors" into which the devout could look to find the moral teachings by which they could adorn themselves spiritually. In one of these mirrors the reader was told bluntly that if he did not forgive others, his own sins would not be forgiven, and that, if he persisted in his cruelty to his fellowman, this would constitute adequate proof that he was a descendant of Gentiles![5]

Edificatory literature for women was written exclusively in Yiddish. It was in this tongue that the women began tearfully to read their *tehinot*, their "supplications" to God on high. Their favorite book—and the favorite of some men, too—was *Go Forth and Behold (Tzeenah u-reenah*, Song of Solomon 3:11), a rather large reworking of the Pentateuch and other biblical books (ca. 1615–1620). Its importance is illuminated by a simple statistic: over 200 editions have been published in Europe, Israel, and the United States since its first appearance. This work, with its fascinating legends, its scriptural lessons and asides, became the Bible of millions of Yiddish-speaking women.

Nineteenth-century German Jewish intellectuals like Moritz Lazarus (d. 1903) and Hermann Cohen (d. 1918) wrote in their native vernacular, German. Lazarus was the author of a study that has also appeared in English translations, *The Ethics of Judaism.*[6] Cohen, a distinguished Neo-Kantian philosopher, published works that touched on the moral teachings of Judaism; one was called *Religion of Reason.*[7] East of Germany, in Russia and Poland, enlightened Orthodox Jewish leaders led by Israel Lipkin (Salanter, d. 1883) developed a *Musar*, or Moral Movement. Abraham Isaac Kook (d. 1935)—no philosopher, as were Lazarus and Cohen—had a profound impact on his disciples in the land of Israel through his writings, which accentuated holiness and repentance. As influential as Lazarus and Cohen were in

5. *Yivo Bleter, Journal of the Yiddish Scientific Institute*, New York, vol. 21, pp. 201 ff.

6. Two volumes (Philadelphia: the Jewish Publication Society of America, 1900–1901).

7. 2nd Rev. Ed., New York: F. Ungar Publishing Company, 1972.

Central Europe, and as Salanter and Kook were in Russia and the Holy Land, they could not reach out to touch the untutored Jewish masses living under the Russian yoke. But this had been accomplished, much earlier, by Israel ben Eliezer (d. 1760), the Baal Shem Tov, the miracle-working Master of the Good (God's) Name. The Baal Shem Tov emphasized ecstatic prayer, devotion, union with the divine, morality, and humility. His followers (Hassidim, or Pietists) in the nineteenth century numbered in the many thousands; even today, in the late twentieth century, Hassidim are found in every corner of the world, wherever there is a Jewish community. Their philosophy of love of life, of humankind, of nature, and their embrace of God Himself, found popularity through the teachings of a German Jewish religious philosopher named Martin Buber, who died in 1965. Hassidic stories and tales, ethical in a social sense, have influenced millions of readers.

Chapter Two

The Ethical Stance in Letters Written by Jews

Departure and Farewell Letters Written to European Émigrés

It will bear repetition: there is a huge and diversified ethical Jewish literature of a social and moral nature. This book, limited to the writings of Americans or their European parents, deals with but one aspect of this cultural legacy that reaches back to the Hebrew Bible. The link to Europe is obvious; American Jewish history began with the departure of emigrants from that continent. Indeed, American Jewry was a European Jewish colony as late as the 1890s, when the multimillionaire Baron Maurice de Hirsch deemed it necessary to help support American Jewish social welfare programs and institutions. When a child, a relative, a beloved friend, or a neighbor left for the New World, those who remained behind were concerned. The American continent was for them Ultima Thule; it was a land that threatened cherished beliefs, a distant shore fraught with danger. One aspect of this danger was implicit in such questions as "What will happen to my dear ones? Will they survive as Jews?" It was believed that for a Jew, a good Jew, loss of identity was death! These concerns are reflected in departure and farewell letters. What were the feelings of those left behind; what were the fearful, anguished admonitions of parents and friends?

An analysis of several such letters sent from Central Europe between 1795 and 1880 throws light on these queries. Although the period covers almost a century, the backgrounds of the writers have much in common. They were all Orthodox Jews; Orthodoxy, on the whole, was unchanging. It is not difficult to summarize the hopes and fears of parents and friends who were saying goodbye to dear ones leaving for the New World. Six of these letters have been reproduced in this work (nos. 4, 14, 16, 20, 21, and 32).

All of these writers, a Netherlander and five Germans, were very probably men and women of some education. The Netherlander wrote in Hebrew; the others, in German. Their message was religious, yet very pragmatic: Fear God, worship Him, follow His dictates, and prosper. The message advocated, after a fashion, a covenantal relationship: Take care of Him and He will take care of you. Try to stay Jewish. Keep far from evil; avoid apostates, gamblers, and prostitutes. The latter echoed a warning against the seductive woman that was issued as far back as the apocryphal Ecclesiasticus, 2,100 years ago:

> Turn away thine eye from a beautiful woman, and look not upon another's beauty; for many have been deceived by the beauty of a woman; for herewith love is kindled as a fire. Sit not at all with another man's wife, nor sit down with her in thine arms, and spend not thy money with her at the wine, lest thine heart incline unto her, and so through thy desire thou fall into destruction. [9:8–9]

The message of these letters could be summed up in the following words: Observe the Sabbath, educate your children Jewishly, stay away from political upheavals. If you can't be as observant as we are here back home, do the best you can. Don't forget to say the Shema: *Hear O Israel, the Lord is our God, the Lord is One.* Don't hate; be humble, grateful, patient, kind, honest, thrifty. If you earn money, remember that God gave it to you.

In addition, the letters indicate that the writers believed in the stewardship of wealth. Help people, they all said, and, incidentally, don't forget us; write, reread this letter, come back if you can. There was an undercurrent of despair: Will I ever see my beloved child again? Immigrants who received such departure letters were never able to cut their emotional ties to the family back home. They would always have one foot in Europe.

There are two farewell letters from East European Jews (nos. 28 and 46). One is written in Hebrew; the other, set in rhymed couplets, is in Yiddish. Jews who lived under the czars in the nineteenth century had few opportunities to advance in secular disciplines. They were, on the whole, an unschooled and oppressed lot. Most Russian Jews, for example, knew no Russian. The emphasis in their letters is not on ethics—that is taken for granted—but on being and remaining Jewish. In their Pan-Slavic world, the Jewish ethos is stressed: ceremonials, rituals, customs, mitzvot will separate you from the Gentiles and keep you Jewish. This was the hope of Meshulam Faitel Goldbaum, an 85-year-old father, as he sat down to write to his two sons in America (no. 28). He did not realize—or did he?—that the battle was half lost when his two boys changed their Jewish names and called themselves Louis and Herman; their wives became Mathilda and Pauline. Acculturation had already set in; the barriers were falling.

Letters Sent by Americans to Children Away from Home

In the previous section I described the feelings of Europeans writing to dear ones who had already left or who were about to leave for America. There are also numerous letters written by Americans, native-born or naturalized citizens, who wrote to sons or daughters leaving home, apparently for the first time; the parents were concerned. In 1797, Jacob Mordecai of Warrenton, North Carolina, wrote to his daughter Rachel (no. 5). Her Mama had died, and Rachel, along with her two little sisters, had found a home with an uncle and aunt in Richmond. Mordecai, always the pedant, was later to open a girls' school. He wrote in polysyllables: Rachel, watch your conduct, he advised. Get an education, and read the book I sent you. Take care of your younger sisters, Ellen and the baby, Caroline. But although Jacob was Orthodox and was hostile to religious change, he wrote nothing of Judaism. We know that he was an ardent Jew, and yet, for reasons best known to him, he saw no need to emphasize Jewish identification. He may well have been the only Jewish father in Warrenton. And Rachel in 1797? She was all of 8 years old. She grew up to be an intellectual, and in her last days she turned to Christianity.

Hannah Alexander of Augusta, Georgia, and Charleston, South Carolina, was also a committed traditionalist (no. 12). She wanted to be buried in Charleston near her late husband so that they would rise together in the resurrection and live happily forever after. In 1838, writing to a son going West, she urged him to stay away from bad women and gambling halls, and reassured him that God would help him.

In 1907, Elias Greenebaum of Chicago sent a letter to his grandson John who was about to leave home for college (no. 43). The grandfather urged the young man to be moderate in all that he did. Two years later, when John passed his twentieth birthday, Grandpa sent him a check—not to spend, but to invest—so that he would learn how to handle money.

Toward the end of the same century another father—Emanuel Rackman, who was to become a distinguished Orthodox rabbi and president of an Israeli university—sent a son away to school (no. 83). Rackman, like fathers before him, preached the gospel of virtue and of premarital celibacy. But more than that, in this post-Holocaust letter, he emphasized Jewish identity. The rabbi was of East European origin; his ancestors had never failed to insist on *yiddishkeit*, Jewishness. Identify yourself as a Jew, he told his son; you belong to your people. Adhere to our Jewish Golden Rule. Live ethically so that your way of life may reflect divinity.

"This I Believe" Letters

In the nineteenth and twentieth centuries, many Jews found themselves turning inward. The urge to express themselves flourished as they became citizens of the lands of their nativity. This push to "be somebody" was manifest in personal documents in which lofty ideas were often vented. Love of one's fellows, at least voiced if not practiced, characterized the intelligentsia, the nontraditionalists, the civil religionists. Ethics were in style. In 1876 Felix Adler, a young American who had trained for the rabbinate, established the first Ethical Culture society. Many of his followers were Jews; some continued to hold membership in Reform synagogues.

Among those newcomers who pontificated in nineteenth-century America was Isidor Bush, a young man who had but recently emigrated from Austria. Freedom here in the United States, he wrote in 1851, challenges us to improve society, to be champions of the light (no. 18). Respect the Bible, he urged; it contains the law of love and morality. Fight bigotry and skepticism; support the public schools; give land to the poor; garner respect for the name "Jew"; don't be a peddler, a clothier, or a moneylender; *go back to the farm* . . . and don't quarrel with one another. This was the program he outlined for his fellow Jewish émigrés coming here from Central Europe.

Two generations later, a young Chicago aristocrat, Rose Haas Alschuler, penned a "This I Believe" type of letter addressed, as it were, to a child (no. 50). Throughout this century many Jews, patterning themselves after cultured Gentiles, have issued moral manifestos. They have begun often, although not always, with the words "This I believe." Moses Maimonides (1135–1204), Jewry's most distinguished medieval scholar, was the author of a thirteen-article credo, each paragraph of which began with the portentous pronouncement "I Believe." His twelfth-century beliefs were all theological; twentieth-century affirmations have been ethical, patriotic, or social. And it was in this spirit that, in 1920, Rose Alschuler began her statement: "This, I believe *today*, " going on to say: Love beauty, be a free soul; in the face of an infinite world, humility is called for; implement your spiritual potential; devote yourself to the welfare of mankind.

In 1947 the lawyer and civil servant David E. Lilienthal was nominated as chairman of the Atomic Energy Commission. Senator Kenneth McKellar, a Tennessean and a friend of the public utilities, opposed Lilienthal's appointment. In a subtle fashion he sought to reflect on the political loyalties of the nominee. Lilienthal responded to the Senator's verbal imputations (no. 67). The state, he said in his "Credo of an American," is not an end in itself; it must be motivated by ethical standards. He was opposed to any type of government that did not respond to the importance of the individual; all men he said, are the children of God.

Just a few years later, in 1951, Leonard N. R. Simons, a Detroit advertising executive, communal leader, and philanthropist, also published a "This I Believe" statement (no. 69). Service to his fellowman was the governing principle of his life, and he wrote that people were put on earth to evince love, respect, and generosity. Like Rose Alschuler and David Lilienthal, Simons specified nothing in his credo to identify him with Jewry or Judaism, yet he was one of Detroit's outstanding Jewish activists in cultural and religious matters. Lilienthal, on the other hand, although he had started out as an ardent Jew, later distanced himself, to a degree, from his people. Alschuler, however, helped establish a Chicago Reform temple and a Sunday School. She was devoted to Israel's Technion and to the Leo Baeck School, both in Haifa. Are Jews compartmentalized in their loyalties to the state, to their ancestral folk and religion? Yes. Definitely. For many Jews—perhaps most—the Jewish and the non-Jewish spheres of thinking and activity are barely tangential, although the Jewish segment may well be the substratum, the continuum, that gives meaning to the "secular"—in this case the *American*—world.

One of the most interesting of these personal avowals was written as early as 1895 (no. 40). It appeared in a Yiddish magazine in Boston. The author was Morris Winchevsky, a Yiddish litterateur, poet, and translator, and above all a socialist. He published a parody of the Ten Commandments. (Pulling the beard of traditional Judaism was at that time a common sport among some East European Jewish secularists.) He called his lucubration "Mammon's Ten Commandments." Its irony and cynicism, and also its naiveté are evident: Mammon rules the world and tolerates no other gods, not even the Goddess of Liberty in New York's harbor. He continued: Never swear falsely unless it is profitable. Avoid adultery; there are always young working girls who are available. Don't be a petty crook, you'll go to jail. Instead steal millions and establish a trust. Winchevsky may seem to have had nothing in common with Simons, Lilienthal, and Alschuler, but this is not so. They had much in common; they were all concerned with social justice and in that sense, they were all compassionate Jews.

The Son to the Father

Letters from fathers to sons are plentiful enough, but how often do sons and daughters write to or about parents after they have left home and are on their own? What do they say? The few letters we have are interesting, even revelatory. In 1809, after Levi Sheftall died in Savannah, his son Mordecai Sheftall, Jr. wrote an obituary of his beloved father (no.7). Sheftall père had been a Revolutionary War veteran, the son of a Georgia pioneer who came to the colony only weeks after Colonel Oglethorpe landed. Levi, said Mordecai, had labored industriously to provide for his family and had been honorable in his business dealings; he was a man without pretensions, a conscientious civil servant, charitable to all, and kind even to his slaves.

On April 26, 1943, Sidney Robins (*né* Rabinowitz), stationed in Tunisia during World War II, sat down to write his father and stepmother a letter (no. 63). He was moving on to the front. If he died in battle, his letter was to be forwarded to his parents. Three days later he was fatally wounded at Hill 609 and died almost immediately. He barely had time to reach into his tunic and pull out the letter; it was found clutched tightly in his dead fingers. Sidney was 21 years of age, an employee of Macy's Department Store. One of his ambitions had been to make enough money to provide for his stepmother and his father, a Polish immigrant worker who had come to the United States to better himself. "You were the best parents in the world," he wrote. And to his father he added, "You'll never know how much I have always loved you." He added that he was giving his life "for the greatest cause in the world—that men might be free."

In 1976 Art Buchwald, the celebrated journalist, published a letter that appeared in the hundreds of newspapers that carried his column (no. 86). His "Letter to Pop" [1] was a tribute to his father, who had come to the United States in 1910 as a lad of 17. Buchwald's father had had the moral courage to undertake a hazardous journey across the Atlantic in order to make a new life for himself in a free land, where he then slaved for fourteen or fifteen hours a day to support his wife and four children. "You kept telling me there was no better place to live than America," Buchwald wrote. "Everyone has dreams for their children, but here it's possible to make them come true."

The Parent to the Child

Parents have never lost the opportunity to write and advise their children. The father reaches out to his son at the bar mitzvah celebration; parents give their children letters when they leave home—letters of advice and warning—and in their old age, parents express their last wishes in formal notes or in ethical wills. One letter, for example, was written by a young woman dying of cancer in Denver. She was deeply saddened, for she feared that her young children would not remember her. She wanted them to be happy, to be honest, to be good Jews. Above all, she hoped they would know that she loved them.[2]

Styles in relating to beloved ones changed with the century, even within decades. Polite usage, not the heart, often dictated the contents of a note to the object of one's affection. In 1793, Simon Gratz, one of the Philadelphia Gratzes, wrote a congratulatory note to his sister, who had just announced her engagement (no.3). He laid down the criteria for a successful marriage: A woman must always be mindful of the precepts of the Lord—whatever that might have meant—and do what her husband tells her. Simon was speaking out of the fullness of his experience: he was 20, and his sister Richea was 19.

---

1. Publishers Hall Syndicate.

2. J. Riemer and N. Stampfer, *Ethical Wills* (New York: Schocken Books, 1983), pp. 183–186.

A full generation later, when Hannah Alexander's son Aaron was undertaking a dangerous trip north—he was traveling on a steamboat!—she sent him a note of love and admonition (no.12). Beware of sin, she wrote. Cursing and using God's name in vain is a mortal evil, a violation of one of the Ten Commandments.

In earlier days, bound by custom in literary exchanges, parents and siblings tended to be formal in expressing affection; in the twentieth century, on the other hand, women and men have had little hesitation in baring their feelings. Jennie Rosenfeld Gerstley of Chicago wrote: "I should like my children to know that I have loved them devotedly. . . ."[3] She wanted them to cherish what was fine and good, she said, and she wanted them to know that their kindness had "sweetened" her declining years. Mrs. Gerstley was writing in around the year 1931. As the century advanced, parents began to address their infant children, even those yet unborn. They were anxious to tear away the veil that masked the future. They were beguiled with thoughts like these: What will happen to this little one? Who or what will help her, him, when I am gone? What can I do to ease the burden for this helpless child? Can I imbue him, her, with my hopes, my ideals?

In 1944, during World War II, Corporal Samuel Furash was stationed in England. A political radical, he was disturbed by the evils that the war had brought in its wake. Lonely without his wife and their baby daughter, he wrote to his child (no.64). She and her mother were "the nearest stars in my heaven," he wrote, "and each night I sing out my love. . . ." It was his prayer that his child would grow up to fight fascism and help build a new world of righteousness, truth, freedom, and economic equality.

In postwar days—it was 1955—Rabbi Louis J. Sigel of Teaneck, New Jersey, wrote a letter to his daughter to be read aloud at her baby-naming ceremony (no.70). The baby had just come into the world; she would give him love, and he offered her love. The sun is shining for you, he seems to be saying. The world is good; use its blessings and become the best that it lies within you to become. We shall always be proud of you, for you are yourself.

When Samuel Furash and Louis Sigel wrote to their infant daughters, they were writing as fathers, entranced by the mystery of birth, the burgeoning of a new type of love; they were thrilled with the thought that a little bundle of quivering flesh would yet implement the fondest hopes of an adoring parent. Sentiment threatened to overpower them. But in 1959, when Dr. Harry Levinson of Topeka's Menninger Foundation addressed his baby son, he was thinking not only as a father but as a Jew (no.75). He was concerned, indeed a little frightened, lest his child be exposed to bigotry. Obviously the doctor had at some time in his life encountered prejudice. His baby, he feared, would grow up to be scorned as a "Christ-killer." I will give you the strength to

3. J. R. Marcus, *The American Jewish Woman: A Documentary History* (New York: Ktav, 1981), pp. 315–320.

survive, he said. If you are conscious of the beauty, the significance of your heritage, you will not be destroyed. Judaism will give you roots and enrich your life with love and mercy. As a Jew, continue to help build America, he wrote to him. Work for the new State of Israel, which has brought hope to thousands; fight for religious freedom; encompass all men and women with love and mercy.

In 1963, Jane M. Bloch of Cincinnati addressed her son Peter on his fifteenth birthday (no.77). What were the thoughts of a highly intelligent and articulate mother as she lay helpless on her mattress grave? (This was her fifteenth year in an iron lung.) What could this magnificent human being say to her son? She gave him a message of hope, equanimity, courage. Her knowledge that she was doomed did not dismay her. The love her family showered on her was ample assurance that there was divinity in the universe.

By the late twentieth century, Jews in the United States were coming to terms with the Holocaust. In the 1980s, Franklin J. Riesenburger wrote a letter to his teenage son, whose great-grandparents and many other relatives had perished when the Germans murdered millions (no.90). Riesenburger (the father) wanted to impress on his young son the obligation to continue the family's spiritual legacy. If the boy's grandfather had not escaped to America, then there would have been no family, no father, no child. It was a chilling thought. Because your parents were born here in free America, he wrote, it is your sacred duty to battle injustice. He urged his son to work to strengthen a society where positive social values would flourish.

Chapter Three

Writings that Advocate American Orthodoxy as a Way of Life

Background of American Orthodoxy

Orthodoxy, the denomination of many of those whose letters were discussed in the previous chapter, is a religion that has survived for twenty centuries. It stands securely entrenched in its beliefs. The Torah of Moses, the Pentateuch, is divinely inspired. As interpreted by the rabbis of all past generations, it governs every aspect of life. One neglects God's ordinances at one's peril; observance invites divine favor. Although its numbers are declining, Orthodoxy is making a gallant effort to remain a vibrant alternative for Jewish religionists in the United States. It can now count but relatively few adherents, for American society powerfully encourages conformity to its Christian-dominated form of civil religion. Although ever mindful of its universalist hopes, Orthodoxy in practice is particularistic. It will never surrender its unique way of life, for it is determined to survive, to preserve its own vision of Judaism. Today, aware that it is different, Orthodoxy emphasizes apologetics; it is compelled to justify its disparities.

But traditionalists were not always a Jewish minority in this country. Ever since the days when the first Jewish worship service was held in seventeenth-century New Amsterdam, until the early 1930s, most religiously affiliated Jews were Orthodox. Despite the fact that all Torah-true Jews have a more or less common prayer book, similar ceremonies, and the same rites of passage, every Jewish community in every land is *sui generis*. American Orthodoxy is no exception; it has a distinct ethos. The historian as voyeur will find nothing scandalous in the letters of Abigail Franks (d. 1756), but he or she will certainly gain knowledge of her innermost thoughts (no.2). In a series of letters written between 1733 and 1748 to a beloved son in London, she says: Do your duty to God and man, for the good we do lives after us; think of what you want, but adhere to tradition. We, too, have our superstitions; we Jews need a Calvin or a Luther. Mrs. Franks hopes, as King George's War rages, that a day will come when men beat their swords into ploughshares. She is shocked and distraught when a beloved daughter secretly marries a Christian; intermarriage is the ultimate disaster.

Benjamin Nones, a Revolutionary War veteran, was attacked in the press as a Jew during the hotly contested presidential election of 1800 (no.6). His answer to his attackers appears more typical of the late twentieth century than it is of the days of John Adams and Thomas Jefferson, for his rejoinder was ethnic; he was proud of his people and its history. Is it possible that his pride was really a defense mechanism, that he was in reality inwardly plagued by a sense of inferiority? All the evidence suggests that, for him, Judaism was a superior faith. His religion, he said, was established by God. It is the mother of Christianity—but Jews, unlike Christians, do not murder one another; Judaism has given birth to an Abraham, a Moses, the prophets, Jesus.

Nones had served several years as president of Philadelphia's Orthodox synagogue, Mikveh Israel. In 1829, three years after Nones's death, Isaac Leeser mounted the pulpit as *hazzan* of this congregation. This German immigrant was to become the most important Jewish religious officiant in the antebellum United States. Leeser was a strict conformist, yet he was to be the harbinger of Neo-Orthodoxy. He believed that Orthodoxy, its customs, its ceremonies, and its traditional beliefs must be maintained; yet he believed also that the Jew must always face the future, and that there must be a complete acceptance of America, its essence, its ethos.

Leeser exercised influence through *The Occident*, a periodical that he founded in Philadelphia in 1843.[1] Judaism, based on the Hebrew Scriptures, was the most reasonable, the most rational of all faiths, he wrote. Good deeds and moral living are no less important than religious practices. In 1860, he edited an American edition of an Anglo-Jewish Sunday School textbook written by a woman named Sarah Harris. There are sixteen chapters—or vignettes—in this vest-pocket booklet. Four of these touch on God's attributes, Moses, the Sabbath, and the precepts (mitzvot); the other twelve speak of truth and falsehood, respect for one's parents, faith, charity, neighborly love, compassion for the aged, meekness and pride, unity, teachers, uprightness, industry, immortality. The emphases here are on ethics and social conduct.[2]

---

1. This was the first regularly published Jewish periodical in America. Until its demise in 1869 it was a mouthpiece for Anglo-American Orthodox ideas.

2. *The Occident* 3:18, 99, 372–378, 495; 4:66.

The thinking of many mid-nineteenth-century American Jews is reflected in the pages of *The Occident*. These Jews were not hesitant about expressing their views; to them, the teachings of Judaism constituted a supreme ethical code. In a published letter to the City Council of Richmond, Virginia, local Jews bragged that, if they were good citizens, it was due to their religion. In 1845, a Jewish New York assistant district attorney noted that there were very few Jews in the country's prisons; another Israelite told his readers that the moral teachings of the New Testament were derived from the Hebrew Scriptures. Baltimore's Rabbi Abraham Rice was one of the most Orthodox congregational functionaries of his time. Speaking at the dedication of the city's first synagogue he declared that, when Jews met for worship, their goal was to urge one another to walk the road that led to righteousness.[3] The last words in the minutes of every session of the Independent Order of the Free Sons of Israel were *friendship*, *love*, and *truth*. The constant emphasis on morals and ethics by mid-nineteenth-century Orthodox Jewry was, after a fashion, an apologia: We are good people, good citizens, because of our religion, because of our very differentness.[4]

Writings that Deal with the Meaning of Bar Mitzvah

Among the rites of passage that most Jews observe, few have been as popular as the ceremony of bar mitzvah. A "bar mitzvah lad" is one who is eligible for the performance of good deeds. When a male reaches the age of 13, he is deemed a man; he is called to the Torah, reads selections from the Hebrew Bible, makes a speech, and is from then on expected to perform the traditional "good deeds," the mitzvot. He has reached the age of legal and religious majority. In earlier times, the bar mitzvah boy often gave his talk at a special dinner held in his home. The bar mitzvah celebration had become a well-developed formal ceremony by the fifteenth century. By the early twentieth century, American Jews could purchase books that contained samples of bar mitzvah speeches in English, Yiddish, and Hebrew. These works have been used by parents, teachers, and rabbis in preparing boys for the ceremony. In his Hebrew monograph on the bar mitzvah, Isaac Rivkind appended a bibliography of 468 such books.[5]

American Jewry has never, ethnically and spiritually, been of one piece. There have been Germans and Russians, Orthodox, Conservatives, and

3. Ibid. 3:365–366, 462, 564; 4: 173.

4. H. B. Grinstein, *Rise of the Jewish Community of New York, 1654–1860* (Philadelphia: Jewish Publication Society of America, 1945), p. 113.

5. *Bar Mitzvah: A Study in Jewish Cultural History* (New York: Shulsinger Bros. Linotype and Publishing Co., 1942).

tradition-minded Reformers. All have encouraged their male youngsters to observe this rite of passage. Isaac Leeser, who was a powerful influence on many in the decades before the Civil War, wrote a bar mitzvah speech for a Philadelphia youngster (no.17). It was brief and to the point: I was an innocent child; now I am responsible for my own deeds. My parents have always protected me; I am grateful. The "Germans," Leeser's contemporaries and his survivors, listened as their sons parroted the talks that rabbis wrote for them: We can survive only through traditional religion and its rituals. Tefillin, which are bound on the head and hand, are important, for they remind us of our Jewish moral teachings. We must be virtuous, kind to all, good Jews, good Americans, good human beings.

This was the dominant, recurrent theme in those generations when Orthodoxy reigned. The twentieth century would not be denied; as the immigrants left Europe behind and were confronted by the demand for conformity to American standards, they sought to combine tradition and modernity, Torah and Enlightenment. A bar mitzvah speech written for a youngster in Hebrew or Yiddish might well take the nineteenth chapter of Leviticus as a text and preach the gospel of social justice. Forms of ethnicism and Zionism have never been absent from Judaism; they were re-emphasized after 1917, when Great Britain agreed to establish a Jewish homeland in what had been Ottoman Palestine, the ancient Holy Land. In 1969 a Denver judge, Sherman G. Finesilver, stressed Jewish pride as he addressed his sons in their bar mitzvah years (no.78). Jewish ritual practices are important, he told them, but you must never forget that we come from a great people. Study the lives of contemporary distinguished Jews; know who they were; share their greatness. Be a Jew; it can make you great. Pride is an integral part of the ethos. When parents mount the rostrum to lecture to a 13-year-old son, they might well tell him: Love God and your neighbor, follow the Mosaic code, work for the coming of a glorious messianic age. Irving Leibowitz of Indianapolis, a journalist and a World War II veteran, wrote a no-nonsense newspaper column in 1958 when his son reached the age of 13 (no.73). Cherish liberty and learning, he advised, and help the oppressed. Show responsibility. Feed the dog! Grow up!

Most bar mitzvah talks have always been rather stereotypical: Now that I am a man, the 13-year-old says, I must serve God and Jewry; I must abhor sin. My thanks are due to my parents, my family, my teachers, my friends, for all their help to me, materially, culturally, spiritually. Pray God they will continue to aid me as I strive to be a good Jew, a moral human being, an exemplary American citizen. In the mid-nineteenth century, the youngster's talk was frequently given in German, the language most often heard in immigrant homes. In later decades, English—the child's native tongue—would prevail. The use of English reflects the Americanization of the parents, too. It was an inevitable change. The parents may have lived on the Lower East Side, but spiritually they, too, were no longer ghettoized. This explains the overriding emphasis on humanitarianism, on universalism. The Jew in the East European immigrant scenes on Hester Street was now a member of the unitary American whole. In a way, the bar mitzvah ritual—with its English-language features, its memorized speech, its gifts, its good food—was attaining the status of an American Jewish coming-of-age rite.

Of course the bar mitzvah youngster understood English, but he could hardly have sensed the full meaning of what he declaimed: I am now a responsible religious individual; I will observe the Law, the Torah, the Jewish way of life. The address he delivered in German, English, Yiddish, or even Hebrew, reflected his parents' sentiments and not necessarily his own. When he read his talk, he was merely mouthing words; it was his parents who were speaking. The rebbe wrote what Papa and Mama wanted to hear. The address reflected the religion and the ethics of the parents. The son played the stellar role, but the ceremony was often a panegyric with the parents as the heroes. They loved to hear their son say that he would be a good Jew, that he would cling to the sacred ritual, that he would never fail to cup his ear when the father spoke. The father, the newcomer with one foot in the Old World, wanted the son to accept the traditional European way of life. The fear of change, of assimilation, was the silent undercurrent in the bar mitzvah address. Its message was: The child owes it to us to live as we have lived. It is not an overstatement to say that the father—through the rabbi or tutor who wrote the speech—was unwittingly seeking to develop a sense of guilt in the youngster so that he would remain Jewish and follow the traditional path. If he did not observe the ancient customs, he would be guilty of betraying his parents—and after they had done so much for him!

The bar mitzvah message is invariably a religious one; at the same time, it has almost never failed to be ethical both in Jewish and in universalistic terms. Implicit always is the thought or hope that virtue not only is its own reward, but that it also brings a mundane dividend. Does the youngster's talk, written by his elders, really reflect every facet of parental thinking? Probably not. The Jewish father is likely to be Janus-faced: a Jew and a businessman. In the son's talk, the entrepreneur is crowded out by the religionist and the moralist. Yet *takhlis* is never completely absent. *Takhlis* is an old Hebrew word given a new meaning by Yiddish-speaking Jews. It means the end, the goal, the result—success, the bottom line. *Takhlis* weighed heavily with Mr. Louis Heilbrun of Washington, D.C. (no.29). Putting himself in the limelight, he laid down an ethical regimen for his son; he drafted nine commandments—but then he added pages of maxims: Be polite, honest, industrious, and temperate; live within your means; pay your bills; watch your expenses; beware of lawyers! The *takhlis* Jew is subordinated in most ethical talks and statements. Perhaps Papa thought that the two worlds were not altogether compatible, but *takhlis* always lurked at the threshold; it was never completely absent; it was banished only when the boy made his speech during the week of his thirteenth birthday.

Writings that Deal with Liberalism, Reform, and the Ethical Avowal

When Judaism was born as a religious system in pre-Christian days, it was frowned upon by the cultures of the Eastern Mediterranean world and thus had no choice but to assume a defensive posture. This was the only way it could survive. Millennia later, too, the French Revolution and the Rights of Man compelled Judaism to reevaluate its philosophy and its stance. Orthodoxy, then coming under increased attack, was moderated radically. The universalistic moved closer to the particularistic. More and more the Jew of the nineteenth and twentieth centuries was to be pushed into the arena of modernity. His former corporate, and disparate, universe began to dissolve; now he was an integral part of a common one-world system. In the United States Dr. Max Lilienthal, although still Orthodox, concluded in the 1840s that a change was inevitable. He made a virtue of necessity; the Jewish people, he wrote, had been preserved in order to teach the nations the Jewish concept of morality. Judaism is the only true system of ethics, he insisted: It is our mission to teach it to the world.[6]

During that same decade, addressing a Jewish Sunday School audience in Columbia, South Carolina, a Mr. L. T. Levin spoke of justice, virtue, temperance, and piety as central to the nature of Judaism, but did not fail to emphasize benevolence to all human beings.[7] And Arthur L. Levy, a religious-minded father congratulating his son on his twenty-first birthday, did not urge him to keep kosher and go to services; what he saw fit to underscore was integrity, truth, and a sense of honor (no. 23). By the late nineteenth century, liberal Orthodox Jews as well as Reformers were turning to the left, theologically and ideologically. By the 1880s, in more than one Reform prayer book, God's blessing was invoked not only on the Jews but on all mankind. This was true in 1892 of the *Union Prayer Book*, the standard Reform service manual, although the original Hebrew—still retained by the Reformers—limited God's favor to Jews alone.

When the brothers Isaac S. and Adolph Moses, both rabbis, published a textbook on ethics in 1889, they said point-blank: The soul of Judaism is ethics.[8] In that same decade, Julius Ochs, a lay rabbi, served as Chattanooga's

6. *The Occident* 3:540–542.

7. Ibid., 4:152–153.

8. Isaac S. Moses, *The Ethics of the Hebrew Scriptures*, ed. A. Moses (Chicago: E. Rubovits & Bro.; Cincinnati: Bloch Publishing, 1889).

minister. His religious views undoubtedly reflected the thinking of many Jewish laymen who deemed themselves intellectuals. Reverence in conduct is more important than the resort to ceremonials, said this innocent rationalist (no.34); every man is my brother; religious practices are useful in that they serve to constrain the evil instincts of the masses! He believed that the eternal verities are best exemplified in Judaism. Ochs's philosophy can be summed up in a few words: Obey the Ten Commandments and be a patriotic American.

In a somewhat liberal congregation in Akron, Ohio, in 1883, Harry E. Leopold, age 13, read the bar mitzvah talk that his rabbi had written for him (no.33). After genuflecting in the direction of traditional Judaism, he told his auditors that he was now ready to fulfill the duties of a good man, and that human love leads to perfection. As the Jews moved into the twentieth century, with all its high hopes, a latter-day Deism was making itself felt. Ritual was in disfavor; there was some rather smug talk of deed, not creed; the Reform rabbis preached constantly on universalism, and finally, in a somewhat laggardly fashion, followed their Christian colleagues in a new emphasis on social justice. Twentieth-century American-born fathers still exhorted their sons: Study, learn, give charity, be a good human being, be a good citizen.

The closing years of the 1960s were marked by student unrest and a degree of mass hysteria; the demand for social improvement was almost universal. It made an impression on at least one bar mitzvah lad—Jerrold Franklin, who apparently wrote his own bar mitzvah speech and spoke maturely of the problems of his day, such as drugs, troubled race relations, faithless politicians (no.80). We young people must make the world better, he said. I shall try to be a good Jew, a decent human being. That was in 1971. Toward the end of that decade, Bertram Wallace Korn, a noted Philadelphia rabbi and historian of American Jewry, left the hospital after surviving a serious illness. His devoted congregation had rallied around him. Faced with eternity, he wrote a general epistle expressing his thanks for their support (no.88). God has not cured me, he said, but the thought of divinity within has sustained me. The Holy One, Blessed be He, gave me the strength to hope, to persevere. There is love in the universe and that love is God.

A decade before this stricken rabbi poured out his thanks to his congregation, the aged Herbert H. Lehman, a former governor of the state of New York and later a United States senator, wrote to a Sunday School boy who had wondered whether Judaism would be a handicap in the pursuit of public office (no.76). The governor was a religionist, a believer in Judaism, a synagogue member. With a touch of ethnicism, Lehman assured the youngster that he could make his way politically if he was a person of character. *Never be ashamed of your Jewish origin*! he wrote in his letter. Despite the push toward the ethical among liberal Jews, ethnocentrism was rarely absent. Jews were very proud of their American Jewish confreres and their achievements. This was no pretense, no psychological maneuver to cover a feeling of inferiority; Jews believed that they were "somebodies," that they were leaving their mark on contemporary America.

In 1943, Rabbi Jacob Philip Rudin was serving as a chaplin overseas, in the Pacific theater. It was his custom to write what he called an Open Letter to parents who had a son or daughter in the armed forces. The theme varied. For example, he wrote on one occasion that on Guadalcanal, in a foxhole, under fire and curled around a rock, a Jewish soldier did not recite psalms; he was not thinking of hearth and home (no.62). Was he occupied with ethics, ritual, faith in the One God? What was on his mind as the shells screamed overhead? He was dreaming about a pastrami sandwich! He was a *Jew*! Ethnos is everything, Rabbi Rudin believed. A sandwich can tie a Jew closer to his people than can a sermon. Every century has its pastrami, its blintzes, its borsht, its kugel. Gershom Seixas, the Revolutionary War rabbi, drooled as he wrote to his daughter Sally telling her of Mother's fritters with Madeira sauce, of her *albondigas* (meatballs).[9] Nostalgia and folkways are as important as the articles of faith. A pastrami sandwich, as Rabbi Rudin noted, is a declaration of allegiance and identification.

But not everyone could feel at one with this declaration. In 1919, almost a decade before his death, Rabbi Max Landsberg of Rochester, an unreconstructed liberal of the old universalistic school, wrote an ethical will of sorts (no. 47). He was an angry, unhappy man who had lived to see brushed aside much—almost everything—of all that he advocated and for which he had fought. He was a Classical Reformer, in the universalism-preaching van. He sensed—correctly—that Classical Reform was doomed by political conservatism in Europe and the United States, and also by the rise of the East European Jews here, by the renewed Jewish ethnicism, by Zionism. I want no eulogy, he said. Burn my sermons.

9. *Publications of the American Jewish Historical Society* (printed in Baltimore), 1939, no. 35, p. 192.

Chapter Four

Ethical Wills

Introduction

The traditional ethical will is usually a letter in which a parent offers a member of the family good advice; hence, it is an ethical instrument. It underlines the values that the writer holds dear. The ethical will is not to be misidentified as the legal document whereby a testator disposes of his material estate. As I pointed out earlier, the Jewish custom of a father formally addressing a member of his family goes back at least to the patriarch Jacob. The caption in Genesis 49, in the King James version, reads as follows: "Jacob calleth his sons to bless them." Many ethical wills are burdened with details relating to burial, the care of the body, the prayer for the dead (kaddish), the lighting of a memorial candle. Because ostentation is decried, such last-moment prescriptions are deemed "ethical."

Who writes ethical wills? Almost anybody, any man or woman who wishes to reach out to a beloved child. Such letters waned in popularity through the years, but became popular again in the late twentieth century. Their writers are always people who have something to say that concerns them deeply. This, so they believe, might be their last opportunity to embrace their dear ones, and they grasp it.

Notables and Their Wills

One is tempted to venture the opinion that, for some writers, an ethical will might be a fad worthy of emulation. A rabbi might well ask his gifted confirmation class members to pretend that they were old and to write wills that expressed their hopes for family and society; women might gather together in workshops where they would practice composing moral testaments. Many notables, people in the public eye, have written such documents in the hope that they would be published and read widely. These testaments may or may not have been contrived. The critic suspects that some were, at least in part, an attempt to seek postmortem recognition. These individuals had enjoyed national or local acclaim for decades; they were eager to remain alive, to be quoted and remembered after death, not only by their families but by thousands of others. A cleverly written will was a guarantee of immortality. This is not to question their sincerity, their devotion to the ideals they espoused. What these celebrities wrote was deemed important; during their lifetimes they had cut a wide swath, and so thousands rushed to read what they had to say.

We may assume that the Jewish notables quoted here were expressing their own views; or is it probable that, with a curtsy to the public, they were merely regurgitating the cherished beliefs of twentieth-century American Jewry? The Reverend Dr. David de Sola Pool (d. 1970) was certainly a man of distinction; for a generation he had been the religious leader of Shearith Israel, America's oldest Jewish congregation. In his spiritual testament he told the world that he was not afraid to die; life had been good to him and he was thankful to the Holy One, Blessed be He, for all of His and man's beneficences (no. 79). The rabbi wrote that he had always been ready to help both Jew and Gentile; if he had hurt anyone, he now sought their forgiveness. He hoped that he would always be remembered with a smile, and like all wise husbands he paid his devoirs to his wife, Tamar. Summing up his religious and ethical philosophy, he cited Ecclesiastes 12:13: "Revere God and keep His commandments." Pool was Orthodox and observant; although his Tamar was the daughter of a well-known scholarly rabbi of the old school, Pool in his will did not underscore the importance of Jewish ritual and the ceremonial commands. It is worth noting that Orthodox Jews—and their leaders, too—emphasized the ethical rather than the ceremonial when they assumed an apologetic stance.

This was true also of the famous humorist Sam Levenson. His stock in trade was nostalgic immigrant Jewish humor; but in 1980, when he addressed a grandchild, he made only a passing reference to the mitzvot, the "commands," the traditional Jewish way of life (no. 89). Levenson made no more than a brief bow to the Bible (Protestants often read it; Jews, rarely). We Jews, he wrote, believe in learning; we plead for compassion, love, mercy, peace, universalism. Sam never forgot that he was on stage: The American Jew wishes to be remembered for his ties to this country, he said, and will always be grateful for what it has done for the oppressed Jews of Eastern Europe. It would have been gauche on Levenson's part to suggest that the "huddled masses" had repaid their host in full measure.

The Punctilious Orthodox and Their Wills

As a rule, writers of ethical wills are in dead earnest. In fashioning their spiritual testaments, the meticulous Orthodox have adhered to a ritual that is stereotypical, prescribing what is to be done when one is terminally ill, and at the funeral and beyond. For example, when Jacob Lopez de Olivera prepared a last will and testament in 1751, he commended his soul to the God of Israel; he repented of the evil that he might have done, asked the Lord to receive his soul, and solemnly repeated the doxology: "Hear, O Israel, the Lord our God is One." With his son in mind, he wrote: "Walk in the fear of God and in the path of virtue. . . ." Many of the regulations for the dying and dead are rooted in practices that are centuries old; they are a mélange of customs, traditions, and ethical practices. For the Orthodox Jew who contemplates death, the ritual is important and sacred; frequently, no distinction is made between the ethical and the ceremonial. The stricken and the ill are sustained by the recital of prayers and the intoning of psalms. The dying person is called upon to repent and to ask for forgiveness.[1]

After death, the corpse is cleansed and dressed in a shroud. Flowers are forbidden. The eulogy is often omitted; custom requires that the ethical testator depict himself as a humble, unpretentious person. Frequently, however, the officiant announces the request of the departed that there be no funeral talk, and then proceeds to wax eloquent. The family mourns for several days; candles are lit; formal religious study is encouraged. The reading of rabbinical classics is held tantamount to prayer. The traditional prayer for the dead, the kaddish, is recited at the funeral and for the following eleven months by the immediate family. Observant Jews remind their dear ones to keep the Sabbath, the holidays, the dietary laws. Women are admonished not to neglect the prescribed monthly ablutions. The customary testamentary instruction is that the tombstone be a modest one. In his ethical will, Rabbi B. L. Levinthal of Philadelphia asked that his daughter's son-in-law, an academician, devote himself to religious studies. This young man, Dr. Samuel Belkin, subsequently became president of Yeshiva University.[2]

The writers of ethical wills nearly always asked their children to live in harmony with one another, to gather together for the death-anniversary prayers, and to give charity liberally. Charity was given before and after death, for "charity saves" both here and in the hereafter. Sometimes eighteen coins were given; eighteen in Hebrew, numerically, is *hai*, spelling life, or living. The medieval and early modern Jew was certainly aware of the

1. Barnett A. Elzas, *The Jews of South Carolina* (Philadelphia: J. B. Lippincott Company, 1905), pp. 38–39.
2. J. Riemer and N. Stampfer, *Ethical Wills* (New York: Schocken Books, 1983), pp. 140–141.

teachings of his Catholic neighbor, who believed that charity to the church could redeem a dear one from the uncertainties of purgatory. If the uncompromising Jewish traditionalist did not harp upon ethical practices, the known virtues, it was because he took it for granted that his sons, his daughters, his grandchildren would live honorably. That was fully implicit in his plea that they be God-fearing.

The Orthodox Accommodator

The Germans and East Europeans who came here and were devoted to the Orthodox way of life knew immediately that their traditions were threatened. They were desperately eager to hold on to the old, but they knew full well that the intense Orthodoxy of their European homes would have scant future here. Grudgingly, they made concessions; this is reflected in ethical wills written by those who respected the ancestral practices. There was no compromise in their ethical standards; compromises, however, emerged in the new–old way of life in the United States. These accommodators did not dwell on the details of burial. Here, under the impact of Americanization, the testators asked that there be no commotion at the graveside, no uncontrolled bursts of emotion and grief. Mourning was to be shortened. The children were enjoined: Stay Jewish, in one form or another; observe what mitzvot you can. Your good deeds will bring you recompense in the World to Come. People will remember you for them. Women were urged: Keep a kosher house; that will make Jews of your sons and daughters. Jewish education was emphasized. Never questioned was the thesis—a moot one—that if one were educated Jewishly, one would remain Jewish. In 1838, in South Carolina, a Jew who had lived with a Gentile common-law wife asked his Christian executor to make certain that his children received a Jewish education (no. 13). A Seattle Jew used his wealth to guarantee the hiring of a rabbi versed in halakah, canon law. A learned talmudist might well keep the community entrenched in Orthodoxy [3].

And money? Here was a land where wealth beckoned! *Takhlis*, material success, was not openly stressed in most moral testaments. (That is not to imply that the writers did not have their eye on the main chance.) Charity? If you can't study the Law yourself, they said, you can at least support those who do. You are only the temporary owner of the wealth that God gave you. And, incidentally, avoid speculation. (There were depressions in the United States in almost every decade.)

Confronting the American way of life, a father wrote: Don't read novels; don't be a doctor or a lawyer—these are onerous professions (no. 42). Instead,

3. Ibid., p. 143.

study Jewish history! Zionism, accepted by most East European Jews, was rarely mentioned; the American agenda overpowered it. In one respect, all the testament writers were in agreement, the Orthodox and the non-Orthodox alike: *Look after your mother!* In a formal legal instrument dated 1706, Isaac Rodriguez Marques was most insistent and detailed as he made provision for his mother (no. 1). If she wished, he wrote, she should be allowed to live with his wife or his daughter, Easter (Esther). And if she tried that and didn't like it, he directed, then she should be allowed to live alone, and a good, serviceable Negro woman should be purchased to attend her.

For the uneasy Orthodox, the stress of life in the United States demanded accommodation. Ritual suffered; the virtues were always underlined, and the belief that the Jew must have a good name. Charity was always stressed—it was to be given because it was good; in addition, it paved the way to Heaven. Before Mrs. Isaac Moses died in 1837 she gave a Gentile, an Irish woman, a gift of money. Then she wrote her will (no. 11). She wanted no stone monument. A wooden headrest and a footpost—without inscription—would suffice:

> Mourn not beyond the hour sanctified by nature and true grief. The tears which spring from the heart are the only dews the grave should be moistened with. The dead receive sufficient honor in being called to face their God.

The Poor and the Nonreligionists and Their Testaments

Poor men also wrote ethical wills. They could not hand out largesse, but they could always express their regrets. They could sententiously hand out advice. Adolph Fisch of Cleveland (d. 1904) was unhappy; he was poor, although he left nominal sums to an orphanage, a home for the aged, and a Jewish hospital. He wanted no eulogy; why encourage falsehood? Forgive me, he wrote, for I leave you so little.[4]

Hayim Greenberg (d. 1953)—Labor Zionist leader, editor of the *Jewish Frontier*, essayist, Yiddishist, Hebraist, English-language writer—asked all those he might have wronged to forgive him; he blessed all those who were dear to him and asked them to forego the eulogy. What then at the funeral? A few psalms, some verses from Job, a Russian song (one by Mikhail Lermontov).[5] David Edelstadt was a fiery, passionate Yiddish poet, a socialist, a communist, a devoted fighter for the oppressed workingman, "hated, driven, plagued, persecuted." His poem "In Battle" roused his followers: We'll

4. L. P. Gartner, *History of the Jews of Cleveland* (Cleveland: Western Reserve Historical Society, and Jewish Theological Seminary of America, 1978), pp. 175–176.

5. Riemer and Stampfer, op. cit., p. 157.

battle, we'll battle till the whole world is free. In impassioned words, he cried out in his "Testament," his ethical will (no. 35): Carry my red flag to my grave and sing of life and love, and I, entombed, will pour out my tears for everyone enslaved, Christian and Jew.

The Liberal Religionists and Their Wills

By the third quarter of the twentieth century, most American Jewish religionists had abandoned the camp of the conforming traditionalists. Conservative Jews still remained within the boundaries of the old faith, but they had long since embraced the critical scientific method. Implicitly, at least, they had rejected the Sinaitic, divine authority of the Law, and in this sense they were definitely reformists. When Dr. Israel Davidson, an eminent Conservative Jewish scholar, sat down (ca. 1939) to write a spiritual testament, he brushed aside the thought of a postmortem eulogy. I will live through my books, he said (no. 59). The Conservatives revered and enjoyed the folkways of their ancestors, but in ritualistic practices they did not hesitate to assert their autonomy. Conservatives like Rabbi Herman (Hayyim) and Esther Kieval of Albany did not find it difficult to summarize their beliefs when they addressed their children: Love Judaism, the Jewish people, the Jewish way of Life, America, and the Holy Land.[6]

Some Generalities Concerning Ethical Wills

A study of many ethical wills reveals that there is no consensus. No two testaments are really alike, because no two human beings are alike. Even so, these ethical documents can supply a thesaurus of beliefs, attitudes, convictions, misgivings, ideals. To be sure, some testators express similar views. As is to be expected, these final words to one's family tend to emphasize ethics: Observe the Ten Commandments; maintain a high standard of conduct; be good, be just; help one another; keep peace in the family; be honest, industrious, thrifty. Don't be too concerned about getting rich; wealth is not ours to keep. Give to charity, and teach your sons and daughters to give. Benevolence brings pleasure and God's blessing. *Prosperity*! Share and share alike what you inherit; by serving mankind you will best serve your family. Don't mourn for me when I am gone; we had a good life together. Judaism, religion, is a consolation. I believe in prayer; God watched over me. There is some form of life after death. Forgive me if I have offended you. Stay Jewish even if you have to change with the times. Say kaddish if you can do so with

---

6. Ibid., pp. 181–182.

good conscience. *Avoid intermarriage*! I have educated you; that should help you make your way. Continue to study and become learned. Nothing is more important than love. Respect yourself; live your own life; participate actively in both the Jewish and the general communities.

Some Specifics Concerning Ethical Wills

In the 1860s, Gottfried Wehle, a native of Prague and a member of the Brandeis–Dembitz–Felix Adler clan, expressed in his ethical will his hope that the Messiah would come and usher in a Golden Age (no. 24). Dr. Abraham Bettmann, a Cincinnati physician, had long since moved away from the Orthodoxy he had treasured as a young man in Germany, but he wished to be buried with his skullcap on his head; he wished to be dressed reverentially when he appeared before his God. Bettmann wrote his testament in 1893 (no. 38). Two years later, Dr. Isaac M. Rosenthal of Fort Wayne made an impromptu recording on a newfangled machine, a sort of gramophone (no. 41). (It was only in 1877 that Emil Berliner, a German immigrant, had invented the first usable microphone.) This is a voice from the unknown beyond, Dr. Rosenthal said in the recording, which was heard posthumously by his family. I am now united with my wife, and this is happiness beyond human comprehension. We who are gone will love you and protect you.

It was in the same decade—a sad one for Henry S. Louchheim, heartbroken because of his losses in the depression years—that Louchheim wrote to his dear ones: Be ready and willing at any time to share your last dollar with your brother. A generation later, a son, Jerome, who had repaired the family's fortunes, told his children: A good American is a religious one (no. 39). The Louchheims were Philadelphians; a fellow Jew from the same city, Leon Dalsimer, assured his grieving descendants that those who live in the hearts of their loved ones never die (no. 56).

Years later, in 1942, Sol Blank, a small-town Illinois merchant, wrote that he wanted to stay alive to do some good. He had two sons; one was teaching at Harvard, the other at the Hebrew Union College. Sol had been reared in a pious Bavarian home; in the United States he had found employment at Bloomingdale's Department Store in New York City, where he was put to work on the Sabbath, breaking up wooden boxes; he shed bitter tears (no. 61). An old man named Harold instructed his dear ones: Bury me so that I will face my wife.[7] Jennie Stein Berman addressed her children in 1956: See that Sam, my bachelor brother, has a place to sleep and a bite to eat.[8] Three generations of Blumenthals wrote and read ethical wills: The best pillow is a

7. Ibid., pp. 171–172.
8. Ibid., p. 169.

clear conscience, said one Blumenthal will. Keep on loving me in memory as I loved you in life.[9]

In 1963, William Lewis Abromowitz assured his wife and four children that a good Jew was a better human being. Say kaddish for me, he wrote; it will echo in your heart. Turning to his daughters he warned them: No dalliance![10] I have tried to be a good father, wrote Allen Hofrichter in the 1970s, "no sacrifice on my part was too great."[11] Jacob (Jack) J. Weinstein, a Chicago Reform rabbi, reminded his children, who had lived through the turbulent 1960s: There is a usable Jewish past; continuity in tradition is a family resource (no. 84).

9. Ibid., pp. 163–166.
10. Ibid., pp. 187–189.
11. Ibid., pp. 167–168.

Chapter Five

Summary of the American Jewish Ethical Stance, 1706–1980s

Introduction

The various types of ethically slanted documents in the archives of American Jewish historians are a challenge to them. These documents serve as an unusual source for the historian who is eager to determine who is a Jew and what is Judaism. In these very personal papers, where emotions, tears, yearning, love, and hope are so intense, the student of the individual psyche is afforded an opportunity to evaluate Jews as they really were. True, some of the wills of notables read as though they had been written by men who were playing to the gallery, but these wills, too, are revealing, particularly if the perceptive and critical reader is ready to take some discount. On a purely historical level, all wills are important; the East European father who wrote to his children reflected the pathos—and the pathology—of the world around him, a world of bigotry, poverty, and misery. The Russian and Polish centuries were, in *some* respects, among the most inglorious in all Jewish history.

What the Documents Do Not Tell Us

These testaments do not place much emphasis on *lernen* —studying the Talmud, rabbinic literature, the codes. The testators knew, intuitively, that there was little future for talmudists in America's Gilded and post-Gilded decades. Careers were to be made by writing in English, not in the dialectics of the Aramaic rabbinic texts. Very little was said about anti-Jewish prejudice, despite the fact that there were few, if any, Jews who had been spared harassment by Gentiles. Anti-Christian statements were exceedingly rare; pettiness and bigotry were brushed aside. Jews in the United States knew that no land offered them more security. Leisure, play? There was no talk of such things when life and death were the subjects of discourse. Sex? Victorianism was still alive generations after England's great queen had departed this earth. References to "sex" were guarded: *Lewd women!* —Stay away from them! Admonitions of this type were not infrequent. In Jewish thinking, universalism was in the ascendant, although it is probable that the Holocaust moved many twentieth-century Jews to the right. Humanism had been jolted. The murder of millions by the Germans and the subsequent rise of the State of Israel stimulated Jewish nationalism and ethnicism. Even some Reform Jews began to wear skullcaps, to sway in prayer, to sing Israeli songs; bar mitzvah tended to displace Reform confirmation. Jews knew, however, that the horror of the Holocaust would fade away; that the horror would be forgotten, if not forgiven. Pride in being a member of the Chosen People? This vantage was not flaunted. No Jew thumped his chest: no Jew proclaimed, in these writings, *I am one of God's elect!* But the constant reiteration of "Be Jewish" is evidence that "Jewish is beautiful." We *are* a superior people! The testators did not have to be convinced on that score.

In the ethical wills and similar statements, the writers made no effort to preach a gospel of financial success. There is not much smugness, not much self-congratulatory pride. The world of dollars and cents has little place in these documents, which often touch on eternity itself. The authors had very probably prepared legal instruments in which they disposed of their possessions. Men and women were at their best when writing an ethical letter: The mundane was suppressed; the world of power and money was glossed over. No one said baldly that wealth was an end in itself. Even in the Gilded Age, people were hesitant to brag of their achievements. Such boasting would have been deemed inappropriate, even vulgar. No one cast himself in the role of a Horatio Alger hero, a successful Ragged Dick.

Writers who dealt with morals, with good conduct, lived in two worlds, the explicit and the implicit. In the explicit world, morals were lauded; in the implicit world, the ethos of the political, the economic, the cultural, the daily give-and-take was neatly and modestly sequestered in other compartments. In farewell letters, the material things—which really dominated the writers' lives—were for the moment pushed aside. Actually, most Jews who had any possessions were very comfortable in bourgeois America. Explicitly, however, they unhesitatingly subscribed to the prophetic teachings, to the Ten Commandments, to the social demands of the biblical moralists: Be honest and upright; pay your hired hands promptly; be just to the stranger in your midst. All of this was expressed or taken for granted when they addressed the family in a final message. There are few overt references to *takhlis* in this moralistic literature, but let there be no question: It was almost always in the back of the mind; poverty was not held to be a virtue in Judaism, except perhaps in the Psalms. All Jews, one may venture to say, would applaud Joseph B. Greenhut when he told his dear ones: I tried to be a good provider (no. 44). The desire to help their children in a worldly sense crops out in gnomic asides: Associate only with good people; be thrifty; don't drink; work hard; be good; be courteous; write home to those who love you and can help you. Many writers avoided the outright statement, but they made their point: God will reward you if you live the good life.

It bears repetition: not many writers of ethical letters acknowledged the importance of riches, possessions, success, *takhlis* – although a few did, quite explicitly. Most rabbis, fully aware of the material leanings of their congregants, were hesitant to reproach them. Most congregational boards would tolerate no real criticism of the economic system. When Gentile notables wanted to flatter their Jewish audiences, they extolled their virtues in the countinghouse: The Jew was honorable in his dealings and prompt in his payments.[1] If Simon Wiess of Wiess's Bluff, Texas, wrote an ethical letter to his sons, it is apparently not extant. Addressing them in the 1860s, he first promised that their mother and he would pray for their happiness and welfare (no. 26). He then advised them, in considerable detail, on how to conduct themselves in business. This is one of the few letters in which a father told his boys how to get ahead: no liquor, no credit, no loafers in the store!

In 1877, Joseph Seligman was excluded from the Grand Union Hotel in Saratoga: Jews were not wanted, he was told. American Jewry was furious. The attack on Seligman was an attack on them. It was a rejection of a rich, respected, patriotic banker. They were shocked that, in an age when success was God's most coveted accolade, wealth brought no security or respect.

In 1910, Isidor Blum published *The Jews of Baltimore*,[2] in which he included about eighty biographies of the city's prominent Jewish businessmen and professionals. A substantial number were asked to account for their success in life. They listed the principles that had moved them as they struggled for affluence. When they gave no answer, the editor himself attempted to assay the qualities that distinguished these solid citizens. Thus the book provides a good sampling of the "virtues" that help us evaluate the factors making for success. The road to *takhlis* can be only inferred from formal ethical avowals; but in these biographies, the characteristics that underlie their subjects' success are explicit: Love your work, master your problems, attend to business, adapt yourself to your needs. Be patient and persevering; be honest, courageous, pertinacious; work hard, be energetic, enthusiastic, and ambi-

1. *The Occident* 3:524.
2. Baltimore, Historical Review Publishing Co., pp. 149ff.

tious; don't play too much; let your word be your bond; be frugal; hustle constantly. Others—and this is interesting—ascribed their success to their work in the local Jewish charities. They said that they had tried to be kind to their fellowman, that they had preached the Golden Rule. Only a paltry few ascribed their success to their faith in God, to religion, to piety, to ritual observance. Still, it is very probable that most, if not all, of the eighty Baltimoreans surveyed were members of synagogues. Baltimore was a very Jewish, a very religious city. It would seem, however, judging by the data in Blum's book as well as in many of the ethical documents, that religion (ethics) and business were planets revolving in separate solar systems. Is it possible to live harmoniously and effectively in two different worlds? What credence can we give the businessmen who wrote ethical wills and guides to moral conduct? Obviously many of them believed that one could be—at the same time—completely ethical and completely aggressive in trade; they were aware of no inherent contradiction.

Is There an American Jewish Ethical System?

The Orthodox, the Non-Orthodox, the Secularist

When we study the genre of American Jewish ethical literature, we are puzzled by these indications that the ethical and the business worlds have been so disparate, so compartmentalized. There is yet another puzzle that confronts us: Is there an ethical system to which American Jewry as a whole has made obeisance? When we turn to the Orthodox, the answer is simple, clear: There is but one Law. God gave it to Moses on Sinai's mount. Moses and the rabbis, vicegerents of God, interpreted it and made it available for all time to come. This is the Oral Law, divine in origin. Through interpretation by qualified decisors, every contingency in life is provided for, no matter how minute and apparently inconsequential. For instance: Don't wear a garment made of cloth woven from two kinds of material, such as wool and linen (Leviticus 19:19, Deuteronomy 22:11). All the prescriptions, the mitzvot, codified by the rabbis must be observed by every Jewish man, woman, and child. God has so ordained. If you conform to the mitzvot—avoiding evil and pursuing virtue—you will be a good Jew and a good human being. Orthodoxy has a perfect, complete ethical system.

On the other hand, it would seem that all non-Orthodox Jewish religionists and secularists have varied beliefs and sanctions, although they share with the Orthodox many concepts of the good and the true. As we have just noted, God, for the Orthodox Jew, is the source of all good. The non-Orthodox religionists, the Reformers and the Conservatives, may well look to divinity for their ethical sanctions, while actually or implicitly discounting the authority of the God-given Law, in whole or in part. In 1895, the members of the (Reform) Central Conference of American Rabbis rejected the authority of the traditional canon law. The Conservatives have never formally repudiated the concept that Rabbinic Law is binding, but they have done so de facto through a policy of salutary neglect. All non-Orthodox Jews, both religionists and secularists, have been indoctrinated by their parents, secular educational institutions, the social-cultural environment, and fortuitous circumstance. A variety of ethical influences have impinged upon them and have been assimilated, but the non-Orthodox have, finally, no single authoritative ethical system.

Golden Threads: Prime Concerns in the American Jewish Ethical Documents under Study

There is diversity in the documents collected in this volume. They reflect the differences in the individuals who penned them, yet they have much in common. Business? They generally expressed the belief, as we have said, that for the nonce there are things more important than "bread to eat and a garment to wear." In the ethical wills, for example, we deal with people in their last reaching out; they are pouring out their hearts as they say an affectionate goodbye. They are frightened men and women striving for immortality through their children. *Don't forget me*, they beg them. I desperately want to be remembered. Through you I remain alive. Say kaddish for me if you can do so in good conscience; that will rescue me from oblivion. (Even the Reformers believed in kaddish.) They say also, *I am an ethical somebody* ; therefore, I am really modest, even humble. Let my funeral and burial rites be simple; I want a plain casket, no eulogy, no excessive mourning. I plead with you; I am your parent; read and remember what I am telling you now; treasure my values. Be a Jew, my kind of Jew. Parents often expressed a well-founded fear that their children would go their own way, Jewishly. Rarely does it appear that a son or daughter was living the life the parent had prescribed. Too often the traditional practices were neglected. A new way of life had developed in the United States, and even the old Orthodoxy was modified. It was not, it could not be, the Judaism of the Bavarian *Dorf* or the Polish *shtetl*.

And, especially as evinced in the letters these men and women wrote, there is no end to the love between them. The parents loved their children; the children loved their parents. Fathers and mothers were desperately anxious to make sure that the family would stay together. This theme recurs again and again. It must be borne in mind that many of the German and East European Jews in the nineteenth-century United States were immigrants, foreigners, uneasy men and women concerned about the quality of family life on these shores. Back home the German Jews had suffered persecution and prejudice; the German people had merely tolerated them, at best. The East Europeans were generally an impoverished lot; their Gentile rulers had abused them. To a large degree all these émigrés were insecure; their American-born children grew up uneasy—they were Jewish! Under these circumstances, unity was imperative. There was also some ongoing contact with parents and grandparents who had not emigrated. The East European Papa who wrote to his family in the United States would have appreciated help, money. Jewish children, sons and daughters of immigrants, grew up in homes filled with problems, with unhappiness. Friction among siblings was very common, and it disturbed the parents. Don't quarrel, they would implore. Please help one another. Was the idyllic Jewish home a myth? It is evident that many families experienced internal hostility and enmity; there is also ample evidence that others knew love and devotion.

Despite the social and ethnic differences among them, Jews had much in common in matters ethical. The traditionalists said: Be good, as God demands. Their moral code was enriched by particularism, folkways, ethnicism, ritual ceremony. But they believed that mankind does not live by ethics alone. The nontraditionalists said: Be good, as religion, rationalism, and the social mores demand. In general, the trend among all Jewish groups, Orthodox and non-Orthodox, was away from strict ritualistic observance; moral conduct was emphasized, at least verbally. All nontraditionalists were, of course, subject to some religious and Judaic influences; the Jewish background to which they were exposed was part of their very being, and a Jewish home and Jewish friends left their impress. Family folkways, the parental language, and a dash of ethnicism colored their lives. One may also venture, cautiously, to suggest—and this applies to practically all the writers—that religion was not an end in itself among Jews as it was in the salvationist mystique of the Christians. For many Jews, religion was a social instrumentality intended to preserve and further the family, the group, and their specific traditions. Theirs was a religion that changed from generation to generation; the basic social teachings, however, remained constant. These teachings were all of biblical origin; they embraced all living things, even the animals in the fields and the beasts in the barns. Were they unique? These universal rules of morality to which Jews paid homage were no different from those espoused by Christians. (Indeed, some Jewish ethical letters and testaments could well have been written by Gentiles.) Because Jews shared so many of the ideals held by their Christian fellow Americans, they found it relatively easy to identify spiritually with them. This pleased them; they wanted to be accepted.

Part II, which follows, contains in chronological order many documents that embody the essence of American Jewish ethical belief. It is my hope that they will help to enrich the reader's understanding of this valuable heritage.

II

The Documents

1

Isaac Rodriguez Marques

Be Dutifull to My Deare Mother

Isaac Rodriguez Marques Signs His Will

October 17, 1706

Isaac Rodriguez Marques, a Danish-born Sephardi, was a highly successful New York merchant-shipper. Already resident in the city in 1695, he became a freeman in 1697, wrote his will in 1706, and was dead less than a year later. As the following excerpts from his testament indicate, he was concerned with the welfare of his mother.

In the Name of God Amen the seaventeenth day of October in the fifth year of his majesties reigne Anno Domino one thousand seven hundred and six, I Isaac Roderecus Marques of the citty of New Yorke merchant, being of perfect remembrance and bound on a voyage to Jaimca in the West Indies, and considering the certainty of death and the uncertaine time of the coming of the same, do make this my last will and testament in manner and forme following, that is to say:

First I doe bequeath my soul to God Almighty and my body to the earth to be decently buryed, and as for the disposall of my worldly estate it is as followeth, that is to say:

First I do desire that all such just debts, as I doe owe, shall be honestly paid in convenient time after my decease.

Item it is my will and minde that my deare mother, Rachell Marques, be maintained out of my estate and live with my wife or my daughter dureing her naturall life, but if she cannot agree with them or like to live by her self that then she shall receive out of my estate, before division be made, the sume of fifty pounds current money of New Yorke, and a god servicable negro woman shall alsoe be purchased for her out of my s'd estate to attend her during her naturall life which at her decease shall fall to my son and daughter, the vallue thereof to be equally divided betwixt them, and I doe give hereby a strict charge to my wife and children be dutifull to my said deare mother.

Item I give and bequeath to my daughter Easter [Esther] fifty pounds to buy her a jewell at her age of eighteen yeares or marreage with her mothers consent.

The rest of my estate, reall and personall, I give devise and bequeath as followeth, that is to say, one third parte thereof to my deare and loving wife, Rachell Marques, to have and to. . . hold the same to her, her heires, and assignes for ever; one other third part thereof to my son, Jacob Marques, to him his heires and assigns for ever, the remainding third part thereof to my loving daughter Easter Marques, her heires and assignes for ever. . . .

Isaac R'cs Marquiz

2

Abigail Franks

I Can't Help Condemning the Many Supersti[ti]ons Wee Are Clog'd With

Abigail of New York Reaches Out to a Son Overseas

1733–1748

In 1712, Abigail (Bilhah) Franks (1696–1756) married Jacob Franks (1688–1769), who had but recently come to New York City. Franks was the son of a German family headquartered in London, where its members engaged in international trade. Once in the United States, Franks, a significant merchant, broker, and army purveyor, worked closely with his English brothers as their North American correspondent. His wife Abigail was the daughter of Moses Levy, one of New York's distinguished merchants. Their oldest child, Naphtali, born in 1715, was sent by his parents to London while still a teenager to work closely with his uncles. A number of his mother's letters to him have been preserved. They are important historically, for they permit us to peer into the very soul of an able and intelligent woman. Fortunately for us, she loved to pontificate. Thus we have the privilege of knowing how she felt about the amenities, religious values, the dietary laws, and the tragedy of death. Her moral pronouncements are often arresting.

The animal symbol of the biblical patriarch Naphtali is a deer, a hart. Abigail, a clever woman, dubbed her beloved son Heartsey.

The spelling in these letters, as in all of the documents, has not been altered, but the punctuation, the paragraphing, and the capitalization have been modernized. All but one of Mrs. Frank's letters that are excerpted here were sent from Manhattan. The one exception was written in Flatbush, where she had fled upon discovering that her daughter had married out of the faith.

July 9, 1733

. . . I have soe offten recommended you to be wary in yr conduct that I will not again make a repetion. But this I must recom[men]d to you not to be soe free in yr discourse of religeon and be more circumspect in the observence of some things especially yr morning dev[otio]ns. For tho' a person may think freely and judge for themselves they ought not to be to free of speach nor to make a jest of wath ye multitude in a society think is of the last consequence. And as you observed to me some time agoe you wondered any one could take amiss if his neighbour did not goe the same road. Pray why are you soe intent by your disputes to think anyone will follow you. It shows in one of your age a self-opinion which quality I would have you carfuly avoid for it will grow opon you with time if not nipt in the bud. You wrote me some time agoe you was asked at my brother Ashers to a fish dinner but you did not goe. I desire you will never eat anything with him unless it be bread & butter nor noe where else where there is the least doubt of things not done after our strict Judiacall method. For wathever my thoughts may be concerning some fables, this [kashrut] and some other foundementalls, I look opon the observence conscientioussly and therefore with my blessing I strictly injoyn it to your care.

June 5, 1737

Dear Heartsey:

I have three of your letters answered. The first of them brought us the melancholly acco't of the death of that worthy and good man Mr. Is[aac]. Franks [his father's brother, d. 1736] wich truly was a very great shock, especialy to your father who for a long while had bin very uneasy on acc't of his indiposision, and, as he very justly fear'd, you had not given him a true information how ill he was. Sam. Myers brought a letter, wich Uncle Asher's [Levy] had inclosed to him, and befor he opened it tould him the sorrowfull contents. Y'r father seemed imovable for some time. At last he broke out in a flood of tears. He was very melancholly for a long time, but now begins to be more setled.

For my part when I find a person has soe great a cause for greife I can say but little by way of releife, knowing nature has its call opon these occassions and nothing but time and reasson to aswage the dolor. You tell me I may geuss the concern you laboured under at the loss of soe tender a parent [his future father-in-law] and friend. I truly sampathize with you, but under that great misfourtune you had the satisfaction of imploying y'r indefatigable endeavours in discharg'g your last dutys to him in such a manner as procoured you the commendations of all his freinds. And I hope you still make it your endeavour in a strickt preseverance of regard and duty to his remains, for that is all wee have left to show our gratitude to the memory of soe kind a benefactor. He was but a very young man, "but in the grave there is noe inquissision wether a man be ten, twenty, or a hundred years ould." All the difference after deth is a man's works here on earth, for that never dyes, and one that has left soe great and good a name may be said to have lived full of days and dyed in a good ould age.

I hope soe great an example of worth may be an emulation to all those that have the happyness to be his relations, to follow his steps in dischargeing theire duty to God an man in the severall stages of life it shall please the All mighty to set them in. . . .

October the 17th, 1739

. . . Pray give my humble service to Mr. Pecheco [B. M. Pacheco, a New York and London merchant] and thank him for the pres[en]t of the book he sent me. Its very entertaining to me for I confess it to be agreeable to my sentiments in regard to our religeon. Whoever wrote it I am sure was noe Jew for he thought too reasonable. . . . I must own I cant help condemning the many supersti[ti]ons wee are clog'd with & heartly wish a Calvin or Luther would rise amongst us. I answer for my self; I would be the first of there followers for I dont think religeon consist in idle cerimonies & works of supperoregations, wich if they send people to heaven wee & the papist have the greatest title too. . . .

Flat bush, June 7th, 1743

. . . I am now retired from town and would from my self (if it were possiable to have some peace of mind) from the severe affliction I am under on the conduct of that unhappy girle [her daughter Phila]. Good God, wath a shock it was when they acquainted me she had left the house and had bin married six months. I can hardly hold my pen whilst I am a writting it. Itt's wath I never could have imagined, especialy affter wath I heard her soe often say, that noe consideration in life should ever induce her to disoblige such good parents.

I had heard the report of her goeing to be married to Oliver Delancey, but as such reports had often bin off either of your sisters [Phila and Richa], I gave noe heed to it further than a generall caution of her conduct wich has allways bin unblemish'd, and is soe still in the eye of the Christians whoe allow she had disobliged us but has in noe way bin dishonorable, being married to a man of worth and charector.

My spirits was for some time soe depresst that it was a pain to me to speak or see any one. I have over come it soe far as not to make my concern soe conspicuous but I shall never have that serenity nor peace within I have soe happyly had hittherto. My house has bin my prison ever since. I had not heart enough to goe near the street door. Its a pain to me to think off goeing again to town and if your father's buissness would permit him to live out of it I never would goe near it again. I wish it was in my power to leave this part of the world; I would come away in the first man of war that went to London.

Oliver has sent many times to beg leave to see me, but I never would tho' now he sent word that he will come here [to Flatbush]. I dread seeing him and how to avoid I know noe way, neither if he comes can I use him rudly. I may make him some reproaches but I know my self soe well that I shall at last be civill, tho' I never will give him leave to come to my house in town, and as for his wife, I am determined I never will see nor lett none of the family goe near her.

He intends to write to you and my brother Isaac [Levy] to endeavour a reconciliation. I would have you answer his letter, if you don't hers, for I must be soe ingenious to conffess nature is very strong and it would give me a great concern if she should live unhappy, tho' its a concern she does not meritt. . . .

Aprill 29th, 1748

As to news I never dable in it. The situation of America with relation to ye war is much as it was. I should be rejoyce'd to see Isaiah's prophecy fulfilld that all warlike instruments where converted to implements of husbandry [Isaiah 2:4].

3

Shinah Simon Schuyler and Simon Gratz

Shinah S. Schuyler: I Would Advise You Not to Be Too Percipitate

December 17, 1791

Simon Gratz: Make It Your Constant Duty and Study to Please

August 5, 1793

Aunt Shinah and Brother Simon Offer Marital Advice

The notable trader Joseph Simon of Lancaster, Pennsylvania, had a large family. Shinah, one of his daughters, married Dr. Nicholas Schuyler of Troy, New York. Although she became a Christian when she married out of the faith, Shinah appears to have been happy. After an initial period of paternal rejection, both she and her husband maintained good relations with the Simons. Shinah's sister Miriam married Michael Gratz, the Philadelphia merchant. Two of the Gratz children, Richea and Frances, became favorites of their childless Aunt Shinah. In the first letter that follows, Aunt Shinah, writing probably from Troy or Lansingburgh, expressed herself on the selection of a husband.

When in 1791 Aunt Shinah Simon Schuyler wrote to her nieces Richea, 17, and Frances, 20, she told them to wait a few years before marrying. Richea took her suggestion to heart. Two years later she was engaged to Samuel Hays, of a well-known family active in the New York synagogue. One of the first things that Richea did was to write the good news to an older brother, Simon (Simmy), then living in Lancaster, where in all likelihood he worked for Grandpa Simon. Simmy, out of the fullness of his wisdom and experience—he was all of 20 years of age—wrote 19-year-old Richea a pompous letter telling her how she was to conduct herself as a matron. As the oldest son in a family of nine younger siblings, he took himself very seriously. Obviously the ideal woman he conjured up was then the commonly accepted concept of what a wife should be. Apparently, however, he failed to find her in his own Jewish circle, for he, like his Aunt Shinah, was to marry out of the faith.

December 17th, 1791

Miss Richea Gratz,
Lancaster.

I received my dear Richea's two aggreeable letters with inexperssable pleasure. . . .

My dear Richea, I sincerly thank [you] for all the news. Why, my dear, your information was quite from the matrimonal budget.

And when, pray, do you enter the list of matrimony? Seriously, my love, I must be your confident; however, my dear Fanny [Frances] must enter her claim first. You have my most cordial prayers for both your happiness whenever that happy period arrives. I would advise you not to be too percipitate, unless an extraordinary and worthy man solicits that honor, and your heart can accompany the gift. Never, my lovely girls (for I address you both), alter your situation but by uniting your selves to a worthy man and one you can love and esteem. Should even adversity be your lot their will be a consolation experienced which your marrying for wealth will never yeild you, and compleat your misery with an undeserving man. Let esteem for virtueous principles be the first basis for love, and then your happiness will be perminant. That both of you, my dear girls, may marry agreeable to your parents, and each have a worthy husband, I sincerely wish, tho' I would still advise you to continue single. Your both young, and two or three years more will be sufficent for to think of altering your situation.

I am in exceeding good health and spirits; indeed, few have less reason to complain. I have a very dear, good husband. I think few, very few, can say they live happier, and, thank God, he's exceedingly hearty and has constant employ in either writing or visiting his patience and chatting to his little wife, for, you know, I will have some attention paid to me. . . .

Your affectionate friend and aunt,
Shinah Schuyler

Lancaster, August 5th, 1793

Miss Richea Gratz,
Philadelphia.

The letter of the 1st instant from my dear sister I now seat myself to acknowledge. Its contents I duly note. The subject it treats on is the most interesting nature, and I hope my dear sister gave it the consideration due.

You are now about to enter into a state wherein I hope and pray you may experiance nothing to give you pain but, on the contrary, enjoy perfect happiness and tranquility. But, my dear, you must remember that to ensure yourself and to the man you love a lasting continuance of happiness, you must ever make it your constant duty and study to please. In short, copy our amiable and virtuous mother; act as she does, and you will ensure to yourself and to all about you contentment. But as a preliminary to all happiness, lett a due sence of relegion, and a proper attention to the precepts and commands of the great God always actuat you, and place your sole confidence and trust in him. . . .

I shall write to you again shortly, but in the intrem, beleive me to be, with constant prayers of your happiness,

Your ever affectionate brother and well wisher,
Simon Gratz

Hyman [their brother] desires his love to you and can't write this week.

4

Moses Hayyim Levy

Don't Forget Your Brothers and Your Sisters

Young Aaron Levy Receives Spiritual Food for the Road

October 15, 1795

In October 1795, Moses Hayyim Levy of Amsterdam wrote an ethical letter that he gave to his son Aaron (1774–1852) who was about to leave for America—specifically, for Philadelphia, which was then the metropolis of North America. The letter was in the form of a Hebrew acrostic poem. Young Aaron was able to understand it; something of a Hebraist, he owned a modest Hebrew library, which included a volume of the Shulhan Aruch, *the standard legal code. Levy landed in the autumn of 1795 and in the course of time was well integrated into the local Jewish religious community.*

The letter that Aaron received from his father was typical of such missives in that it called upon him to live the Jewish life, to cherish the ideals of his faith, and to do what he could to help those left behind. After arriving in the New World, Aaron turned to his uncle, Aaron Levy, Sr., a well-established land agent and the founder in 1786 of the town of Aaronsburgh in Pennsylvania.

---

2 Marheshvan, 5556, shorter reckoning (Oct. 15, 1795)

This is the will which I, your humble father, Moses Hayyim, the son of the honorable Aaron of blessed memory, give to my son Aaron, the son of Moses Hayyim:

You shall fear the Lord and cleave to Him
In order that you may prosper on the way.

Serve the Lord with your heart
  In order that He may protect your soul completely.
Your strength lies in that you will throttle the evil within you;
  And the Lord He will help you.
Open your doors to the poor
  In order that God, blessed be He, may enrich you.
Lift up your eyes unto the Lord
  And He will be with you wherever you go.
Observe the Sabbath
  In order that you may prosper in all that you undertake.
By all means remember the Lord your God
  And He will give you length of days.
Practice love and truth throughout your life
  And the Lord will be gracious unto you.
Good shall you be in all that you do
  In order that He may protect you wherever you go.
May the impulse to do good possess you in all your thoughts;
  Then God will watch over you in all your trials.
Honor your father with all your strength
  In order that the Lord may open up his treasures and be generous unto you.
Don't forget your brothers and your sisters;
  They are orphaned without a mother.
Give money to the poor
  In order that God, blessed be He, may favor you in all that you do.
Direct your eyes to God continually;
  And He will watch over you in all your goings and comings.
Turn aside from evil and do good;
  Then God will forgive you for all your sins. . . .
Bestow charity on all those who are close to you
  Because they have helped rear you since childhood.
Don't forget to say kaddish after your father has died. . . .
Cleave closely to a good companion
  And he will always be nigh to advise you.
Peace be unto you, and may you reach your uncle in a happy state,
  For he will always look after you.
Be perfect with the Lord your God in all your thinking
  So that He may favor you.

May He bless you in all that you do, prosper you, and protect you from every misadventure, every adversary, every evil eye, all misfortunes, all sicknesses and diseases, in order that your days may be long. Amen. Selah.

This letter your father has given to you in order that you may not forget what I have written to you today, the 2d of Marheshvan, 5556. You are leaving me; let it be a reminder that you should serve the Lord your God with all your heart, with all your soul, and with all your might. Do not forget your brothers and your sisters and all who are associated with you. . . . They were with you in all your troubles ever since your mother died, and they helped rear you unto this day. May you prosper in all the works of your hand and achieve length of days.

5

Jacob Mordecai

Examine Your Conduct

Jacob Mordecai, The Pedagogue, Writes to Daughter Rachel, Age 8

August 13, 1797

In August of 1797, Jacob Mordecai (1762–1838) of Warrenton, North Carolina, sat down and wrote a letter to his daughter Rachel who was then 8 years old. She and her two younger sisters were living in Richmond with relatives; her mother had died and her father found it difficult to rear his younger children himself. Jacob was nearly always the pedagogue. He would later open an academy for girls in Warrenton, which explains his writing such a ponderous, didactic note to this little girl telling her how to behave, what to do, what to say. She was to be courteous, he advised, even to the domestic, a Negro slave. Despite his frequent misspellings, the American-born Mordecai was a cultured man who knew Hebrew and read widely. If he was a pedagogue, how could he write such heavy polysyllabic letters to his Rachel? A total waste? In Russia and in Galicia, it was not unusual to start boys of 7 or 8 reading the Hebrew–Aramaic Talmud. What is more, they understood the meaning of this abstruse legal code! Rachel grew up to be an intellectual. Thus it appears that Papa Mordecai, when he donned his hat as a pedant, could write a letter fit for a child.

Warrenton, August 13th, 1797

My dear Rachel must not suppose from my long silence that I have been unmindful of the promise I made to acknowledge the letter she delivered me in Richmond.

I have received it with pleasure. It assures me of your affection and convinces me of your improvement. The former I will always endeavor to preserve, for you are very dear to me; and I am certain you will merit mine, by attending to the advise I may occasionally give, and strictly observing that which you frequently receive from your dear aunt and uncle.

Inattention to the council of our friends who are zealous to promote our welfare is at all times and in every situation inexcusable. It is a species of ingratitude that will tend to alienate their affections, for when their well meant endeavors to form the mind, cultivate the manners, and improve the person are either obstinately opposed or carelessly attended to, their attempts ceasing to be a pleasure, disgust ensues, and we become almost indifferent to the welfare of any one capable of making an unkind, improper, and painful return for our good intentions.

Those general observations will, I trust, have your attention. Examine your conduct. If they apply, correct your errors. The goodness of your heart will ensure you success and secure the esteem of your kind patrons. Be obedient to their councils. Impress them upon your mind. Persevere in attempts to improve your personal carriage, so justly the object of animadversion. Difficulties always decrease when we encounter them with firmness, and what at first view appears very difficult, soon becomes familiar, easy, and agreeable.

Cultivate the affections of your sister. Be kindly attentive to that dear blessed infant, my Caroline, and whilst under one roof, daily attend to my former request. Let politeness distinguish your conduct to every one. Nothing excuses rudeness, even to a domestic.

Your brothers are well and send a great deal of love to you, their sisters, and friends. They have not time to write by this opportunity which leaves town immediately. I send you a book; it is well spoken of. Peruse it with attention; give me your opinion. Read it for Ellen, to whom my love, which I would confirm with many kisses. . . .

My affectionate regards to grand ma, aunts, uncles, etc. God bless you, my dear Rachel. In haste, I am

Your,
J. Mordecai

6

Benjamin Nones

I am Accused of Being a *Jew*

Benjamin Nones Answers a Bigot

August 11, 1800

During the bitterly contested presidential election of 1800, from which Thomas Jefferson emerged victorious, the editor of the conservative Federalist newspaper, the Gazette of the United States & Daily Advertiser, *published an article belaboring Benjamin Nones, a Revolutionary War veteran. Nones, who was reproached in that article as a Jew, a political liberal, and a poor man, answered the attack in a liberal democratic newspaper, the* Philadelphia Aurora. *In the following excerpt, Nones defends himself as a Jew.*

I am accused of being a *Jew*. I *am a Jew*. I glory in belonging to that persuasion, which even its opponents, whether Christian or Mahomedan, allow to be of divine origin—of that persuasion on which Christianity itself was originally founded, and must ultimately rest—which has preserved its faith secure and undefiled, for near three thousand years—whose votaries have never murdered each other in religious wars, or cherished the theological hatred so general, so unextinguishable among those who revile them. A persuasion whose patient followers have endured for ages the pious cruelties of pagans, and of Christians, and perservered in the unoffending practice of their rites and ceremonies, amidst poverties and privations, amidst pains, penalties, confiscations, banishments, tortures, and deaths, beyond the example of any other sect, which the page of history has hitherto recorded.

To be of such a persuasion, is to me no disgrace; though I well understand the inhuman language of bigotted contempt, in which your reporter by attempting to make me ridiculous, as a Jew, has made himself detestable, whatever religious persuasion may be dishonored by his adherence.

But I am a Jew. I am so—and so were Abraham, and Isaac, and Moses and the prophets and so too were Christ and his apostles. I feel no disgrace in ranking with such society, however it may be subject to the illiberal buffoonery of such men as your correspondents.

7

Mordecai Sheftall

The Indigent Never in Vain from Him Sought Charity

A Son Writes His Father's Obituary

January 1809

The Sheftall clan was one of the pioneer families of the United States. The Sheftalls were Germans who came to Savannah in July of 1733, just a few months after James Oglethorpe cast anchor in the Savannah River, bringing with him Georgia's first white settlers. Levi Sheftall, American-born, was a butcher, tanner, merchant, and rancher. The old Georgia records tell that his cattle brand was the L◇S, and undoubtedly he combined his cattle business with that of a butcher. At times he was in partnership with his older brother Mordecai, the outstanding leader of the Savannah Jewish community and one of the most prominent Georgia Whigs in the early days of the Revolution. Levi himself was a tireless worker, a hustler who made and lost two or three fortunes before death carried him off in 1809. During the Revolutionary War, as we know from a memoir that he left for his children, he was in the thick of battle and survived many harrowing experiences: "Several guns . . . cocked, ready to fire at my breast." Yet despite his patriotic services to the new government and his labors as an army supply officer, he was falsely accused by one of his personal enemies and punished as a Tory.

One of his sons—his name was also Mordecai (1783–1856)—wrote a necrology of the father. This beautiful, if florid, tribute bears witness to the son's affection and at the same time records the cherished moral values that he saw reflected in the life of a beloved parent.

Died at Savannah, in the State of Georgia, my venerable father, Levi Sheftall, Esquire, "United States agent" and "Agent for Fortifications in the

State of Georgia." He was born on the 12 day of December, in the year 1739, and departed this life in the morning of the 26 day of January, 1809, age sixty nine years, one month and fourteen days. He had been confined to his bed for upwards of ten days with a severe cold. The day prior to his decease, he was so far recovered of his then late indisposition that he sat up and mentioned to his family that it was his intention to "go down stairs." He went to bed in good spirits and passed several jests while in bed. It is the opinion of my sister Judith that he must have died about the hour of 4 o'clock in the morning, as she heard him snore and draw his breath with unusual difficulty about that time. Her opinion is supported by that of the physician, Doct'r Borguin [Henry Bourquin] who, as soon as he was discovered to lie lifeless, was called in. He was interred on Friday afternoon about 1 o'clock, in his family burial ground, attended by the Union Society [a charity organization that included Catholics, Protestants, and Jews] and a vast number of other citizens.

If it is "a virtue to be industrious," my father possessed it in an eminent degree. In a short history of his life written by himself, he has said: "From my early years to the age of twelve or thirteen, I had taken a resolution to try and endeavor to do something or other to earn a little money, as my turn was industrious and mechanical." This "resolution," the offspring in him of nature, he carried into consummate execution. Those who were acquainted with him can bear evidence of the fact, neither the scorching sun or chilling winter detered his industrious pursuits. Actively alive to the welfare of his affectionate wife and dutiful children, his heart palpitated with a generous ardor to accumulate sufficient property to make them easy and satisfied in life. They composed the Polar Star to which his felicity and warm affection were directed. His purse was ever open to their wants, and his bosom beat in unison with theirs. In domestic life he possessed all those qualifications which are necessary to embellish humanity and render it a peculiar blessing. His manners were pure and chaste, and not of that complexion which is characterized for studied deception, pretended ease, and external show. His were the flowings of a heart sensitive of virtue. The indigent never in vain from him sought charity; his objects were widely selected and as liberally releaved. Many, very many, received his money, but none never heard his tongue lisp their names.

As a friend he was peculiarly sincere, as a member of civilized society, obedient; as a man of business, upright and punctual, as a master [of slaves] kind, indulgent, and benevolent. In the offices with which he was honored by the United States, he was active, industrious, and always ready to discharge demands that were legal. None had reason to complain of delay of payment; he was invaluable as an officer of government, invaluable as a private member of society. Integrity in life secured to him a popularity that could not be impaired. Tho' jealosy and envy generated the gale of slander, yet it was ephemeral, for his unshaken correctness and veracity succeeded to the gale, as a calm to boisterous weather. His superiors in office approved his numerous accounts, and in a manner gratifying to his children. In them his memory will be ever embalmed and recollected with tears, the effusions of hearts, melting with the warmest, keenest, and most piercing affection for the bereavement of an ever to be lamented parent.

8

Jacob Henry

Will You Bind the Conscience in Chains?

Jacob Henry of North Carolina Pleads for the Right to Hold Office

December 6, 1809

On December 6, 1809, Jacob Henry delivered an address defending his right as a Jew to sit in the State Legislature of North Carolina. (Because of its length, only excerpts from the address are included here.) He had already been elected and was seated in the legislature when another member of the State House of Commons pointed out that, according to the state constitution, only a Protestant and a believer in the divine authority of the Old and New Testaments was eligible to take the oath of office. The House, meeting as a Committee of the Whole, allowed Henry to retain his seat and ignored the requirement that he take a Christian oath. The members argued—and this was casuistry—that a Jew could constitutionally occupy a legislative office but not an executive one! Henry's appeal was, in all probability, actually written by John Louis Taylor, the North Carolina attorney general. Taylor, a Catholic, had a vested interest in defeating the intent of the Protestant-motivated constitution. As early as 1814, Henry's address was included in a collection of great American orations. In 1868, after Christian blacks were allowed to hold state office, Jews, too, were permitted, as of right, to sit in the State Legislature.

. . . If a man should hold religious principles incompatible with the freedom and safety of the State, I do not hesitate to pronounce that he should be excluded from the public councils of the same; and I trust if I know myself, no one would be more ready to aid and assist than myself. But I should really be at a loss to specify any known religious principles which are thus dangerous.

It is surely a question between a man and his Maker, and requires more than human attributes to pronounce which of the numerous sects prevailing in the world is most acceptable to the Deity. If a man fulfills the duties of that religion, which his education or his conscience has pointed to him as the true one, no person, I hold, in this our land of liberty, has a right to arraign him at the bar of any inquisition. And the day, I trust, has long passed, when principles merely speculative were propagated by force; when the sincere and pious were made victims, and the light-minded bribed into hypocrites.

The purest homage man could render to the Almighty was the sacrifice of his passions and the performance of his duties. That the ruler of the universe would receive with equal benignity the various offerings of man's adoration, if they proceeded from the heart. Governments only concern the actions and conduct of man, and not his speculative notions. Who among us feels himself so exalted above his fellows as to have a right to dictate to them any mode of belief? Will you bind the conscience in chains, and fasten conviction upon the mind in spite of the conclusions of reason and of those ties and habitudes which are blended with every pulsation of the heart? Are you prepared to plunge at once from the sublime heights of moral legislation into the dark and gloomy caverns of superstitious ignorance? Will you drive from your shores and from the shelter of your constitution, all who do not lay their oblations on the same altar, observe the same ritual, and subscribe to the same dogmas? If so, which, among the various sects into which we are divided, shall be the favored one?

I should insult the understanding of this House to suppose it possible that they could ever assent to such absurdities; for all know that persecution in all its shapes and modifications, is contrary to the genius of our government and the spirit of our laws, and that it can never produce any other effect than to render men hypocrites or martyrs. . . .

Nothing is more easily demonstrated than that the conduct alone is the subject of human laws, and that man ought to suffer civil disqualification for what he does, and not for what he thinks. The mind can receive laws only from Him, of whose divine essence it is a portion; He alone can punish disobedience; for who else can know its movements, or estimate their merits? The religion I profess inculcates every duty which man owes to his fellow men; it enjoins upon its votaries the practice of every virtue and the detestation of every vice; it teaches them to hope for the favor of heaven exactly in proportion as their lives have been directed by just, honorable, and beneficent maxims. This, then, gentlemen, is my creed, it was impressed upon my infant mind; it has been the director of my youth, the monitor of my manhood, and will, I trust, be the consolation of my old age. At any rate, Mr. Speaker, I am sure that you cannot see anything in this religion to deprive me of my seat in this house.

So far as relates to my life and conduct, the examination of these I submit with cheerfulness to your candid and liberal construction. What may be the religion of him who made this objection against me, or whether he has any religion or not I am unable to say. I have never considered it my duty to pry into the belief of other members of this house. If their actions are upright and conduct just, the rest is for their own consideration, not for mine. I do not seek to make converts to my faith, whatever it may be esteemed in the eyes of my officious friend, nor do I exclude any one from my esteem or friendship, because he and I differ in that respect. The same charity, therefore, it is not unreasonable to expect, will be extended to myself, because in all things that relate to the State and to the duties of civil life, I am bound by the same obligations with my fellow-citizens, nor does any man subscribe more sincerely than myself to the maxim, "Whatever ye would that men should do unto you do ye so even unto them, for such is the law and the prophets" [Matthew 7:12].

9

Judith Cohen

Do Not Forget the Aged Parent You Have Left Behind

Judith Cohen Prescribes Rules of Conduct for a Younger Brother

April 20, 1815

Levy I. Cohen was born in Lancaster, Pennsylvania, in 1800. Fifteen years later his father Joseph, then living in Charleston, South Carolina, sent him to London to live with a half-brother, Solomon, a stationer. Before leaving on his voyage, Levy's half-sister Judith gave him a set of "Rules" meant to serve as a guide to conduct on the journey . . . and thereafter. They are reprinted here.

Cohen remained in England for only four years and then returned in 1819 to his native land on the bark Susan and Mary. *He now called himself Lewis I. Cohen. The switch from Levy to Lewis was common among the English Jews. Lewis had a keen mind for business. As he sailed into New York harbor, he noticed a Florida schooner loaded with cedar logs—and, as a skilled pencil-maker, he realized the value of cedar for his purposes. He bought the cargo and immediately arranged to have it sent to London as ballast in the hold of the* Susan and Mary *on her return trip. He and his brother Solomon turned the logs into pencils and made a handsome profit on the deal. One of the logs he reserved for himself; he cut it into pencil lengths and made what his family claimed was the first lead pencil in the United States. In the stationery store that he soon opened at 71 William Street in Manhattan, he sold his famous pencils and soon introduced steel pens and four-colored printed playing cards to an appreciative clientele. His highly successful business grew in the course of time into the New York Consolidated Card Company.*

RULES

For Levi Cohen's Perusal When He Has Leisure

Fear God and keep His commandments and He will ever protect and guard you from evil. Honor your superiors and they will love you. Be particular in keeping the Law you were brought up to. Keep truth in all your doings and you will never be brought to shame. Let your actions be such that you will always deserve praise without pride. Keep no vicious company. If you can not keep company with your superiors or equals, keep none at all. And be sure when, please God, you arrive at Liverpool to inquire for one of your own persuasion, and go to them, or him; tell without falsehood your story. Ask the Captain's permission as soon as you arrive to let you go ashore, and be careful of your cloaths, and do not be too communicative to inquisitive people.

The first house you get to, be sure to write to your brother [in London] and wait for an answer to know how you are to come to him. Be grateful to your benefactors, and treat them with that respect that is due to their reverence.

Do not forget the aged parent you have left behind, but keep in your memory the many troubles he has undergone for you, the anxiety he will be in untill he hears of your arrival.

Do not forget to write to us by the first opportunity; make yourself as agreeable to your shipmates as you can be, and do anything in your power to oblige them.

Let virtue be your guide, and remember these are the sentiments of your affectionate sister.

April 20th, 1815

Judith Cohen

10

Grace Nathan

My Full Approbation of Your Deportment toward Me

Grace Nathan Expresses Her Gratitude to Her Son

1827–1831

Grace Nathan (1753–1831), the wife of Simon Nathan, a businessman, was the sister of Gershom Seixas, the rabbi and Revolutionary War patriot. A number of her descendants were notables: Emma Lazarus, Maud Nathan, Annie Nathan Meyer, Robert Nathan, Benjamin Nathan Cardozo. Although her education had probably been limited to a few years in an eighteenth-century elementary school, she developed literary interests. She is the first American Jewish poet of whom there is any record. Her poems reflect the aspirations of a sensitive soul reaching out for the infinite and the beautiful.

Some time before her death she wrote a farewell note to her son, her only child. This letter was given to him after she had died. The son, Seixas Nathan, was a prominent New York City businessman and Jewish communal worker.

To My Son

This effort will speak to you from the tomb. Years of infirmities lead to the reflection that we must soon part. I am perfectly resigned to meet the last earthly event, grateful to God for the blessings he has given me.

I *die* in the *full faith* of my *religion.* I leave you in the bosom of a virtuous wife, surrounded by a numerous offspring who give promise of comfort.

Long may they live to shew *you* the same filial duties that I have uninterruptedly received from you. Now in this solemn moment when I am taking an eternal earthly farewell let me express my full approbation of your deportment toward me. It has been exemplary; as you have devoted your kindnesses so may be your great reward; more I could not say. Need I exhort you to the cultivation of your endearing children and give them a just idea of their religious and moral principles, these being the corner stones of all *good*, and on which the basis of life here and hereafter may be supported. You my son will live in peace and bear a kind manner to those who have shown it to me; by this they will cherish my memory; and I shall live.

Now thou my son who wast the joy of my younger days and the balm of my declining age, let me thrice bless you and say may peace rest with you forever and ever. Amen.

Your mother

Grace Nathan

Keep the seven days of mourning and no more, for that time *only* you will keep your beard.*

Began, November, 1827
[completed, 1831]

*Pious Jews do not shave while in mourning.

11

Deborah Moses

The Dead Receive Sufficient Honor in Being Called to Face Their God

Deborah Moses Makes a Final Request

November 14, 1837

Deborah Moses (1776–1848), the wife of Israel Moses, Charleston businessman, was the daughter of Hazzan Jacob R. Cohen of Philadelphia's Mikveh Israel synagogue; Abraham Hyam Cohen, who served as rabbi of Beth Shalome in Richmond, was her brother. Excerpts from her will that include her final injunctions to her family are included here. She was a strict conformist to all Jewish customs. Her son, Major Raphael J. Moses of the Confederate Army, said of his mother that she was "as pure a spirit as ever dwelt in human form." Her will was signed in 1837; she died in 1848 in St. Joseph, Florida.

The State of South Carolina. In the name of God, Amen.

I, Deborah Moses of the city of Charleston and State aforesaid, being deeply impressed with the conviction that the Almighty had blessed me beyond my deserts, I feel bound in humble gratitude to avail myself of the full possession of all my faculties to regulate and dispose of my worldly effects in a way that I deem most advantageous to those exclusively dear to my heart, and who claim both from nature and affection every effort on my part to secure my property which I hold and have possessed as a free dealer, to them and for their interest and future welfare should the will of God so ordain (which with humility of spirit I hope may be the case) that they should survive me. . . .

I request that no pomp or parade whatever may be exhibited over my last remains. A plain coffin of the most simple materials and in due time a wooden head and foot post without any inscription whatever are all that I require. The wisdom of God has mingled us indistinctly with the earth; why then shall we take from the living to arrogantly perpetuate an ephemeral name. To be forgotten is the lot of all. I therefore require no mark of outward woe. Lay the earth quietly and with respect on me; I leave the rest to conscience, feeling, and duty. Mourn not beyond the hour sanctified by nature and true grief; the tears which spring from the heart are the only dews the grave should be moistened with. The dead receive sufficient honor in being called to face their God. . . .

Witness my hand and Seal this fourteenth day of November, One thousand eight hundred and thirty seven.

Deborah Moses

12

Hannah Alexander

Shun the Brothel and the Gaming Table

Hannah Alexander's Son Leaves for the West

1838

In 1838, Hannah Alexander of Charleston, South Carolina, wrote a letter to her son Aaron who was leaving for the West, quite possibly New Orleans, that "emporium of wine, women, and seegars." Hannah, the daughter of a Dutch Jew, Levi Aaron Van Blitz, was born in South Carolina in 1789. In 1865 she died, a Civil War refugee, in Augusta, Georgia. She had become blind, and she suffered a fatal fall down a flight of stairs. She wanted to be buried in Charleston, near her husband, so that at the resurrection—in another and better world—they could be together forever. Her husband, Abraham Alexander, Jr., had been a hardware merchant more interested in reading English literature than in waiting on his customers, whom he simply ignored.

Hannah's tombstone informs us that she was "amiable, pious, charitable." Her son Aaron, to whom she wrote, was warned by his mother of the evils he might well encounter. She loved him very much, and, even though he married out of the faith, she did not disinherit him.

My dear son:

You are going to leave us perhaps forever as human nature is frail and we do not know how long it may please God to spare us but we must hope to meet again, please God.

I hope dear son that you may always remember the advice given to you by one that you are more dear to than life, for what would be life to me without my children.

Do not, my dear child, follow a multitude to sin but shun the brothel and the gaming table for they have brought many a good young man to shame and death finally. Do not think dear Alexander that I am not aware of your sober habits at this time but youth is soon led away by example and very often caught into meshes that they would otherwise shun but I am incapable of writing all I think. So pray God to keep you under his special care.

I subscribe myself

Your affectionate mother,

H. A.

13

Hyam Jacobs

Continue the Religious Worship of My Children in the Same Jewish Faith as Myself and My Ancestors

A Father Provides for the Jewish Education of His Children in an Intermarriage

September 17, 1838

On the above date, Hyam (Hyman) Jacobs of Charleston, South Carolina, signed his last will and testament. Jacobs, it would seem, had arrived in the city as early as 1800. Decades later his common-law wife, Susan Smith, gave him four children, three boys and a girl. In his will, which follows here, Jacobs asked his executor, a Christian, to make sure that the children were reared as Jews. One of the boys was named Isiah. Records indicate that a Lieutenant Isaiah Jacobs, commander of Company D, Second South Carolina Regiment, was killed at Chickamauga. He had been promoted from the ranks.

Charleston District. I, Hyam Jacobs, in the name of God, Amen. Know all men this to be my last will and testament. And to be acknowledged by all courts of justice and equity in this state. I do hereby will and ordain that after my death, that after all my just debts are paid, that all my property of whatever description be equally divided amongst my four children. The eldest Isiah, the second a girl named Meriam, the third named Joseph, and the fourth named Israel. And I hereby appoint Mr. Albert Happoldt as my lawful executor, and direct that the said executor to apply Susan Smith of the aforenamed children Isiah, Meriam, Joseph and Israel for their support and maintenance. And further the said executor is authorized my negro wench named Minto, either to sell her or hire her out to bring in wages to be applied to the support of the children. I do further request my executor to continue the religious worship of my children in the same Jewish faith as myself and my ancestors. I do deliver my soul to Almighty God and depart in peace with mankind. Done on Charleston Neck, September 17th, 1838.

Hyman Jacobs

Witnesses:

Elias Jones Gottlieb Meyer H. M. Hertz

Proved before Thomas Lehre O.C.T.D. on the ninth day of October, one thousand eight hundred and thirty eight, and at the same time qualified Albert Happoldt Exor.

14

Lazarus Kohn

Withstand This Tempting Freedom: Remain Good Jews

Lazarus Kohn Alerts Jews Going to America

March 5, 1839

On March 5, 1839, Lazarus Kohn, a teacher in Unsleben, Bavaria, signed a letter addressed to two friends, a man and his wife, who were leaving for the United States. The letter, written in German, was really intended for a party of nineteen Jews who were setting out together across the seas to seek their fortune in "the land of freedom." These Jews were determined to establish a congregation, a community, in the town where they hoped to settle, Cleveland. One man, a skilled ritual slaughterer and circumciser, also owned a Scroll of the Law (Sefer Torah). Thus the group was equipped to hold divine services.

Accompanying the letter was a list of over 230 Jews, men, women, and children, who remained behind. This German-language roster, a substantial packet of over forty pages, was more than a statistic. It was a reminder, an appeal, an admonition reinforced by the contents of the letter: Remember your Jewish friends, remember your roots. May God protect you on your journey; keep the faith!

My dear friends Moses and Yetta Alsbacher:

I give you by way of saying goodby a list of names of the people of your faith with the fervent wish that you may present these names to your future heirs—yes, even to your great-grandchildren, and under pleasant economic circumstances.

I further wish and hope that the Almighty, who reigns over the ocean as well as over dry land, to whom thunder and storms must pay heed, will give you good angels as travel companions, so that you, my dear friends, may arrive undisturbed and healthy in body and soul at the place of your destiny, in the land of freedom.

But I must also, as a friend, ask a favor of you.

Friends! You are traveling to a land of freedom where the opportunity will be presented to live without compulsory religious education.

Resist and withstand this tempting freedom and do not turn away from the religion of our fathers. Do not throw away your holy religion for quickly lost earthly pleasures, for your religion brings you consolation and quiet in this life, and it will bring you happiness for certain in the other life.

Don't tear yourself away from the laws in which your fathers and mothers searched for assurance and found it.

The promise to remain good Jews must never and should never be broken during the trip, not in your home life, nor when you go to sleep, nor when you rise again, nor in the rearing of your children.

And now, my dear friends, have a pleasant trip and forgive me for these honest words to which the undersigned will forever remain true.

Your friend
Lazarus Kohn
Teacher

Unsleben near Neustadt on the Saale,
in Lower Franconia,
in the Kingdom of Bavaria,
the 5th of March 1839.

15

Kitty Cohen

Let All Your Movements Be Dictated by a Strict Sense of Propriety

Kitty Cohen Sends Her Daughter Rachel to School

June 25, 1840

On June 25, 1840, Mrs. Benjamin I. Cohen of Baltimore sent her daughter Rachel off to boarding school in Burlington, New Jersey. Rachel (1825–1913) was given some "food for the journey"—detailed instructions on how to conduct herself. These parental admonitions are interesting, for they mirror the mores of a cultured, wealthy banking family. The Cohens of Baltimore were the outstanding Jewish clan in town, highly respected and politically influential. That very year the Misses Pallache had opened a Jewish girls' boarding school in New York City, but the Cohens preferred to send their daughter to a Gentile institution. It is very likely that Rachel attended St. Mary's Hall, an Episcopal school for girls. The Cohens were loyal Jews, but their associations were Gentile; they moved in the highest Christian social circles.

There is no evidence that any school catering to the public at this time limited the number of Jewish applicants; the Jewish population in the antebellum United States was simply too small to inspire any wish for a Jewish quota.

It is curious that nothing is said in this rather admonitory note about religion. However, if cleanliness is next to godliness, then this is indeed an ethical letter.

A few words of parental advice for my Daughter Rachel on her first absence from home—Balt. June 25th, 1840.

Make it your habit no matter what may [be] the habits of others to rise early; enquire the hours of Breakfast, Dinner etc., and be sure that *in this and in all other respects you conform to the ways of the house.* Let the family of which you are an inmate be thereby not inconvenienced else their time and y'r own is rendered unpleasant and your absence will be desired.

Let me again inculcate as I could wish to do most urgently: *cleanliness* in *appearance* and *in fact.* Keep your body pure, the surface of your skin free of blemish; use (during the summer season especially) *water* freely on *rising* and on *retiring,* besides the good which in all respects is the result of such habit, health is vastly promoted.

You are to recollect after y'r arrival in Burlington that you are under Mrs. Emory's guidance and responsible to her for all your actions. Nothing must be done without her knowledge and *consent,* and let all your movements be dictated by a strict sense of propriety.

If at any time whether at home or abroad you meet with *disappointment,* bear it with patience and without murmur, *no pouting*; reflect that 'tis for the best and that exhibitions of temper (which I regret to say I have seen latterly rather too much of) do not mend the matter. Patience under good government is evidence of a kindly disposition and of sound sense.

In your intercourse with society recollect your youth; with the youthful be animated and say as you please; in the presence of mature age do not be prominent; *converse* when y'r conversation is sought, and, when had, let it be in moderate tone, not so loud as to annoy those who may be near and do not desire to hear.

Your host or hostess must not be put to expense on y'r account without return. I refer of course now to the *direct* expenses, that is to say, for instance, for *postage,* porterage etc. Make it y'r business always in such cases to repay the amount expended for you *no matter how small the amount.* The greater y'r attention to small matters the more do you evidence your conscience of propriety.

16

Joseph Rosengart

You Will Find a Real Home Land

A Country Teacher Instructs an Emigrant

April 16, 1846

Bavarian-born Herman Kahn (1828–1897), whose sons founded a textile empire, was only 17 years old when he left Germany for the United States in 1846. Arriving in America, he joined his sister, Elise Kahn Hirsch, and her husband in Richmond, Virginia, where he changed his name to Cone and became a peddler. A few years later, Herman began a wholesale grocery business in Jonesboro, Tennessee, and in 1856 married Helen Guggenheimer, a Virginian. Some four decades later, in the 1890s, his sons established the Cone Mills of Greensboro, North Carolina.

Although in 1846 the immigrant teenager brought with him to America little of material value, he did not arrive on these shores with nothing, for—as one of his sons, probably Julius W. Cone, was to write proudly of him—Herman Cone did include among his baggage the "intangible possession" of a "vitalizing heritage." That heritage was eloquently embodied in a letter written to young Herman by his brother-in-law Joseph Rosengart. Originally written in German, this letter was given to Herman upon his departure for America.

Place your full trust and confidence in God who will send his angels to guard you. So, do not be discouraged, and do not be afraid of leaving or of the voyage, but consider your fate a good fortune, designed for you by God.

You may shed tears because you are leaving your parents' house, your father, brothers and sisters, relatives, friends, and your native land, but dry your tears, because you may have the sweet hope of finding a second home abroad and a new country where you will not be deprived of all political and civil rights and where the Jew is not excluded from the society of all other men and subject to the severest restriction, but you will find a real home land where you as a human being may claim all human rights and human dignity.

Be careful of your voyage and pay attention to your health as well as your belongings. Avoid the company of all but respectable and educated people. Be modest and polite to everybody. Thus you may surely expect good treatment for yourself.

Every evening and every morning turn to God with sincere prayers; do not be afraid of anybody and do not let anybody disturb your devotions. Even if some people should make fun of you at first, they will understand later and show their respect.

I recommend to you the faith of your fathers as the most sacred and the most noble. Try to follow all the Commandments most painstakingly and thereby attain actual happiness. Do not sacrifice your faith for worldly goods. They will disappear like dust and must be left behind in due time.

Remember particularly the Sabbath day, to keep it holy, for it is one of the most important pillars on which our Faith is established. Do not disregard this day and do not let gold or silver make you blind and do not let any business, however tempting, induce you to violate the Sabbath, but at least on this day think seriously about your existence and your work.

It is not man's destiny to accumulate worldly goods just to be wealthy, but to acquire them to be used as means for the attainment of eternal happiness. I am, therefore, giving you as a keepsake an excellent religious book for your instruction. Make it your sacred duty to read one chapter on each Sabbath and holy day with serious devotion and meditation. Do not lay it aside when you have read it through, but keep it and read it again from time to time.

You will thereby learn your religion thoroughly, act accordingly and thus be honored by God and men. It will be your counsel in good times and bad, and will preserve you from all evil.

Honor your father and your mother, that your days may be prolonged. Even in that distant country you can show your respect and love towards your father by always remembering his good advice and by frequently writing him loving letters, thus giving expression to your devotion to him and your brothers and sisters.

Although your sainted mother is now in Heaven and although you never knew her, you can show her your greatest respect and love by following the Faith as she did. You will thus be able to know her and be with her in Heaven.

Your sister and brother-in-law in America will surely receive you in their home with loving care. Consider their home as your father's house and be respectful and modest toward them, show them your filial devotion and be attached and faithful to them, as you have always been toward us. Follow their advice and their suggestions and, whatever you may undertake, first ask them for their counsel. They will always give you the best advice and you will derive benefit therefrom, I am sure.

If you should be lucky enough to become wealthy in that distant land, do not let it make you proud and overbearing. Do not think that your energy and knowledge accumulated that wealth, but that God gave it to you to use it for the best purpose and for charity. Do not forget that you are also under obligation to assist your relatives and to help them to get ahead.

However, if you should not become wealthy, be satisfied with what you do have and try to be as comfortable and happy as if you had the greatest treasures.

Follow the middle way between avarice and waste. Do not be stingy, but live according to your position and your finances and be particularly liberal toward the poor, and charitable to the needy. Be glad to help and give part of your bread and give assistance to the distressed.

Do not let anybody call you a miser, but be known as a philanthropist. On the other hand, do not be extravagant or a spendthrift. Even if the necessity should occasionally rise to spend more than usual, never feel obliged to squander. It is of utmost importance that you keep account of your expenditures and live within your income.

I am closing with the quotation:

"Do right, trust in God, and fear no man."

Joseph Rosengart

Buttenhausen, April 16th, 1846

17

Isaac Leeser

Every One Must Go Forward to Meet His Destiny

Isaac Leeser Writes a Speech for a Bar Mitzvah

1850–1860?

It was probably in antebellum days that Isaac Leeser (1806–1868), America's most distinguished Jewish clergyman of his time, wrote a bar mitzvah address for a very intelligent youth. Leeser disapproved of the high-flying lucubrations that eager clerics wrote for young bar mitzvah aspirants. He was determined to compose something simple on this occasion. If this talk, reprinted here, does not reflect the views of a 13-year-old Philadelphia lad—and it probably does not—it certainly voices the strong religious and ethical convictions of the Neo-Orthodox Leeser.

My dear Parents and Friends!

To-day I am numbered among the responsible sons of Israel; till this day I was an innocent child, protected by the kind hand of parental authority, watched over by its care, and restrained by the fear of giving offence and pain to those who laboured for my welfare. Even the eye of the Almighty looked mildly down on my doings, not exacting from me punishment for transgression; as I was still under the guardianship of those appointed by Him to watch over my dawning life. But from this hour I am a man in responsibility, though yet a child in years; I stand here on the entrance of manhood, and I shall have to pursue the road which all mortals tread, to the end of my earthly existence. Joy and sorrow stand ready to accompany me on this pilgrimage, and good and evil will ever be there to claim my choice. O, how deeply do I feel the new responsibility! God bids me to listen to his command, in order that it may be well with me; while pleasure and sin invite me to partake largely of the enjoyments of the earth, which so many around me will choose as their portion. Well may I tremble in view of the fearful struggle, which awaits me like all others, and of the danger which threatens me, that through haste, passion, or ignorance I might lay hold of the evil and its sorrows, neglecting religion, its trials and its ultimate reward.

Could I make the years of my childhood last forever, could I hope to go down to the grave without testing of the trials to which mankind are destined; I might wish myself again into the midst of infancy, so that my innocence and unconsciousness of evil might still continue. But this cannot be, every one must go onward to meet his destiny, while he has the means placed before him, by God's mercy, to enable him to distinguish between good and evil. Knowing this, let me entreat our Father in heaven that He will give me a knowledge of his law, that as I am now a bar mitzvah, a child of Israel through the capacity of a religious majority to be one of the chosen people, entitled like them to participate in the privileges and burdens of our brothers, I may also have the mental enlightenment to understand my duty and the will and the power to observe it all the days of my life.

This day shall not be only one of rejoicing to me, but one also to be remembered always, to remind me, when I shall be tempted to transgress, that to-day I have thanked God, amidst the assembly of his servants, the house of Israel, that He has given us the law of truth, and planted everlasting life in our hearts; and that I would commit an offence against that truth, if I permitted myself to forget the parents who gave me the earthly existence, the glorious ancestors from whom the Israelites have sprung, and the beautiful religion which we have received from the Creator of the world. Yes, I will endeavour to live so that my faith shall have a true follower in me, and that those, who feel in my welfare the interest of blood-kindred, shall rejoice to call me their relative. Much is not in the power of a child, such as I am as yet, to accomplish; but this I can do. I can resolve to be good and dutiful, and I will trust firmly in the mercy of the God who chose us as his heritage to be with me in my pilgrimage, to strengthen my resolve for good, so that I may acquire the dominion over the desire for transgression, to which our natural inclination might otherwise lead me.

The future is truly before me like a sealed book, which I shall only be able to read slowly with advancing years, and a greater knowledge of things than I possess now. But I will learn daily from those who are wiser and better than myself; I will listen to the voice of religion which admonishes me to depend on God and not on human aid, and not to follow the example of sinners; and, in short, I will labour hard to obtain the approval of the Lord our God, and the good-will of those who are mortal like me. You, however, kind guardians of my infancy! Do not abandon me at once in this period of my transition from childhood to manhood; guide me yet longer; admonish me when I am in danger of going astray, and encourage me to do what is right, when doubt and indecision might otherwise prevent my advancement in goodness. But believe me, that it is my earnest desire to testify to you and all others, that it is my full determination to remain always a faithful son of Israel, and that, as I entered today into the congregation of Abraham, Isaac, and Jacob, I will prove that the ancient faith of our fathers has at least one true disciple in him who now claims fellowship with the house of Israel.

And may God bless you all and myself with his spirit of benevolence and wisdom, and consider us worthy to be accepted servants in his temple. Amen.

18

Isidor Bush

Let Us Openly Avow that We Are *Jews*

Isidor Bush Challenges American Jewry

August 7, 1851

Prague-born Isidor Bush was only 29 years old and had been in the United States for scarcely two and a half years when he took it upon himself—with consummate self-assurance—to pronounce on "the task of the Jews in the United States." What could this young immigrant have known of American Jewish life? But, in fact, young Bush knew a great deal. His youthfulness and inexperience notwithstanding, he was probably one of the best-informed Jews in America. His family in Bohemia had been part of high society, and Bush had had contact with such leading European Jewish scholars and writers as Leopold Zunz, Samuel David Luzzatto, Ludwig Philippson, and Leopold Kompert.

During the 1840s, Bush had won an impressive reputation for himself in Vienna as editor of the scholarly Kalender und Jahrbuch fuer Israeliten *as well as the liberal* Organ fuer Glaubensfreiheit. *When the Revolution of 1848 proved abortive, Bush's liberal sympathies made it necessary for him to flee the Hapsburg monarchy, and he arrived in New York in January 1849. Three months later he had begun publication of the first Jewish weekly in the United States, the short-lived German-language* Israels Herold. *The summer of 1849 found Bush settled in St. Louis, where he would remain for the rest of his life—he died there in 1898—and where he would fashion for himself a varied career as banker, politician, communal leader, and viticulturist.*

The remarks reprinted here are part of an address written by Bush on the 9th of Ab, August 7, 1851, traditionally the anniversary of the fall of the Jewish state first in 586 B.C.E. and then again in the first century of the Christian era. It was then, said Bush, that Jews lost political rights and immunities; and it was here in the United States that we have regained them—we are emancipated. But it is not enough to enjoy emancipation: Jews must work to elevate society spiritually and culturally. To accomplish this, he believed, we must prepare for leadership by improving and perfecting ourselves so that we may indeed become "champions of light."

The pioneers of the New World had to work, and a hard task it was, for the first introduction of civilization. They had to protect themselves against the inclemency of wild nature, and yet wilder men; they had to lay the foundation for our political and material existence, and they have done it bravely and more successfully than any progress human genius can boast of elsewhere.

Let us hope that on this prosperous foundation, under the best hitherto known form of government, corresponding more closely than any other of our days to the spirit of our own Holy Scriptures—let us hope that, from now and hereafter, the progress in the region of spiritual knowledge, of philosophy, and religion, and in the reforms of social life, will be equally great, rapid, and propitious; and let us also hope to find our Israelitish brethren in the foremost rank of those who strive and struggle for it.

That this is really our task—that we are to be the "champions of light"—a "blessing for all the people on earth," we could easily prove by a hundred Bible texts and by history; but it would be far more difficult, and beyond the scope of this periodical, to discuss the ways how we shall execute it.

Let the following short rules, or rather hints, be sufficient, therefore, and I sincerely believe that every one who reflects upon them, and who has an earnest will to do his part, will find out the remainder for himself.

1st. Let us openly avow that we are *Jews*; never be ashamed of this long-persecuted name, and bear it with pride. It is a name that has lasted more centuries than any people's name in history; for who can show us now the Romans, the Trojans, Spartans, etc.? It is a name that has to be respected by every one, and dare not be insulted in this country, even by its most powerful foes.

2d. Give honour to yourselves; when the rose graces herself, she is the ornament, too, of the garden, says a German poet. Make yourselves respond, beloved, and avow yourselves as Jews, and this very name will receive part of this respect and love, without taking any from you. Do this particularly by choosing different and honourable trades and pursuits. The clothing business and peddling, which the greatest part of you have adopted in some cities, are neither very profitable, nor calculated to give us the honourable position we should endeavour to possess among our fellow-citizens.

3d. Give to the Bible the full veneration that is due to these Holy Scriptures, and which the wisest of all nations and times, and our great philosophers, even sceptics, could not refuse to them. You live among a

Bible-venerating people; let them never forget that you have been its bearers to mankind, and when their fathers were heathens, that you knew the Bible in its originality and purity; and the gospel even does not contain any moral law, any doctrine of love, that is not already contained in the older and only Holy Scriptures. But do not act like the men who, repudiating the doctrines of those false priests, who have hypocritically or fanatically corrupted the pure idea of the sole God of the Universe, go in their hatred and criticism so far as to deny all, and build new systems, which, in the best case, are no less a perversion of that pure, simple, and eternal doctrine of our Eternal God and Father.

4th. Support as much as you can the public school system, and lend no help whatever to [Christian] sectarian institutions; do not send your children, neither your sons nor your daughters, to such and don't complain about heavy [public] school taxes. Establish no Jewish school except only the one branch of your religion, history, and Hebrew language.

5th. Employ the word of defence whenever requisite; but use it only after mature reflection. Jews have always been distinguished for soundness in criticism and encounters of wit, and solidity in debate. Oppose frankly, but with dignity and apparent scorn, those who strive to calumniate us, or to transplant hither the hatred and injurious legislation employed against us in the old countries.

6th. Be brother to each other; preserve this good reputation which your deadliest enemies have never ventured to take from you—that you are, and act, brotherly to each other. Assist the brother in need above your means; form societies for this purpose; and, if you have such, do all in your power to procure for those societies the high esteem of all your neighbours. This tends not to any social exclusiveness, like some pretend, just as little [as] (and less perhaps than) a German emigrant society.

7th and lastly. Study and keep in your mind the principles of the Bible, as regards interest on money, the distribution of the country to the landless or real cultivator, the promotion of agriculture, and prevention of land usury. Thus you may go hand in hand with our noblest social reformers (protected from the errors of the communist and others), sure to advocate an object that must at last be victorious, and a blessing to the world, that all may exclaim, "Indeed, a wise and intellectual people is this great people of the Jews."

19

David De Moses Sarfaty

Undeserving of So Precious a Charge

David De Moses Sarfaty Welcomes a Newborn Son

November 7, 1851

David De Moses Sarfaty (1828–1854) was a native of Kingston, Jamaica, where his father was a pillar of the island's Jewish community. The Sarfatys were a famous Sephardic family with branches in Morocco and various parts of the British Empire. Sarfaty *is Hebrew for "Frenchman," and the family claimed to be descendants of the great French Torah commentator Rashi (1040–1105). David married Phoebe Elizabeth Da Silva, who was on her mother's side a Westchester Hays. They had a boy within the year and named him Moses David Sarfaty (1851–1923).*

Answering a congratulatory note from Rabbi Isaac Leeser of Philadelphia, author of an earlier document in this book, David expressed his joy at Moses David's birth. He prayed that God would help him rear the child to become a worthy son of Israel. He and Phoebe were determined to educate the youngster to be a good human being. It is a pity that David did not live to watch his son grow up. The father died when he was a young man of 26. Moses was but 3 years of age.

New York, November 7th, 1851

The Reved Isaac Leeser

Dear Friend:

Your appreciated favor of the 30th ulto I received last Sunday; the sentiments therein contained are such that cannot fail to produce the effect on those for whom you desired. Indeed when the happy hour arrived it made me a father. My heart oer flowed with gratitude to the God of our Brethren for the Bestowal of a gift, the which I almost felt I was incapable of guiding safely to its future haven, or undeserving of so precious a charge. Yet I prayed secretly and fervently to my Heavenly Father to cause me to possess a sufficient knowledge of my duty as a parent, so as to lead my child in the true paths of our blessed religion, and rear him to become a worthy son of Israel. My dear wife and myself will never cease to inculcate such morals in him as the best of our abilities will allow. My dear wife joins with me in the appreciation of your kind letter, and desires me to say will prize it highly. I am happy to write that she, as well as the boy, are doing well. . . .

With kind regards and trusting to have the pleasure to have a visit from you when you come over here, I remain

Yours sincerely,
David De Moses Sarfaty

20

Lena Roth

Only Those without Religion Fall into Wicked Ways

A Mother's Letter to a Son Going to America

ca. 1855

Some time around the year 1855, Lena (Mrs. Benjamin) Roth of Hechingen, Germany, wrote a letter to her beloved son Moses (Morris) to take along with him as he set out for America. Such departure letters were not uncommon. Many anxious parents gave their departing children such spiritual nourishment for the journey. Moses was named after a grandfather of the same name who was given a special license to marry after he had courageously strangled an attacking wild dog. He had apparently been subject to the Matrikel Gesetz *(registration law) that limited the right of Jews to marry. The year after Moses emigrated, Solomon, a younger brother, left for America to join him. Solomon carried with him a departure letter from his father, Lena's husband, which is the document that follows this one. Below is Lena's letter to the older son.*

[Hechingen, 1855]

My dear Moses,

Although your dear father told you everything that a young man should take to heart and although I hope that you will follow his advice and observe his instructions, still I cannot keep from adding my own guidance. Be patient and content even if things don't always go your way.

Often in life things happen which cannot be foreseen. Then you need to gather all your patience and strength to be able to bear the burden. Believe me, dear, I speak from experience. So often, among strangers, I suffered more than I ever thought I could endure. I took faith in my trust in God, Who is my refuge, and did not succumb to grief and sorrow; I have always had His help. He never deserts those who have faith in Him. Believe me, only those without religion fall into wicked ways. No one respects those who abandon their religion. Many who do, return to it later. You could bring me no greater happiness than by keeping your faith, for you know there is no joy for me on this earth except to see good things for my children.

Now I have said enough of that, and just want to make one important point for you to remember: never underestimate yourself or those who seem beneath you. Be your true self whether with man or woman. Do not misunderstand me. Don't think I am overly proud. I don't think I have ever been that. I do not refer to people who are poorer than you; the poor often have as much integrity as the richest. A reliable and decent person is just as good as anyone in the so-called elite. I mean this in a way that you may not understand now, but which you will as you get older.

The main thing is, value your good name. When one is looked down on and has a bad reputation, he stays that way forever.

But, I have said enough. When you are on your own and have had more experience, you will realize what your parents hoped for you. Your father sacrificed all he could for you, and for that reason I must hope all the more that you will listen to our advice. And so at last I ask you to take the time to read over what I have written so that you will not forget it—you don't have a great memory, you know. That is the wish of your devoted mother.

Lena Roth

21

Benjamin Roth

No Sacrifice is Too Great for a Father's Love

Papa Benjamin Lays Out a Life Program for a Beloved Son

June 1856

Young Solomon Roth (1837–1911)—all of 17 years of age—embarked for the United States in 1856. Believing that 17 was not the age of discretion, his father Benjamin gave him a long letter telling him how to live his life for the next fifty-seven years. This is one of the best of the ethical letters carried by youngsters as they listened to the siren cry "On to America!"

Young Solomon was met in Philadelphia by his older brother Moses, who was already settled in this country. Together they traveled west to Milwaukee, where Solomon became a peddler. Later he opened a store in a Wisconsin village, went into the leaf-packing business, and then moved on to Cincinnati where he became an affluent cigar manufacturer. Apparently, Papa Benjamin had advised him well.

My Dear Son:

It is doubtful whether we shall see each other again in life; and from afar I cannot warn you against such dangers as often threaten youth. Yet, even from the furthermost distance I shall think of you only with fatherly love and tenderness, and will at all times do everything in my power to help you. No sacrifice is too great for a father's love to bring willingly. In whatever situation you may find yourself, turn to me; and I will always show you that I am yours with an unending love, now and forever. Always have confidence in me. Before you give your confidence to a stranger—trust your father.

At this moment of our parting, since I can no longer be near you, let me give you the following precepts for life to take with you. Obey them, follow them, and you will never be unhappy. Whatever situations you may enter into, you will be able to take hold of yourself, to comfort yourself; and God to whom I pray daily for your welfare, will let it be well with you.

1. Always seek to keep your conscience clear, i.e., never commit an action which you will have to regret afterwards. Think carefully about everything you contemplate doing before its execution and consider its consequences, so that you will act only after due consideration. A true test of a clear conscience is an unclouded temperament and a cheerful spirit. Since you have received both from nature, seek to preserve them.

2. Consider what you possess as a trust given you by God. Be thrifty with it, and seek to enlarge it in an honest manner. Consider it just as much the possession of your brothers and sisters, and therefore. . . let no sacrifice appear too great for you. Wealth should never come to diminish your honor and your clear conscience. Also, never say in the manner of the cold Englishman or American: "Help your own self!" Instead, aid rather to the full extent of your powers every poor man and anyone who needs your help. In short: be thrifty for yourself, that you may be able to aid a suffering humanity with your wealth.

3. Never leave the religion that is yours by birth, the faith of your parents and ancestors. Neither wealth, nor friendship, nor the possibility of a brilliant career in life, nor seduction, nor even the love of a girl should move you or have the power to make you change your religion. Should you be forced, partly through circumstances, partly because of the dictates of reason, to omit the ceremonial observances, you must nevertheless under no circumstances depart from the basis of religion: "The Eternal, your God, is one, unique, single being." Reason and conviction can never force you to desert Judaism, since the Jewish religion is really the only one whose basic teachings can be brought into harmony with philosophy. Therefore, desertion would be for worldly advantages, and these are never valuable enough to sacrifice the Eternal One or our conscience. I feel I must recommend this to you doubly, since you have a tendency towards frivolity which could lead you to an easier acceptance of this type of seduction.

Also, never have any contact with missionaries. You do not have enough knowledge of the Holy Scriptures. That way, you cannot engage in disputations with them; for they could easily lead you astray. Consider them therefore only as self-seeking cheats, or as ranting visionaries, as I have come to know them. And, indeed, in my conversations with them I frequently exhibited them as such in the presence of company, something I could do since I have studied Scripture from my childhood days. And yet, even then it was a difficult task.

4. Do not become acquainted—not to mention closer relationships—with

women. Be polite and well-mannered towards them; for the rest, as far as it is possible, keep your distance. Consider them like a sharp, pointed toy, with which one can play only occasionally—and then with the greatest of care. Seek to keep your heart free; guard it, and be not seduced by the tempting, destructive speech and actions of your contemporaries. This last demands your closest attention.

Have no relations with a prostitute. Her breath is poison, her word the bite of a snake; and they are all alike. However, let me add here, in praise of Jewish womanhood, that with a few exceptions they have preserved much purer morals than the girls of other races; and they have contained themselves from selling their charms for money.

I recommend the above to you in particular as injunctions to be followed. With your fine appearance and cheerful temperament you will be exposed to many temptations and opportunities in regard to women. And I do not want to say much on this point, leaving it rather to your wisdom and unspoiled instincts. My deepest prayer is that you may guard the latter; and, if it is your firm intention to remain pure, the good Lord will aid you in this task.

5. Do not trust a stranger; and, certainly, do not confide in him, particularly if he flatters you. In general, be reserved and discreet towards all. For many a wolf wears lamb's garments, and a true, honest friend can be recognized only after years of close acquaintance, and after he has passed many tests. But then, value him as a jewel—and a rare jewel, at that. If someone confides a secret to you, guard it; but do not make him your confidant in return. Again, this is a point which I must emphasize to you, since you are a trusting soul. But you yourself have already had experience of this nature in your travels. Young as you are, you yourself know that men do not always mean what they say.

6. Never exhibit money or articles of value in front of a stranger, at an inn, or in any public place where strangers may be found. Even when you are with your acquaintances, do not act boastfully in regard to your possessions. On the contrary, rather claim to be poorer than you actually are. For there is no greater lure to crime than the god Mammon; and needless bragging has brought misfortune to many a man.

7. Throughout life, whether you are in good or evil circumstances, keep your parents and your home in your mind. Guard firmly your resolution to return to them, even if only after many years (unless they are able to come to visit you). No matter when, no matter what the circumstances surrounding you, they long for you; and they will receive you with open arms.

8. Do not try to see everything because of an overwhelming curiosity. Avoid any locations or places that threaten danger. Do not place yourself in danger through willfulness, carelessness, or excessively brave or needless action. However, be brave and determined where danger cannot be avoided, and, at the critical stage keep your presence of mind. For presence of mind

has often turned away the gravest dangers and has saved others when the danger seemed overwhelming.

9. Avoid the company of drunkards and merrymakers. Should you, by accident or because of unavoidable circumstances, find yourself in their presence, leave the room and the location they occupy. Suffer an insult rather than get into an argument with them, for such people cannot really insult a man of honor. As a general rule, let yourself be insulted rather than insult others. Be particular to avoid all quarrel and argument. Meet everyone in a polite and friendly fashion. If you believe that someone has slighted you, lock your sensitivity and your anger into your heart; and forgive the offender.

10. Avoid gambling; and seek to occupy your time with useful things. Any occupation is better and more honorable than gambling; for before one becomes aware of it, one may become an inveterate gambler. Gambling is the most destructive of vices. Much as I must criticize the excessive reading of novels, which damages one's sensibilities and the heart, and makes one weak and womanlike, if time must be killed which could be used for so many pleasant and useful occupations, such reading is preferable to gambling.

11. Be frugal and economy-minded. Save each heller as you would a gulden, for he who needlessly spends a kreutzer will never save a gulden. Seek to acquire wealth in an honest manner; and preserve it through economy. But let not this economy turn to miserliness. Be very saving in regard to your own needs, and limit your needs to the utmost. Avoid unnecessary luxuries, unless it be a matter of doing good. If you save without being miserly, no one will be able to entice you into acts of dishonor or crime.

12. Be meek and patient, and seek to acquire the character and patience of your mother. Through many years of continual suffering and pain she showed herself, in this manner, to be a true angel of patience. Be, as she was, forgiving when injustice or misfortune seeks you out; and strive in this to emulate your all-forgiving God.

13. Sunlight and moonshine are powerful lamps. But the light of your reason must eclipse them, i.e., do nothing in haste, nothing without due thought.

14. Passions are the mightiest of all tyrants. Give them one finger, and they will at once take all of your body and soul. Seek, therefore, to keep free of them; and give them no opportunity to rule you.

15. Those who hate and envy us can bring much evil upon us; but the greatest evil can be brought upon us through our own soul when it walks the paths of foolishness and error. Therefore, seek to avoid them in every way of life; strive to set yourself against their power.

16. Great tribulations bring us into bad habits; and once we become accustomed to a habit, it becomes second nature to us. Therefore, do not learn any vices; and let no habit become a passion to you.

17. The lying tongue of viciousness can do us great damage; but our own

tongue can be still worse. Therefore guard your mouth and tongue. Consider each word before it crosses your lips, for he who guards his mouth and lips is exposed to no danger. Particularly guard yourself against saying what you think during revolutionary times no matter to which faction you belong. Do not enter into political discussions, and always remain in the background on such occasions. Live a private rather than a public life.

18. Do not count too much on the favor of a personage, whether he be highly placed or of low rank. But least of all rely on the favor of a great man. Their promises are an empty sound, their words a gust of wind. They prefer you as long as they need you; once the need is gone, they do not know you any more.

19. Give in to necessity, and patiently bear what fate has in store for you. That which is done cannot be changed, and what has been decided on high cannot be nullified or avoided.

20. Despise and avoid the man of invectives, the calumniator, and the hypocrite. They would entice you and then use your words against you; and avoid a fool the way you would avoid a mad dog.

21. Long have I pondered, searched, and examined as to what constitutes man's true happiness. I have found only one bliss for him; virtue and fear of God. Hold fast to both of them, if you desire to attain happiness.

And thus I transmit to you, my beloved son, these rules for life. Seek to follow them. I particularly recommend to you that you seek to emulate your brother Moses and that you obey him; partly because he is your older brother, partly because he has an excellent, steadfast, and firm character. I do not censure you for the fact that big-city life and your growing up among strangers have in some ways been detrimental to you. This is the reason why you have almost discarded by now that steadfastness of spirit which you took with you from your parents' home. It remained longer in Moses, who stayed at home till he was seventeen, and whose character could therefore develop further. Really you could not give me more pleasure than by living together peacefully and in brotherly harmony; as you could also give me no greater pain and sorrow than by not doing this. I do not doubt that both of you will follow my wishes, and in that way you will also fulfill the words of our sage: "How good and how pleasant it is for brethren to live together in unity. . ." [Psalm 133:1].

I assure you that my whole happiness exists in the happiness of my children. Believe me, no sacrifice would be too great for me to bring willingly if I could make you happy. It was a great inward struggle for me (and I had to conceal my feelings from you as from Mother) to send you away from me while you were yet so young. But it was your firm desire—and I did not want to take it from you. For all eternity my feelings toward you will be those of the deepest love.

And with this I give you, now, my blessing; may it follow you on all your paths with the words . . .

> The angel who hath redeemed me from all evil bless thee; and let my name be named in thee, and the name of my fathers, Abraham and Isaac; and mayest thou grow into a multitude in the midst of the earth.
>
> The Lord bless thee and keep thee.
>
> The Lord make His face to shine upon thee and be gracious unto thee.
>
> The Lord lift up His countenance upon thee and give thee peace.
>
> God make thee as Ephraim and Manasseh, like Moses in his humility, like Solomon in his wisdom, like Samson in his strength, like Absalom in his beauty, like Hezekiah in his righteousness, and like David in his reverence.

B. M. Roth

Hechingen, June 1856

22

Anna Marks Allen

Diligently Study Our Holy Laws

Anna Marks Allen Congratulates Her Nephew, a Bar Mitzvah Boy

June 28, 1858

Anna Marks Allen (Mrs. Lewis Allen, 1800–1888), granddaughter of a Revolutionary War soldier, was one of Philadelphia's best-known Jewish communal workers. She was active in the Female Hebrew Benevolent Society, the first Jewish Sunday School, and the Jewish Foster Home. In 1858 she wrote a congratulatory bar mitzvah letter to a nephew, Lewis Arnold. Accompanying the note were some religious articles that the 13-year-old confirmand was expected to use: a prayer shawl and phylacteries. Although a fourth-generation American, Aunt Anna was no assimilationist. She was respected for her piety and strict conformity to Jewish traditional practices. Her religious views are reflected in this letter to her nephew.

Phila., June 28, 1858

My dear Lewis,

Accompanying these few lines, you will receive articles suitable for a boy soon to become *bar mitzvah*, and with them accept the love and blessings of your aunt who sincerely congratulates you on your attaining so important an epoch in your life.

May you live to be a credit to yourself, a comfort and blessing to your dear parents, and the pride and protector of your sisters. As your God Mother, my dear Lewis, I may be allowed the privilege, perhaps, of speaking to you of the many *duties* and *responsiblities* which every *day* and *hour* of your life, encreases, and assumes a more important character.

In the first place, my dear boy, let the duties you owe your *Maker ever* predominate over every other. Diligently study our *holy* laws and ordinances, so that when you look upon the sacred emblem of faith (the tzitzith) you may be reminded that no temtation that the world can offer may induce you to forsake your God, and when you bind upon your body the *tephillin*, you must remember that it is not *only* intended to commemorate the chief commandments of the Mosaic Religion, but that we must *obey* and *do* them, so that the mantle that envelopes you when in the House of God may not prove a covering for *vain thoughts* and *evil imaginations*.

Next comes, my dear Lewis, your *duty* to your parents. I cannot point out a more impressive and beautiful passage by which to govern your actions than that contained in the fifth commandment: "Honor thy father and mother." What a vast amount of duties do these emphatic words contain! To define them, my dear nephew, would take a more able pen than mine, but let us hope as you advance in youth and manhood that the instruction you receive from your dear parents and teachers, and your own good sense, may develop them. And may the *Holy One* of *Israel* enlighten your *eyes* and impress them on your *heart*, that you may "do *always* that which is right in *His light* " is the prayer of your

Aunt Anna

23

Arthur L. Levy

You Are All a Fond Parents Heart Could Desire

A Birthday Letter to a Son Coming of Age

November 4, 1861

Arthur L. Levy of New York congratulated his son in a formal letter when he reached the age of 21. Obviously the father was very pleased with the character and conduct of young Joseph Levy, for he listed with pleasure – if not without a degree of unction – the virtues that characterized the young man. The tone and contents of this letter indicate that the father was a man of culture and breeding. In addition, although the words Jew *and* Judaism *are not mentioned specifically, Arthur Levy was a religionist.*

New York, Nov. 4, 1861

I am at a loss my dear boy for words in which to convey to you (and yet I cannot allow this day to pass, without endeavoring at least to express on this the anniversary of your birth and of your attaining the age of 21 years) my unbounded satisfaction of your conduct and the very great satisfaction I experience in having a son such as you, and for which blessing I am truly grateful to the Giver of all Good, for as a son or brother, you are all a fond parents heart could desire, possessing as you do, every good quality that can adorn mankind. Combining such a reverence for your parents, strict integrity, a nice sense of honor, a love of truth and religion, and who can ask for more? I need not urge you to continue on the same path, for your principles are too strongly rooted ever to be eradicated, and I can only hope others will follow your bright example, thereby proving a blessing to their parents and ornaments to society.

These feelings are shared in by your dear Mother, who joins with me in invoking Heavens choicest blessings on you, praying our Heavenly Father to shield, guard, and protect your footsteps from all and every evil. May this be his Divine Will. Amen! Selah!

Wishing you many, many happy returns of the day, and all a fond parent can wish for the welfare of a dutiful son, I enclose you a small token of my approbation, and

Remain
Your affectionate Father

To my dearly beloved son
Joseph A. Levy

24

Gottfried Wehle

They Were Seeking for the Spirit of Religion

Gottfried Wehle Writes of His Belief in Existence after Death

1863–1864

Reprinted here are excerpts from the ethical will of Gottfried Wehle (1802–1881). It differs from the others in this collection, for Wehle was a cultist, a believer in the teachings of the seventeenth-century messianic pretender Shabbetai Zevi and his "reincarnated" successor Jacob Frank (d. 1791). Zevi had in 1665 been proclaimed the long-awaited Messiah. These eighteenth- and nineteenth-century "Believers," Sabbataians, or Frankists—as they were sometimes called—believed in personal immortality. They were mystics who treasured the kabbalistic literature and looked forward to the early coming of the Messiah. Influenced by the Enlightenment and Deism, they were antinomian, unsympathetic to talmudic casuistry and ritualistic Orthodoxy. Thus they had something in common with early Hassidism and the burgeoning Reform Judaism of the nineteenth century.

Wehle, a native of Bohemia, came to the United States in 1849 in a family migration that included the Brandeises and the Dembitzes as well as the Wehles. Louis D. Brandeis's maternal grandfather was a member of Wehle's cult. Wehle lived in Madison, Indiana, and later in New York City. He was at first in the dye-import business; in New York, he bought and sold leather and hides.

In the name of God, the Ruler of Human Destiny!

My dear, beloved children,

I start today a document, the commencement of which I put off for many years. With every year, however, it is more pressing. Alas, far too often the frailty of the human being becomes more evident, so that it eventually appears impossible to make arrangements which before would have been only too easy. . . .

It is well known to you, my dear children, that, influenced by the repeated popular demonstrations in Prague against the Jews, I decided to leave the Continent, the country and the town where I and also you were born, where my ancestors throughout the centuries lived an honourable life agreeable to God, where they suffered innocently and so greatly for their belief and their nationality. It is not granted to me to share with them the clod of earth where they rest in peace. . . .

The pedigree of my parents is known in Prague since centuries—all these ancestors were noted for their biblical and talmudical learning, for their practice of charity, their honest and blameless way of living, their wealth and inoffensiveness. . . . To these gentle-folk who had a clear conception and a higher urge, the dry study of the Talmud, the aim of which was only sophistry and mental acuteness, did not suffice. That portion of the Talmud, which deals with morals, metaphysics and religion, was neglected by the greatest part of their contemporaries; the systems and opinions concerning these theological principles remained unnoticed! Now your ancestors declared all the old and new writings concerning the Talmud as wrongly exploited by sophistical and astute commentators, that they were only the outer shell and peel of the true Judaism which instead represented doctrines that were the quintessence and symbol of Judaism, higher than the discussions, debates, questions and solutions of old and long forgotten laws about offerings and food. In consequence your ancestors were decried as heretics by many hypocritical, so called public educators, who called themselves rabbis. They were slandered and persecuted by them. Those hypocrites dared even from the pulpit to stir up the people against them, under the pretext that the principles and doctrines of this "sect" as they called them, had much in common, even the same tendencies as the Christians. They mesmerised the listeners, even publishing pamphlets containing the most impudent and gross calumnies, which were distributed with lightning speed throughout the greater part of Europe. Persecuted by these hypocritics and zealots, these "heretics, Soharites and Sabatians" endured the intolerance with gentle resignation, without asking the authorities for their proffered protection. Strangely enough, even the most fanatical opponents had to admit their high intelligence, blameless way of life, strict morality, honesty, and charity; in fact all the virtues of a good citizen.

With pious and gentle resignation the persecuted ones suffered this intolerance. They were moved by their resolve to establish the principles of revealed religion, its high purposes and the future destiny of their nation. They gladly resigned their perfect knowledge of the Talmud because they were seeking for the spirit of religion. They arranged their theological studies in the spirit of the Bible and various other old theological scriptures known under the generally ill-reputed name of cabbala. They placed higher the doctrines of this secret lore than the dead ceremonies, and tried to revive the spirit contained in them.

That man, being an image and masterpiece of God, will again return to the perfect state, as he was when he left the Creators hand; that he will be free from all sickness of body, mind and soul, that he will be again innocent as before the Fall, free from vice and sin—this was roughly the programme of their endeavours and perception of God, the aim of their studies. Moreover, as God acts only indirectly, a chosen, consecrated Messiah is necessary as deputy of his highest Master. As now, according to the cabbalistic principles, man is only the tool of Providence through which it acts, therefore the smallest act of one chosen for this highest charge may be of greatest importance. Thus these ill-reputed gentle-folk endeavoured to prepare and qualify for this great aim and purpose by the highest moral standards. They welcomed this misinterpretation of their belief as an opportunity for bringing a sacrifice for their high aspirations, and indeed did so on the altar of their creed. . . .

Indeed, I still deem it necessary sometimes to think of the moment when I will have to leave you all, my beloved ones. And perhaps it may come so quickly, or may be I will be in a mental and physical condition when it may be impossible for me to express to you my last wishes. Why should I go from out of your midst without saying my last "farewell," without taking a kind leave, as it is usual if one parts even for a short time?

As on the occasion of every farewell, I shall, at my last parting, look to another "Meet Again." I am, my dear children, absolutely sure of it; I have no doubt to overcome. I would maintain with mathematical certainty—if that expression were acceptable: There is a God and man is His image. This image, Man, cannot be condemned to destruction and putrefaction! When you will be reading these lines and perhaps, to my sorrow, some of you with sceptical thoughts, then I will have realized my aspirations, I will know and perceive that the Creator has not endowed man with mind and soul only to let him live and die unhappy, yes unhappier than the lowliest animal! Should it be the only privilege of man over an animal, that he may develop his mind, to embellish the world, eventually to transform it by inventions into a paradise only to leave it after a short sojourn without any hope of a life after death? Or should it be only by accident that the best and most gentle people, without their fault, drag with sorrow and anxiety through this life during the few years of their existence and then with the ending of life disappear into nothingness? An inner voice—if we do not suppress it forcefully—tells us: there is a life after this life. How this mental life is constituted we do not know—but the faith in a further life implies the capacity for eternal life. My dear children! I believe firmly in the true and blessed faith, without it you will be always unhappy, with it never.

Do not be ashamed of this happy faith of your great ancestors. Say with pride that you feel the germ of this eternal life in you. He who wishes to deprive you of this faith which forms my firm conviction, would rob you of your greatest treasure. He is certainly not your friend. He is not the man who would dare fix his gaze on a future existence. It would mean that he would have to spend his life earnestly on improvement and repentance. But this inclination to good is lacking with most men, and they find it easier to throw a veil over their past and their future.

25

Max Lilienthal

Courage, Courage, Courage—and No Fear

Papa Max Lilienthal Lays Down Rules of Conduct for His Son Theodore

1865–1869

One of America's best-known rabbis in the mid-nineteenth century was Bavarian-born Max Lilienthal (1815–1882). In 1837, he had earned a Ph.D. degree at the University of Munich. He was then called to Russia by government officials, who hoped to introduce a modern school system for the ghettoized Jews. Realizing finally that he could not trust the Russians, who were unsympathetic to the Jewish masses, Lilienthal sailed for New York, where he served as a rabbi for a time and subsequently as the owner of a private school. Finally he was invited to Cincinnati to lead Congregation Bene Israel, the oldest synagogue west of the Alleghenies. Rabbi Lilienthal was well received by the general community and for a time was a member of the city's board of education. He also served on the board of directors of the local university.

Many Jews, like others in this mid-nineteenth-century patriarchal age, had large families. The Lilienthals had seven children, some of them destined to have great careers. The oldest boy, who was not the most distinguished of the sons, was Theodore. As a teenager he had been apprenticed to a pharmacist, who rapped him sharply over the knuckles every time he dropped something. The severe discipline to which he was exposed compelled him to quit. He then went on to New York, where he got a job in a large cloak-manufacturing company owned by a brother-in-law. Theodore made his home with an uncle, Dr. Samuel Lilienthal, a well-known physician widely acclaimed for his contributions to the field of homeopathic medicine. Shortly after the 18-year-old Theodore left Cincinnati in 1865, his father wrote to him—in German, of course—telling him how to conduct himself in the big city. Later, when his son reached the age of 21, Max Lilienthal wrote to congratulate him on reaching his majority. The vigorous individualistic spirit that characterized these two letters documents the complete Americanization of the German-born father. The formal closing was typically Germanic; it certainly does not indicate any lack of affection. Following are the two letters.

Cincinnati, June 30, 1865

My dear Theodore:

The unpleasant incidents connected with your leaving home, had I not known how to overcome them, would almost have deprived me of your farewell kiss. I had no time to give you my paternal blessing, for the bell rang for the train to leave. I send it to you now from the bottom of my heart: "The Lord bless and protect you; the Lord let the light of His countenance shine upon you and be gracious to you; the Lord turn His countenance toward you and give you peace. Amen."

The pleasure of the trip and your entrance into the metropolis will already have made you forget the unpleasant facts of your departure. You will have a new home in the house of dear Uncle Sam who, in addition to dear Leopold [Theodore's brother-in-law], will be as father to you. Therefore, do not let homesickness overcome you. While you must retain forever the love, the sweet memory, and the duties of filial gratitude toward the paternal home, you must know that we cannot remain together forever; therefore, take you place courageously, and with faith in God, in the new circle where your duties call you.

I want to give you a few rules of conduct, which the older you grow the more you will value, and realize their importance. They are well tested, practical maxims; impress them on your heart and try to regulate your life according to them.

1. Courage, courage, courage—and no fear. The world belongs to the brave, and those who venture nothing never win.
2. Be modest and obedient, but do not let others dominate you. He who loses his self-respect loses the respect of his fellowmen.
3. Do not imagine you know everything better than others. Older people have more experience; make use of their knowledge and learn wisdom.
4. Learn to bear contradictions and do not become morose if everything does not go according to your wishes.
5. If you are given an order to do something it is your business to find the means to accomplish it. Accomplished it *must* be, and a clever head and good will are shown by the way in which the desired result is brought about.
6. Do not shut yourself off from the world and do not always remain in the same small circle. You are at times socially shy, due probably to your nervous

headaches. The change of climate and dear Uncle Sam will overcome the latter; then the former too will disappear. The merchant must have acquaintances if he is to succeed in his business.

7. Be friendly and polite to everyone. Fine manners have made the fortune of many a man. Be cheerful and good-humored, but do not indulge in childish folly.

8. Make good use of your time and do not postpone until tomorrow what can be done today. Work, when it is finished, affords satisfaction and confidence.

9. Continue to learn, when and where you can; one never knows enough. While the merchant must devote most of his attention to his business, nevertheless give several hours of your leisure each week to books, and try to continue to educate yourself.

Enough for today, for dear mother wishes to add a few lines. Write me full details of your trip, of your arrival in New York, and remain the good lad that you now are.

Your father who blesses you,
Dr. M. Lilienthal

[Cincinnati, 1869]

Dear Theodore:

My best wishes on your birthday; it is my fatherly blessing and my innermost prayer that your future may realize all the anticipations and hopes of your parents.

You were a good child, an industrious, obedient youth, the joy and pride of your family; now be a man in the full meaning of the word. The time draws near in which the law considers you of age and entitled to all rights. Strive, as you have always done, that not only the letter of the law, but your actions may prove that you are entitled to be called a man. The years will come when you, like all mortals, will have to fight the battle of life. May success, with all its crowns of joy and rich harvests, come to you without effort.

Prepare yourself for it. Patience, perseverance, uninterrupted effort, and persistence assure success. "Stick to the rock and you will get fat on it." "Try again and again; there is nothing like trying." "Mind your business; if you neglect it, it will neglect you." These are practical and good American proverbs. Try to satisfy not only others but yourself; preserve your independence and your own well-considered opinions; listen to all well-meant advice, but then ask yourself if it is suited to your interests and situation.

One cannot please everybody. Whoever tries to meet everybody's wishes satisfies no one, and does himself the greatest injustice. These sentences do not mean that we should become egoists, that the whole world should revolve around our dear selves, and that everything that is not to our advantage and that does not serve our pleasure is worthless. As we belong to the world we live in . . . so we must, in return, live, work, and strive for it. The middle way is always the best, and heart and conscience, if we do not fail to listen to them, will lead us, like Heavenly guides, on the right road to virtue and success. Once again, my heartiest congratulations. . . .

May the Lord bless you is the prayer of your loving

Dr. M. Lilienthal

26

Simon Wiess

It Is My Duty to Give You a Little Advice

Simon Wiess Was a Texas Pioneer

January 1, 1866

A little less than three years before his death, Simon Wiess (Weiss? 1800–1868) wrote a letter to his sons giving them some sound business advice. It is not quite an "ethical" letter, although ethics are implied. (The father took it for granted that his sons would act honorably.) The intent of the note was to help them succeed as merchants; in later years they became very successful. The town of Wiess, in Hardin County, Texas, is named after them.

Wiess, a Polish Jew, had left home early and traveled over Asia Minor, Europe, the West Indies, and much of North, Central, and South America before settling in the Republic of Texas in 1836. Four years later, he made his home in what was later to be called Wiess (Wiess's) Bluff, Jasper County. A large-scale merchant who shipped cotton and developed commercial traffic on the rivers of eastern Texas, Wiess was a linguist, self-educated, a devotee of Masonry, and an ardent exponent of American institutions. Simon was also something of a Napoleon buff and named his youngest son Massena after the emperor's foremost marshal.

Wiess Bluff, Jan. 1st, 1866

My Dear Boys:

As you have just started in business, I think it is my duty to give you a little advice and with the hope that you will take it, observe it, for your own good. 1st, do not force or persuade anyone to buy your goods; 2nd, have but one price; 3rd, open no liquors to be drunk in your store; 4th, credit no one; 5th, don't make your store a harbor for loafers and idlers; 6th, spend your leisure hours in reading and in the best society; 7th, don't be discouraged even should the times be dull—hold on and you will prosper in due time; 8th, stand to all your contracts. I have committed (in business) several errors which I wish to prevent in you, if you will avail yourselves of my advice. 9th, you will lose custom and character if you permit drinking in your establishment. These are my injunctions as well as well as Judge Wingate's to you. Should you fail or not, heed our advice which is all intended for your good.

In conclusion, I will say to you that my anxiety for your welfare and prosperity has prompted me to give you this advice—I show this to your mother and she joins me in these admonitions to you and we will pray for your happiness and welfare.

It is my desire that you preserve these lines as a token of admonition.

And wishing you a happy New Year and may God bless you is the prayer of your

Affectionate Father,
S. Wiess

P.S. Don't hesitate to say No on all proper occasions, as it will save you many dollars and much disappointment.

27

David Appel

Spiritual Fulfillment Is Itself the Highest Goal

David Appel's Bar Mitzvah Address

March 3, 1866

David Appel of Philadelphia became bar mitzvah on March 3, 1866. His parents had his Confirmationsrede *printed (this was the speech he gave, in German, on the occasion). Obviously, the elder Appels were immigrants. David began with a prayer and ended with a prayer. It was a beautiful address, and certainly the work of a competent person, probably a rabbi or a teacher. If the talk does not represent the thinking of the 13-year-old David—and surely it does not—it certainly reflects the views of the rabbi and the parents. They had the boy say what they wanted him to say—what they wanted to hear. Thus they were voicing their own hopes and affirming their own religious beliefs.*

The Appels by this time were a well-established Philadelphia clan. More than one served in the Civil War; later Appels were surgeons in the United States Army.

Honored guests:

The observance of my bar mitzvah, which I celebrate with you, my family, and friends arouses my deepest feelings. I thank God from my heart for my happy childhood which is now completed; I thank my parents, the guardian angels of my life, for the deep love with which they have brightened my beginnings, my beloved grandparents whose gentleness has always been of great comfort to me, my teachers who instructed me, my relatives and friends who have always harbored the most supportive thoughts of me and who today share warmly in my holiday joy.

But among these grateful emotions are also woven the sincerest wishes for the future, whose gates open for me today and offer promise for my course in life. The most suitable expression of these expectant wishes, feelings, and promises is reflected in the short prayer which our teacher Moses offered with ardent emotion to God, as illustrated in this week's Pentateuchal portion: . . . *O Lord, make known your ways to me.* This beautiful and meaningful prayer expresses my innermost feelings today and reflects my deep convictions at this moment's consecration and significance. With Moses, I pray: *O Lord show me your ways to perfection and supreme bliss.*

I

Above all, it is my innermost and holiest wish that God will show me the way to perfection. Perfection is the first and highest object as well as goal for the granting of my wishes today. In my spirit lives the drive toward the perfection of my inner being. I have the firm conviction that spiritual perfection is itself the highest goal to which man can aspire in his lifetime. Thus the Creator made man, implanted within him a ray of His divine being, crowned him with superior worth, and gave him emotions and reason so that he would strive for inner enlightenment and elevate his spirit for the further development of his inner powers and talents. I would pay any price to ensure that my powers do not lessen in my moving along the road to perfection.

Until now, my dear parents guided me in the path of righteousness. They were always seriously concerned for my intellectual and religious education. They had me taught the word of God and encouraged me to attain universal knowledge. Through their pious examples they sowed the seeds of virtue and fear of God in my character. But would not this training be dissipated unless I myself began to aspire seriously toward further education? An ancient sage said: "*Whoever does not increase in learning, decreases what he knows* " [*Avot* 1:13].

Therefore, today it is my firm decision and I express it here among you, the circle of friends, with heartfelt joy to struggle *always and ardently, for the knowledge which assures men of a worthy place in society, as well as toward that which earns God's good will.* How could I otherwise repay my dear parents for the many pains they took in my upbringing except to nurture to ripeness the seeds that they planted in my soul? The worthiness of the children is the best reward for the parents! Thus I lift up my heart and eye to God and pray that he enlighten me and show me the ways which lead to *perfection.*

II

My heart also beseeches God to teach me the ways which lead to happiness. God has created man to be happy. The need for happiness is natural and spiritual. But I must ask what leads humanity to this wonderful goal? Should I, as so many in our day, seek success and prosperity only in material possessions? To attain these is not always possible, and even attained do they satisfy one's heart's desire? No. Earthly goods do not make man happy in a lasting way. That happiness in life can be achieved by man only if he follows God's ways—the ways to virtue and piety. These refresh the heart and soul and soften the storms, the unbridled desires, the violent passions in our breasts, and inspire the soul with peace and contentment without which no man on earth—though he may possess the richest treasures—can be lastingly and truly happy.

So today my heart beseeches God to show me the right way always and to permit me to travel it. May a believing conscience always guide me so that I never consider the physical as more important than the spiritual, and never sacrifice my eternal soul for temporal things. May I never be misguided to go on those byways which one perceives so many do in these times, and which disdain everything that is Godly and which pursue vile gains and physical satisfaction. As it says in this week's portion: You are my God, *God in heaven, who in thy grace guides me, I will always love you above all things. I will serve you according to your commandments, walk in your ways, and devote my heart and soul to you all of my life. Amen.*

28

Meshulam Faitel Goldbaum

I Always Wanted to Learn the Customs of America

Meshulam Faitel, in Poland, Urges His American Children to Live the Jewish Life

1875

Disturbed by reports that the Jews of the United States were lax in observing the age-old Law, Meshulam Faitel Goldbaum of Kuznitzkah, Poland, sat down and wrote a letter in Hebrew to his children in the United States, urging them and their wives to maintain the ancestral injunctions. This letter was sent in 1875; Meshulam died that same year on October 4, at 85 years of age. Thus, these are the views of a man born in 1790. Whether his sons living in postbellum America hearkened to his plea is not known. At all events, his letter, prefaced by a note giving the date of his death and marked "Jahrzeit," was framed and hung on the wall alerting them: Say kaddish!

The children's preface and the father's letter follow here.

IN MEMORY OF

The soul of our father, our guide, a righteous and a pious man, the renowned master Meshulam Faitel, son of the Rabbi Jacob Kopel (May the mentioning of a pious man be a blessing), who departed on the fifth day of Tishri in the year 5636 (Oct. 4, 1875) in the city of Kuznitzkah in the province of Poland. He was eighty-five years of age at his death ("His eye was not dim nor his natural force abated"—Deuteronomy 34:7).

And this is a transcription of his letter which he sent to his children in America before his death. Let this letter be remembered forever by his children; may they live happily and peacefully.

May the One who has made a way in the sea and paved a road in the strong waters watch over you and keep you from all hardship and trouble, my children, who are brothers and friends—none other than the master Nehemyah (Herman) and his younger brother the master Jehudah Lev (Louis). May they prosper as the sun shines in midday.

I always wanted to learn the customs of America and I could not arrive at the truth concerning how people act about religion, the observance of the Sabbath, and other customs, for not all those that write letters tell the truth. Just recently I met a stranger of beautiful appearance, good stature, and garbed in the most honorable attire; and I greeted him and he returned greetings, and I said, "I see that you are not rich and therefore I will ask you where you come from and where you are bound for." He answered me, "I am going to my birthplace, the town of Polotsk. I have just come back from America because the Jews do not observe their religion. They desecrate the Sabbath and eat unkosher food." I said to him, "My honored guest, come to my house and your needs will be upon me, even a lodging place." And he came to my house and I offered him a chair and a light. And when he was comfortably settled at rest I asked him please to relate to me the ways and manners of America, and on the morrow we would drink and be merry. "Only please tell me the truth—how do they observe the Sabbath and Holy Days?"

And he answered, "The Sabbath observers are in the minority and those who profane the Sabbath are in the majority. There are three sects in America. One consists of the poor who understand religion very little, and they do their work on the Sabbath just as on any other weekday.

"And the second sect consists of Jews who have lived in America for many years and have become rich citizens. They work and conduct their business transactions on the Sabbath, not heeding its sanctity. But these people work half the day only. The latter part of the day is spent in non-Jewish enjoyments—smoking and walking, and flirting with non-Jewish girls.

"And the third sect consists of Jews recently arrived from abroad, from Europe, who work on the Sabbath because of fear of being without employment. They work in factories the entire day of the Sabbath. There are also in this group Jews who observe their religion according to the laws of Moses as recorded in the Bible."

My children, do not go astray after the majority who desecrate the Sabbath. Though they be strong and successful, do not join their group and follow in their ways, because the wicked serpent is in their path and bitter will be their end. But always be on the side of the observers of the Sabbath who may seem to be weaker; there is a hidden compensation for them.

My children, observe the Sabbath with fine clothes, Sabbath candles, good food, and songs of glory to the Almighty, as it is commanded. Also, on the Sabbath day do not read any secular books that recount new events. Only the Book of Psalms which the poet of poets composed shall you read. You shall also read that chapter in the Bible apportioned for the week, following the chant according to the notes.

And you too, the wives of my sons, Blumah (Pauline) and Maitah (Matilda), observe the precepts pertaining to women as expounded in special female prayers. Then you will succeed in everything you do and have great joy from your children.

May the teachings of this letter to you be remembered and observed by you all. I am eighty-five years of age now; who knows whether I might write to you again.

Unto you, the wives of my sons I lay the responsibility of maintaining peace and happiness and of sustaining the love for the Jewish religion, for the house wherein peace reigns is the abiding place of the blessing of the Almighty. Wherever peace reigns is the abiding place of the blessing of the Almighty. Wherever ye shall turn ye shall succeed. These are the words of your father,

Meshulam Faitel

29

Louis Heilbrun

Be Temperate and Learn to Subdue Your Passions

Louis Heilbrun Addresses His Son on His Confirmation

July 8, 1877

In July 1877, Louis Heilbrun of Washington, D.C. (d. 1908) prepared an elaborate program for the bar mitzvah–confirmation of his son Morris. He then published an account of the ceremony in a twenty-one-page pamphlet entitled Religious Teachings: Morals and Maxims.

The confirmand, young Morris Heilbrun (b.1864), began the rather lengthy ceremony with a short address, undoubtedly written by his father or the rabbi. In it he asked his father for guidance. Then, in a formal fashion, the son submitted to a catechistic examination on Bible and Jewish theology. He concluded with a recitation of the Ten Commandments. Following this, he vowed formally and publicly to be faithful to the Mosaic religion. The father then took over and addressed his son. This speech is reprinted here. In the published brochure, Morris's father also included two pages of maxims of his own, which indicate that—for Louis Heilbrun—religion, morality, and the acquisition of wealth were all of a piece. These proverbs, also reprinted here, are in the tradition of Benjamin Franklin and the Gilded Age. Indeed, they are followed by extracts from Franklin's Way to Wealth, *published in 1758.* The last two pages of Louis Heilbrun's booklet are a reprint of an ethical letter from a mother to her son, although there is no indication that the author was a Jew; these pages are not reproduced here.*

---

*In Albert Henry Smyth (ed.), *The Writings of Benjamin Franklin* (New York, 1905), vol. III, pp. 407ff.

Address

Delivered by Louis Heilbrun at the Confirmation or Bar Mitzvah of His Son, Morris, July 8, 1877.

My son, thou hast now declared thy intentions of becoming a member of the Jewish faith and church; thou hast proven thyself worthy of the teachings of the Holy Scriptures. We accept your promises of trying to become efficient in the Holy Law, and that you will live in accordance therewith, as it becomes a good and moral Israelite. We accept you as one of Israel's children, and enrol you as member of the true believers in "One God" under the banner for which our forefathers have fought, and thousands of good men have sacrificed their lives and property.

As you have wisely said: the time is now coming when you need paternal advice more than ever, I will give you a father's advice on your journey through life. It is the following:

My son, hear the teachings of your father, and reject not the advice of your mother [Proverbs 1:8]. Let the Law be ever thy guide, and thy firm faith in God thy consolation and trust.

First. Be grateful to your Creator by imitating His great attributes, and by living up to His Laws.

Second. Be grateful to your parents, for they are the agents of God; to them you owe next to God all you know and possess. . . .

Honor, love, cherish, and protect thy father and mother, more especially when they are sick, old, or feeble.

By being kind to your brothers and sisters, by giving them advice and a helping hand, you will please your parents and God. Children must also honor their parents after death, by saying prayers on the day of their demise, according to Jewish custom, and by living up to their wishes.

And here I would remind you that it has pleased God to remove from our midst your mother in the prime of her life, but God in his mercy has given you another mother, who is kind and good to you, and to her you owe the love of a good son. Love, cherish, and protect her unto death.

Third. Be grateful to your teachers and all persons who enlighten you, give you good advice, or assist you otherwise. Remember an ungrateful son or man is the meanest creature on earth.

Fourth. Be kind and polite to all persons, more especially to the poor, fallen, or helpless. Even to your enemies be kind, forgiving, and charitable, as the Bible says: "Thou shalt not hate or take revenge on thy neighbors or fellow-men; but fear God" [Leviticus 19:18].

"Hate, jealousy, envy, and ambition will shorten man's life" [Avot 4:28].

Fifth. Be honest and just in all your doings and dealings with your fellow-men.

Practice truth and honesty through all thy earthly days,
And turn not one hair's width from God's holy ways.

Sixth. Practice simplicity and industry, as by the practice of these virtues our forefathers have preserved themselves to an old age, and Judaism to the present day.

Seventh. Be temperate and learn to subdue your passions. Who is a hero? One who knows how to govern his passions and resist temptations.

Eighth. Be faithful to your country. Live and act in accordance with the laws and customs of the country in which you are a citizen or domiciled. In time of danger or war help to protect your country—your government under which you live—even at the risk of your life and property.

Ninth. By the practice of these virtues you cannot fail to gain the love and respect of all good men. You will enjoy paradise on earth.

Having placed your trust in God, your faith is well-founded, go hence and fear no danger; but before you depart, let me invoke the blessings of God: . . .

"The Lord bless and preserve thee, the Lord cause his countenance to shine upon thee and be gracious unto thee; the Lord lift up his countenance unto thee, and grant thee peace" [Numbers 6:24–26]. Amen!

Maxims by Louis Heilbrun

I have always had and always shall have an earnest and true desire to contribute as far as lies in my power to the common stock of healthful cheerfulness and enjoyment. I believe that virtue shows quite as well in rags and patches as she does in purple and fine linen. I believe that she, and every beautiful object in external nature claims some sympathy in the breast of the poorest man who breaks his scanty loaf of daily bread:

Prudence is the mother of all wisdom.
Caution is the father of security.
He who pays beforehand is served behindhand.
Creditors have excellent memories.
If you would know the value of a dollar, try to borrow one.
Great bargains have ruined many.
Be silent when a fool talks.
Never speak boastingly of your business.
An hour of triumph comes at last to those who watch and wait.
Word by word Webster's big dictionary was made. Speak well of your friends, of your enemies say nothing.

Never take back a discharged servant.
If you post your servants upon your affairs, they will one day rend you.
No man can be successful who neglects his business.
Do not waste time in useless regrets over losses.
Systematize your business, and keep an eye on little expenses.
Small leaks sink great ships.
Never fail to take a receipt for money paid, and keep copies of your letters.
Do your business promptly, and bore not a business man with long visits.
Law is a trade in which the lawyers eat the oysters, and leave the clients the shell.

Rothschild, the founder of the world-renowned house of Rothschild & Co., ascribed his success to the following:

Never have anything to do with an unlucky man.
Be cautious and bold; make a bargain at once.
Mind your own business; let others attend their business.
An agreement without consideration is void.
Signatures made with a lead pencil are good in law.
The act of one partner bind[s] all the others.
Contracts made on Sunday cannot be enforced.
Principals are responsible for the acts of their agents.
Each individual in a partnership is responsible for the whole amount of the debts of the firm.
A note drawn on Sunday or by a minor is void.
An endorser of a note is exempt from liability if not served with notice of its dishonor within 24 hours of the non-payment.
Do not endorse or go security for others, unless you intend to pay for it.
Notes bear interest only when so stated.
It is fraud to conceal fraud.
A note obtained by fraud, or from a person in a state of intoxication, cannot be collected.
Pay as you go and go as you pay.
Do not live above your means, as that is the sure way to bankruptcy.

30

Raphael J. Moses

Would You Honor Me? Call Me a Jew

Major Moses Rebukes a Judeophobe

1878

During an 1878 political convention in Georgia, an anti-Jewish politician attacked Major Raphael J. Moses, a Confederate veteran. Moses defended himself as a Jew in an oft-quoted letter, reprinted here. The major was known throughout the South as a brilliant lawyer and a gifted orator.

I have taken time to authenticate a report which I heard for the first time on the evening of the last day of the convention. At West Point [Georgia], during your congressional campaign, and in my absence, you sought for me a term of reproach, and from your well-filled vocabulary selected the epithet of Jew. Had I served you to the extent of my ability in your recent political aspirations, and your overburdened heart had sought relief in some exhibition of unmeasured gratitude, had you a wealth of gifts and selected from your abundance your richest offering to lay at my feet, you could not have honored me more highly, nor distinguished me more gratefully than by proclaiming me a Jew.

I am proud of my lineage and my race; in your severest censure you can not name an act of my life which dishonors either, or which would mar the character of a Christian gentleman. I feel it an honor to be one of a race whom persecution can not crush; whom prejudice has in vain endeavored to subdue; who, despite the powers of man and the antagonism of the combined governments of the world, protected by the hand of deity, have burst the temporal bonds with which prejudice would have bound them, and after nineteen centuries of persecution still survive as a nation, and assert their manhood and intelligence, and give proof of "the divinity that stirs within them" by having become a great factor in the government of mankind. Would you honor me? Call me a Jew. Would you place in unenviable prominence your own un-Christian prejudices and narrow-minded bigotry? Call me a Jew. Would you offer a living example of a man into whose educated mind toleration can not enter—on whose heart the spirit of liberty and the progress of American principles has made no impression? You can find it illustrated in yourself. Your narrow and benighted mind, pandering to the prejudices of your authority, has attempted to taunt me by calling me a Jew—one of that peculiar people at whose altars, according to teachings of your theological masters, God chose that His son should worship.

Strike out the nationality of Judea, and you would seek in vain for Christ and his apostles. Strike out of sacred history the teachings of the Jews and you would be as ignorant of God and the soul's immortal mission as you are of the duties and amenities of social life. I am not angered, but while I thank you for the opportunity which you have given me to rebuke a prejudice confined to a limited number distinguished for their bigotry and sectarian feelings, of which you are a fit exemplar, I pity you for having been cast in a mould impervious to the manly and liberal sentiments which distinguish the nineteenth century. You are not created without a purpose; nature exhibits her beauties by the contrast of light and shade; humanity illustrates its brightest and noblest examples by placing its most perfect models in juxtaposition with the meanest specimens of mankind, so that you have the consolation of knowing that your mind has been thus deformed in the wisdom of the great architect, that you might serve as a shadow to bring forth in bold relief the brighter tints of that beautiful picture of religious toleration engrafted in the constitution of the United States by the wisdom of our fathers.

I have the honor to remain, sir, your most obedient servant.

Raphael J. Moses

31

Morris Goldwater

Obedience to Your Parents and a Careful Selection of Your Companions

Bar Mitzvah Advice on the Arizona Frontier

May 8, 1879

Early in May 1879, the sedate London-born Morris Goldwater of Prescott, Arizona Territory, 27 years old, wrote a congratulatory bar mitzvah note to his 13-year-old brother, Baron, then in San Francisco. Their Father Michel ("Mike") was a native of Konin, Poland, where he had received a Jewish education; his mother tongue was Yiddish. Baron was born in 1866 in Los Angeles, in a community of between 100 and 200 Jews. Father Mike had moved from Konin to Paris, to London, to San Francisco, to the Sierras, to Los Angeles, to the Arizona Territory. The Goldwaters were merchants, with stores in Prescott and Phoenix. Morris, who had a hankering for public office, served for many years as a mayor of Prescott and as a grandmaster of the Masons. When Baron grew up, he managed the Goldwater branch in Phoenix. Although the family was Orthodox, Baron married out of the faith; his Episcopal son, Barry Morris Goldwater, was elected to the United States Senate in 1953 and ran for president on the Republican ticket in 1964.

The original family name was Goldwasser. Hirsch Goldwasser, Mike's father, had been an innkeeper. The name? Goldwasser was a German alcoholic liquor with gold-like flakes. It was distilled in the German–Polish port of Danzig, about a hundred miles north of Konin. Mike changed his name to Goldwater in London. Since the early eighteenth century, many European Jews passing through London on their way to British North America anglicized their names.

Prescott, May 8th, 1879

Mr. Baron Goldwater

My dear brother:

Although not too well versed in Jewish theology I know that there is a special importance attached to ones thirteenth birthday among our people.

It is with pleasure that I congratulate you on having attained this, your religious majority. I trust that the years which will pass, ere you can claim to have arrived at man's estate, may prove free from care and trouble as those through which you have come. If on that day you can on looking back to the present time, find as little to reproach yourself with, as you can find by a retrospection of the past, you will indeed have passed a most praiseworthy life. It is such a consummation that I trust awaits you but it is not without great effort on your part that this can be achieved.

I am sorry that from my own experience I can not give you rules that would safely guide you to this much desired goal. But I am too well aware of my own defects to think that I could do ought than serve as a buoy on your course to mark some shoal to be avoided.

Nor do I wish to send you a string of maxims cut from some Poor Richard's Almanac which may be read, thrown aside and never (from some reason or other) acted upon.

Let me rather urge on you the steady continuance in the course already begun.

Obedience to your parents and a careful selection of your companions are the only rules which I would urge on you. By a strict attention to those you cannot help being polite, temperate, truthful, and industrious, and possessing these virtues you will have all that the world can give of any worth.

It is because I have so strong a belief that by doing all this you will bring pleasure to your parents and those who are dear to you, and honor to yourself, that I so heartily and sincerely congratulate you.

Trusting that He who has guarded you thus far through life may continue to bless and preserve you and endow you with all those virtues which make life worth having, I am

Your loving brother,
Morris Goldwater

32

Getty Bechmann

The Pangs I Suffer at the Thought of Your Going

Heinrich Goes to America

September 30, 1880

With tears in her eyes, Getty Bechmann wrote a letter—in German, of course, although with some Hebrew—saying good-bye to her son Heinrich, who was leaving for distant America with two trunks and high hopes in September of 1880. The trunks contained his clothing, winter- and summer-weight, including red flannel underwear. In the United States, in Cincinnati, his hopes were realized: as Nathan Henry Beckman (d. 1940), he became a wealthy clothing manufacturer. When he retired in 1910, he devoted himself to good deeds in the communal and religious fields. He became president of a Reform synagogue, treasurer of the Union of American Hebrew Congregations, and a member of the board of the United Jewish Social Agencies. In 1909 he endowed a clinic at the Jewish Hospital in memory of his parents.

His mother Getty's letter to Heinrich, translated and reprinted here, reflects the ethics, the piety, the idealism that characterized many a mother who sent a child out into the world. Be assured that N. Henry Beckman attempted to rear his children in the spirit that had moved his beloved mother. His daughter, Mrs. Martha Ransohoff, was a highly respected Cincinnati educationist; her children and grandchildren were also distinguished citizens.

---

11 P.M., Sept. 30, Night, eleven o'clock, 1880

My dear good Heinrich, may you live to be a hundred [written in Hebrew]:

The long expected has come to pass, your trip to America. You realize, my dear son, the pangs I suffer at the thought of your going. But it is your wish and so shall it be. May the Almighty guide and protect you from all evil and be with you always. Put your trust in Him and everything will work out. Be good, as you always have been, good and kind, and you will get along everywhere. Dear Heinrich, do not forget your beloved religion. It will bring you comfort and consolation, patience and endurance in trials, whether it be your fate to be rich or poor. Always keep God before you and in your heart.

You are going out into the wide world far from parents and family. Don't be discouraged, for you are endowed with so many good qualities, and my heart tells me that God's blessing will accompany you in all that you propose to do. Commit your way unto the Lord and you will be successful. Be careful in all that you undertake, and particularly in your associations. Guard your health, know that it is the greatest gift on earth.

I would like to and I could say much more to you, dear Heinrich, but it is very hard and distressing for me. Therefore I can only say, finally: Go with God and may it be well with you. Be very cheerful and put to good use all that you have been taught. Always consider very carefully what ever you do. Though a great distance separates us, my parental worry, my motherly thoughts of you will never cease as long as my loyal heart beats. The thought that our separation will be of short duration is my only consolation in my great pain.

And so, my dear Heinrich, I bid you adieu. Write me and let me know everything that you experience and that happens to you. Do not play with the idea of settling so far away from us, and let me live in the expectation of not being without you too long. Tears come to my eyes; you will therefore have to excuse my poor writing although you know I have such good intentions.

Your ever faithful mama,
Getty

Amen, good luck, and blessing [written in Hebrew]

P.S. Tomorrow marks the advent of your twentieth birthday and the start of your big journey. May everything be for the best. Good luck, blessing, and prosperity!

33

Harry E. Leopold

I Wish Them to Know that I Love Them

Harry E. Leopold Becomes a Bar Mitzvah in Akron, Ohio

May 20, 1883

Harry E. Leopold was born on May 20, 1870; thirteen years later he became a bar mitzvah in Akron, Ohio, in the Akron Hebrew Congregation. Tradition has it that his bar mitzvah ceremony was the first to be held in this synagogue, whose members were affiliated with the Reformist Union of American Hebrew Congregations. The approach in this speech is not stereotypical; observance and other duties are mentioned, but love is the overriding theme.

My friends!

In accordance with the custom of our holy religion, I today step out of the ranks of childhood and accept those higher duties, which according to our Torah must be fulfilled by every good man and woman. I know that I am little more than a child, that I do not fully understand all the duties which I ought to fulfill. But until now, the loving guidance of my parents, the instruction of my teachers, and the encouragement of my friends have helped me to find the right way; and I hope that they will continue to help me. I understand that the object of life is to become perfect, and that the road to perfection is alongside of the stream of human love. God makes little children so happy, because he wishes them to cling forever to this stream of affection, because he wants their bodies and their souls to be strengthened by the loving kindness of parents and friends.

In this important moment when it seems as though my childhood was passing away from me, I thoroughly appreciate the unselfish love of parents and friends. Now when I feel that God and the world will hold me responsible for all my acts, either good or bad, now I first seem to know what the love of my parents has been worth to me. I feel that their love has kept trouble and sorrow away from me, and has made my childhood seem like an endless day of happiness. For all this I wish to return thanks, first to God for his goodness, to my dear parents for their love, their forbearance, and their watchfulness, to my teachers for their attention and patience, to my relatives and friends for their kindness and encouragement. I wish them to know that I love them, that I feel the importance of this step in my young life. I wish them to hear that I shall try to be a source of happiness to my parents, a pleasure to my friends, and an honor to myself and my religion. Amen.

34

Julius Ochs

Why Did I Preach the Dogmas of Judaism?

Squire Ochs Theologizes

1888

Julius Ochs (1826–1888), a Bavarian who came to the United States in 1845, was a musician, a linguist, a soldier in the Mexican and the Civil Wars, and finally a civic and Jewish communal activist in Knoxville and Chattanooga. He served in both these towns as the voluntary rabbi. Above all he was a kindly, cultured gentleman with theological views of his own. Ochs may well have been influenced religiously by the famous rabbi Samuel Hirsch of Philadelphia, a scholar of philosophic caliber. Hirsch believed that the Jewish ceremonies served to embody important ideas and ideals. Ochs's son, Adolph S. Ochs, was the publisher of the Chattanooga Times *and later of* The New York Times.

At the "urgent request" of his family, Ochs wrote a memoir, shortly before his death in 1888. Part of it is reproduced here.

My religious convictions should more properly be expressed as my "religious ideas." A settled conviction of concrete postulates regarding the unfathomable mysteries of the Unknown cannot be expressed in dogmatic terms. Is there a living soul who can penetrate the veil which divides the finite from the infinite? Is there a living soul who can conscientiously exclaim "I know." We may fortify our belief, our ideas, our convictions by a form of faith that persuades us that we think we "know," but positive knowledge of what lies beyond has never been accorded man by Our Supreme Being. . . .

And how shall we worship this Divine Essence? Not in idle forms, ceremonies or by lip service. No. His worship should be rendered by living a reverent life, by the practice of charity, benevolence, right living, and morality.

This is my religion. I believe with all my soul and with all my reason, with all my heart that there is a Supreme Being, a Supernal Power which brought into existence the mighty Cosmos, who rules and governs it with wisdom and justice and mercy and loving kindness. No human intellect can divine the form or conceive the character thereof. This Supreme Being is neither the God portrayed by either the orthodox Jewish or Christian theology, nor by any other theology known to us. Nor will it ever be vouchsafed to human intellect to know or understand the infinite character and majesty of Him who rules the heavens and the earth. God the Infinite cannot be confined within the limits of synagogue, temple, cathedral or church, be it ever so lofty. The vast stretches of the earth, the infinite spaces of the universe, these are my temple and my Book of Revelations. There I learn my lessons—the lessons that teach me to look upon every man as a brother, to walk humbly before my God, to fear Him, and to love Him, to worship Him and extol Him, to practise morality, benevolence and charity.

The question may be asked: If such are my beliefs, why did I preach the dogmas of Judaism from the pulpit, why do I maintain a Jewish religion, support a Jewish congregation, occupy a pulpit in a Jewish synagogue, encourage my daughters to teach Judaism in Sunday School and to a degree practise and observe Jewish rites and ceremonies?

My answer is that formal religion is a necessity to the masses. Without it there can be no morality, no sense of responsibility or higher obligation. One endowed with culture or education has moral restrictions and inhibitions developed in youth by environment or example. Though in later years the dogmas of specific theology may be discarded, the sense of moral values remains fixed and conscience exercises a controlling influence. But to the uncultured, the uneducated, morality and reverence, the fundamentals of clean living and the perception of duty of one's fellowman, require the precepts and the ceremonial rites of religious training. Morality, justice, the standards of a righteous life as prescribed in the Ten Commandments are not intuitive in frail humanity, but must be inculcated by training, precept and example. Religion, with its solemn environment and its ceremonial rites, is the sole influence that can serve as a restraint against passion, violence, and sinful acts.

The great mass of humanity does not indulge in introspection, does not investigate, does not reason, does not endeavor to penetrate the subtle mysteries of theology. Most people give their entire thought to material affairs, the struggle for existence, and the perpetual quest for pleasure or entertainment. To such as these, the eternal verities must be associated with religious ceremonial and prescribed forms in order to find a lodgment in their thoughts.

The mission I undertook as shepherd of my flock was to impress the members of my congregation to do their duty as good Americans, to live a virtuous life, to fulfil their domestic obligations faithfully and conscientiously, to practice charity, to assist the unfortunate. I urged them to observe in their personal conduct the rules set forth in the Decalogue, wherein are comprehended moral teachings and ethical standards unparalleled by all the theologies and ecclesiastical tomes produced since Moses proclaimed the undying commandments amid the thunders of Mt. Sinai. I endeavored so far as possible to divest our worship of superficial surroundings. I preached the brotherhood of man, the kinship of the human race, the benevolence, omnipotence and all-pervading and all-pervasive mercy of Almighty God.

I believed, and my faith is firmer than ever today, that the teaching of religion is essential to the safety, the happiness and the purity of the human family; that it is essential to the formation of the character of the immature, that our children find in religion the surest and the sanest, the purest and the safest influence to mould their habits and conduct. So believing and feeling in my conscience that in the Jewish religion these eternal truths are more clearly and more logically found and expressed than in any other faith, I expounded our doctrine from the pulpit. If my teachings sowed fruitful seed in any hearts, I am content.

35

David Edelstadt

I Will Sing to My People from My Grave

David Edelstadt's Testament

1889

David Edelstadt (1866–1892) began publishing Russian poetry when he was a child of only 12; Russian was his mother tongue. After the 1881 pogroms in his native land, he fled to the United States in 1882 and finally settled in New York City, where he helped edit a Yiddish anarchist journal, Die Freie Arbeiter Stimme (The Free Voice of the Workers)*. Suffering from tuberculosis, he moved on to Denver. However, because he was impoverished, he lacked the means to secure the care that might have saved him, and he died there at the age of 26.*

This Yiddish poet was an anarchist, a revolutionary who desperately yearned for a new world and a new society that would bring hope to the poor and the oppressed. To inspire the workers, he wrote impassioned, lurid Yiddish pleas; his verses fired the hearts and souls of the men and women bent over their machines.

The poems became songs. Among them were "In Battle" and "My Testament." The latter, reprinted here in a rather literal translation, first appeared in 1889 in Die Warheit*, a New York anarchist paper.*

Is this song justifiably seen as an ethical will? It is an appeal that clearly transcends ethnic boundaries, an appeal for compassion, for justice.

My Testament

Oh, good friend, when I die
Carry our flag to my grave,

Freedom's flag with its red colors,
Sprinkled with the blood of workers.

And there under the flag, that red one,
Sing me a song, my song of freedom,
My own song, "In Battle,"
Which rattles like the chains
Of the enslaved Christian and Jew.

Even in my grave will I hear
My song of freedom,
My battle song.
Even there will I pour out my tears
For the enslaved Christian and Jew.

And when I hear the swords clashing,
In the last battle of blood and pain,
Then will I sing to my people
From my grave,
And will inspirit their heart.

36

Abraham Wolf Edelman

Bring Some Sacrifice to Assist Each Other

Rabbi A. W. Edelman's Will

August 17, 1891

Abraham Wolf Edelman (1832–1907) was the first rabbi of Los Angeles. This native Pole, who came to town in 1862 when Los Angeles was little more than a pueblo, served as a sort of omnibus factotum: rabbi, cantor, preacher, teacher, beadle, circumciser (mohel). *In his role as circumciser, he traveled as far south as Mexico and as far east as Arizona. His initial salary was $75 a month. Orthodox in training and inclination, he moved reluctantly–or was pushed–toward Reform and resigned in 1885 when his congregants sought a more "modern" clergyman. Edelman signed his ethical will in 1891; he survived for sixteen more years. Rather apologetically, he told his children that he was not wealthy. (Actually, he was! The rabbi had bought some city land for $350; by the time of his death in 1907, it was worth about $160,000.) His charities–and they were substantial–embraced Catholic and Protestant as well as Jewish institutions.*

Although entrenched in Orthodoxy, Edelman disregarded the traditional injunction that required immediate burial.

The orthography, capitalization, and italicization in this document are his own.

My Dear Wife and Children:

It is my last wish that you should not be in a hurry with my interment: if possible, let at least forty-eight hours elaps before I am taken to my last resting-place, and that you should follow out these directions:

First. Let my funeral be conducted without any commotion or disturbance; let none of you cry any more than possible, for those who have done their duty to their parents need not cry at their funerl.

Second. I wish to be Methar (washed) according to the old Jewish costom. Before commencing, let some one who is competent to read Hebrew read that prayer which is usually read for those who are engaged in attending the dead.

Third. I desire to be dressed in a white shroud and a talet [praying shawl] around my shoulders. Let my coffin be dark and plain, no *trimings or decorations*, but you may allow a glass on the face of the coffin if you so desire. [The departing soul can be cleansed in the water.]

Fourth. I do not wish for any display of oratory, praise, or to be *Eulogized in either English or German, at the house or at the grave.* (But if you so desire, the Masonic Fraternity may perform the funeral service at the grave.)

After the grave is filled, let the officiating Rabbi, or any one who is competent to read Hebrew, read the Hebrew burial service, *Tzedak Haddin* [God's judgment is right], after which you shall all say the "Kaddish." Let none of you ever wear excessive mourning. You may even be satisfied with a simple *black tie around your neck or hat;* but as I think much of the "Kaddish Prayer," it is my wish that you shall, as far as possible, say the "Kaddish" for eleven mounts, and in latter years, keep the "Jahrzit."

Fifth. I do not wish for any display of *flowers*, rather give that much for charity, nor do I desire a costly muniment or any flowery epitaph. My name. The time of birth (August 17th, 1832). The time of death, and some words like these: "To the Eternal, a perfict Unity, did I gave up my spirit. The Lord hath given, and the Lord hath taken away, praised be the name of the Lord forever and ever."

And last but not least. I do aske and pray of you, dear children, that you shall continue to honor your dear bereved mother, lighten for her the burdens of her distressed and lamented widowhood, help her as you can, and do not disturb her in anything. Everything will surely fall to your lot after her demise. I do not leave you much, but the best which my humble power could offer you, you have already received, and that is my name and the limited education which I have given you. Strive to keep harmoniously together and let no one disunite you, rather bring some sacrifice to assist each other, for the example of six children linked together by a strong love and affection is a more precious ornament to a father's grave than the finest of flowers and the highest monument ever erected or planted in his honor.

A few words more, my dear children, and I have done. I know that you cannot practice our religion as I did. This, however, you can do, and that is, to *remain Jews and to live as Jews as far as possible.* Be ever charitable to the poor. Make it possible to join some synagogue or temple; contribute towards it your little mite; and never stray away from the religion of your fathers, and from the One and only God. For the time will come when the whole world will acknowledge that the Eternal God is One and that His great and mighty name is One, forever and ever.

A. W. Edelman

Los Angles, Monday, August the 17th, 1891

37

Liebman Adler

Remain Jews and Live as Jews

Testament of Liebman Adler, Chicago Rabbi

January 1892

Liebman Adler (1812–1892) was born in Lengsfeld, Saxe-Weimar, Germany. Like many other German Jewish lads of his day, he received a Hebrew education supplemented by training in a Jewish teacher's college. After serving a congregation in his native town, he came to the United States in 1854 and officiated initially in Detroit. Then, in 1861, he moved on to Chicago, where he ministered to Kehillath Anshe Maarabh (or Ma'ariv), the Congregation of the Men of the West, until 1882, when he was pensioned. His will—in German—was written in January 1892, about a week before he died. German was the language in which he preached, and many of his sermons were published in a three-volume German work. Some of his talks appeared in English translation in 1893.

Adler appears to have been a courteous, benign gentleman who spurned sham and polemics. His modesty is reflected in his last instructions to his wife and family. Adler fathered fourteen children, eleven of whom survived. One of them, Dankmar Adler, became a notable architect associated with Louis Henri Sullivan. Frank Lloyd Wright worked in their office for many years.

MY LAST WILL

I desire that there be no haste in my interment. If there are no signs of decomposition sooner, the funeral should not be until forty-eight hours after my death.

If the physician who treated me should find it desirable in the interest of science to hold a post-mortem examination, I would like that he be not interfered with.

My coffin shall not cost more than $7.

No flowers.

My funeral to be directly from the place of demise to the cemetery.

Dear Hannah: In view of your delicate health, I desire that you remain at home and not join the funeral if the weather is the least inclement.

Not more than three days' mourning in domestic retirement.

I justly value the kaddish of my sons and daughters, but I do so only if you, after the expiration of the year of mourning, do not omit attendance at the synagogue without necessity [compulsion].

If financial conditions permit, each of my married children should join a Jewish congregation, the fittest being the Kehillath Anshe Ma'ariv.

Those children who do not live too distant should, if the weather permits, and if it can be done without disturbing their own domestic relations, gather every Friday evening around the mother.

My children, hold together! In this let no sacrifice be too great to assist each other and to uphold brotherly and sisterly sentiment. Each deed of love you do to one another would be balm to my soul. The example of eleven children of one father who stand together in love and trust would be to his grave a better decoration than the most magnificent wreath of flowers, which I willingly decline, but leave to your judgment. The small savings which I leave will come to you only after the death of the mother.

I know you; I may trust that you will not meet in an unfilial way about possession and disposition. The heritage which is already yours is a good name and as good an education as I could afford to give. It does not look as if any one of you had a disposition to grow rich. Do not be worried by it. Remain strictly honest, truthful, industrious, and frugal. Do not speculate. No blessing rests upon it even if it be successful. Throw your whole energy into the pursuance of the calling you have chosen. Serve the Lord and keep Him always before you; toward men be amiable, accommodating, and modest, and you will fare well even without riches. My last word to you is: Honor your mother. Help her bear her dreary widowhood. Leave her undisturbed in the use of the small estate, and assist if there should be want.

Farewell, wife and children.

But one more word, children. I know well you could not, if you would, practice Judaism according to my views and as I practiced it. But remain Jews and live as Jews in the best manner of your time, not only for yourself, but also where it is meant to further the whole.

38

Abraham Bettmann

I Leave My Loving Children Behind with Great Reluctance

The Last Will of Dr. Abraham Bettmann

May 17, 1893

Abraham Bettman, born in Bavaria on January 26, 1806, studied Talmud in his youth at a German yeshivah, but later turned to medicine and in 1837 received his medical degree from the University of Munich. Four years later, he was licensed to practice medicine in a restricted number of Bavarian villages. Probably impelled by the failure of the liberal revolution of 1848 and unhappy under the civil disabilities to which he was subject, he immigrated to the United States, settling in Cincinnati, where his wife's brother had made his home. Bettmann worked as a physician in that city until his retirement in 1887. His will, in German, was written in 1893 in Chicago, where he may have made his home temporarily; he died in Cincinnati on January 14, 1901. It is not surprising that, as a cultured German and a university graduate, Bettmann had literary interests and wrote poetry.

Chicago, May 17, [18]93

It is perhaps not too early for me, in my eighty-eighth year, to write down a few instructions with regard to my burial. It is my wish that after my death I shall not be placed in ice or embalmed. It is, furthermore, my wish not to enter into my final dwelling-place until signs of decomposition are perceptible. When I bid my last farewell to life here, Dr. Kuh will perform the final service for his old colleague, that of examining my corpse several times in order to become convinced that it is in genuine earnest, and not a simulation. Should I die in Cincinnatti [*sic*], I shall expect this friendly act to be performed by my beloved nephews, Fred and Robert [Forchheimer]. My burial garments should consist of my everyday clothes and a skullcap. Mr. Hermann Mack, who should be informed at once about my death, is indeed not to know anything about this travel-habit. [As an Orthodox Jew he would have insisted that Bettmann be buried in a shroud.] A death notice can be published in any newspaper, but not the time of my burial. This is to be strictly private. Quietly and peacefully as I have always lived, just so I desire to enter also upon my last journey.

On the reverse side of the monument, which marks the grave of our dear Mamma, my name and the day of my birth and that of my death are to be engraved. I do not desire any separate gravestone. As greatly and as deeply as I always deplored the loss of my noble wife, your good mother, just as much am I glad now that the warmest rays of the sun of my life can not accompany me. Death has nothing frightening for me, but I leave my loving children behind with great reluctance. A Norwegian also sees the setting of the sun, even though it still shines for him at midnight. My absent sons are not to be informed of the death of their father until after my burial. With tears in my eyes I now take my eternal departure from you and I kiss each of you repeatedly. So then farewell, farewell forever! May peace and love always prevail among you!

Your loving old father,
A. Bettmann

39

Henry S. Louchheim and Jerome H. Louchheim

I Love You All So Devotedly

April 2, 1894

Keep Up Your Religion and You Will Be Better Americans

1933

The Louchheims of Philadelphia

German-born Henry S. Louchheim came to the United States in 1852 and, after a generation, made a fortune in clothing and woolens. He then turned to banking. In the panic of the 1890s he lost almost everything; he was bankrupt, and the blow shattered him. His anguish, his lost hopes, the consolations of religion, his perception of himself as an honorable man are all reflected in the first letter partially reprinted here.

A generation later, in 1933, Jerome H. Louchheim, the youngest of Henry's three sons, wrote an ethical letter to his family some time before his death. This letter appears after his father's in the following pages.

Philadelphia, April 2d, 1894

. . . Since I cannot leave you, dear boys, riches I wish to give you my fatherly advise, and I do hope that you will pay attention to it. . . . First of all honor and obey your dear mother; always be a loving good son to her, as she has been a true, loving and self-sacrificing mother to you. I beseech you to do everything in your power to make her happy and contented. My aim was that she should have everything that her heart may desire, for she of all the women of the world would have deserved it and been worthy to enjoy herself. My financial situation has taken such a turn that I had to refuse her many little things that often my heart blet that I was obliged to refuse it, although she was satisfied with everything and endeavored so often to have me feel satisfied. I cannot express myself what a true and good wife she has been to me, and my heart aches when I think that I provided so badly for her. Therefore, I implore you, leave nothing undone to make her life happy. Should either of you be married or single always be a good affectionate son to your dear good mother.

And now, my dear beloved sons, I have some other matters which are weighing so heavy on my heart, for I love you all so devotedly that I cannot express myself, and I have to stop so often to whip the tears from my eyes that I am not able to write. Always live in peace and harmony together. . . . I hope that should, God forbid, anyone of you three sons ever come in such a situation [bad financial trouble], that you will be ready and willing to share at anytime the last dollar with your brother as long as he is worthy of it.

Something else presses heavy on my mind and heart. To judge from all sorounding circumstances, I shall not live to see one of my sons married, a wish which I so ardently in silence prayed for. While it is not my desire to dictade [to] any one of you whom to select for life as your companion, I do charge you that you never will marry outside of our religion, never think of marrying any other but a Jewess, out of a respectable family. I emphaticaly request that you will never disobey this my request and I know I voice the request of your dear mother if I ask this of you.

I could go on and write page after page, yet I don't wish to burden neither of you with unreasonable requests. Had I been successful in business or never went in this unfortunate business of which I did not understand anything, we should have been one of the most happy families in the world, for I was blessed with a true good wife and three sons all of whom I fairly worshiped. Yet the great change in my financial situation brought so many changes about which I cannot explain but deeply feel, none of which either of you are responsible for. All the fault is mine and I suffer for it, for more than even your good mother or either of you can imagine. I was proud of my name, proud that I was situated to give my dear children as good a education as they could embrace, proud that I was in a position to do good to others which where not situated as well. And now robbed even of my name this hurts me far more than the money lost. . . .

Something else comes in my mind. Always, dear boys, remain in correspondence with my dear brothers and sisters in Europe as well as with your cousins, and if you are able to assist any of them that may need aid, particular Cousin Sophie and her children, do all you can for your father's sake.

Should I be called away suddenly from you all, I wish my funeral as plainly conducted as can be. I never believed to make a show; particular in death all are alike. If you can conscientiously say *kaddish* do so. Always hold up our religion, for I have learned that without religion to consol me I could not have lived any more in this great trouble of mine. . . .

Henry S. Louchheim

1933

To my dear Wife and Sons,

Besides the charities taken care of in my will, I have been contributing to other hospitals, etc. Also sending money to relatives in Europe and some here who require assistance. I leave it entirely to your judgment as to whether you continue any or all of these payments.

I have only one request to make. I want you to keep up your seats in synagogue and attend services whenever possible. Keep up your religion and you will be better Americans. You will realize this more and more as you grow older. You will get more pleasure out of your lives, attain greater success, and have the respect of the community in which you live by being true to your religion.

Do not think that I want to lecture you by leaving this letter. I merely want to try and make it clear that any success I might have had during my life, and surely the pleasures, I attribute to my faith in God as taught me in the synagogue.

If the officers and directors of the congregation would grant permission, I would like the services conducted at the synagogue.

May the good Lord bless you and keep you well.

Your loving husband and father,
Jerome H. Louchheim

40

Morris Winchevsky

I Am the Lord Thy God and Mammon Is My Name

Morris Winchevsky, the Socialist, Parodies the Ten Commandments

1895

In 1894, one of Jewry's eminent socialists made his home in the United States. This Russian had several names. He seems to have been given the name Benzion Novakhovichi at birth, but he is best known by one of his pseudonyms, Morris W(V)inchevsky (1856–1932). Called "the grandfather of Yiddish socialist literature," he published the first socialist Yiddish periodical while living in London in 1884. As a socialist, a philosophic materialist, he was opposed to supernaturalism and religion. Winchevsky employed his talents as a poet and essayist to caricature sacred Hebrew religious documents. He wanted to emancipate Jewry from Judaism, which he deemed to be an oppressive cult without humanitarian goals. That is why he parodied the Mosaic Ten Commandments. The parody was published in Boston in 1895, in a Yiddish paper called The Truth. *An abridged translation is printed here.*

Mammon's *Ten Commandments*

I. *I am the Lord thy god* and Mammon is my name. Heaven and earth, hear my word! Capital, I am thy soul and thy conscience. I cause starvation and I can bring gratification. I can make bitter or I can make sweet every bite you eat. I rule alone down below and up above. I can bring you peace or rivers of blood. I make the sun to rise and the snow to fall. I am the King and I am above all. Mammon is my name and Money is my Eternal Flame.

II. *Thou Shalt Have No Other Gods* . . . Don't dare to set up any other gods in my temple–it will hurt my feelings. I permit no other gods–or goddesses! A goddess makes me uneasy, especially the goddess of Liberty–she is an obstacle to the enforcement of my laws, which are needed to protect us against our foes. And the goddess of Equality is a troublemaker. Her place is more properly in the graveyard than in my temple! In a Word, thou shalt have no other gods before me–and don't you forget it!

III. *Thou Shalt Not Take My Name* . . . Never swear falsely unless by doing so you are adding to your bank account. In your business dealings you may do what the millionaires do so charmingly–tell a lie and then swear to it. . . .

IV. *Remember the Sabbath Day* . . . One day a week your employees shall do no manner of labor for you–and that includes your horse, your ox, your cow. If they protest, tell them to behave or you'll give them *seven* days a week rest. Get my meaning?

V. *Honor Thy Father and Mother* . . . Especially if you have inherited all your gold and silver and oriental rugs from them. In this respect, the worker is luckier than you–he does not have the burden of this commandment, because after all, what does he own for which he should be thankful to his mother and father?

VI. *Thou Shalt Not Murder* . . . No matter how vast your treasures, this is too heavy a sin to bear, my son. On the other hand, do not upset yourself if someone brings you the news that one of your workers has had his head split open by a machine in your factory. This is no worse than happens in a war–whether it be for gold or for revenge or even for a medal of honor.

VII. *Thou Shalt Not Commit* . . .Avoid amorous interludes with women of your own kind–it interferes with your ability to augment your fortune. What do you need it for? There are many young women in the labor market who are willing to sell their talents–and some of them can dance and sing too. But don't go boasting about it all over town, lest the world begin to doubt you are the upright and Mammon-fearing citizen you're supposed to be.

VIII. *Thou Shalt Not Steal.* Don't stoop to common thievery–it will lead to nothing but prison. And don't get involved with underworld characters–a partnership means your cut is only half. Stick to the big bankruptcies. If you play according to my rules, you'll stay out of trouble. Furthermore, you can swim in gold up to your neck if you set up trusts in the U.S. of A. Free countries let themselves be skinned alive without uttering a peep. They even help you weave the ropes to tie them up. On pain of death I command you: Don't be a petty crook!

IX. *Thou Shalt Not Bear False Witness.* Don't bear false witness against your business associate. Don't tell tales out of school. You both have a common interest: to stand united for the status quo. But if you find yourself in court with him don't let him off easy simply because he's your friend. Don't take undue advantage of him either, if you hold the better cards, because you may both want to get together afterward and testify against the socialists who are trying to tear down my temple.

X. *Thou Shalt Not Covet* . . . Do not covet your neighbor's servants, nor his mistress, nor his children. Avoid that like the plague, if you want to be the founder of new temples of Mammon. If you must covet, covet his millions, covet Vanderbilt's estates or Pinkerton's spies, covet Venezuela's oil or the tin of Bolivia. Don't waste such powerful emotions on unprofitable trivia. . . .

41

Isaac M. Rosenthal

A Voice from the Unknown Beyond

Dr. I. M. Rosenthal Makes an Ethical Will on a Gramophone Record

August 30, 1895

On August 30, 1895, Dr. Isaac M. Rosenthal (1831–1906), visiting Mackinac Island in Michigan, stepped up to a recording device and dictated an ethical will. It was an impromptu speech. During the 1890s the talking machine was coming into its own. The German Jewish immigrant Emile Berliner had invented a workable microphone in the 1870s, thus speeding the development of the telephone and what he later, in 1887, called the gramophone.

Dr. Rosenthal was depressed; he had just lost the wife he adored. This mood is reflected in his talk; actually, he lived for another eleven years. He was well known as a surgeon in Fort Wayne, Indiana, where he played an important part in the general and Jewish communities. He was chief of staff in the local Catholic hospital.

My dear ones all:

My last will and testament you will find to be an expression of my impartial love and my desire to be just to all. If I failed, it is but through the limited, very limited wisdom given to all that is earth-born. My soul soars higher. This is to be to you as a voice from the unknown beyond. I will and bequest that you do not mourn for me, but rejoice after my bereavement. I still love to be with you and for you; but to be united again with that true loving pure soul is happiness beyond human comprehension. Think of me as we do of your dear Ma, that we in spirit are with you to love, guide and protect you. Remember all that was good and noble in my earthly career. Do not forget but forgive all the errors, evils and shortcomings of my ways upon earth. Follow the good and avoid all evil. Love and protect one another, thereby giving eternal joy and bliss to your parents in the unknown beyond as you did when we dwelt in body with you. Peace on earth, good will to all. . . . May He who bringeth peace to pass in the highest give peace to us and to all Israel and say *Amen.*

42

Abraham Isaac Saklad

Do Not Forever Strive to Be a Doctor or a Lawyer

A Bostonian Writes an Ethical Will

1906

While in Turkish-ruled Palestine, Abraham Isaac Saklad (d. 1909)—a Bostonian, born in Slonim, Russia—wrote an ethical will in rhymed Yiddish for the edification of his children and grandchildren in the United States. Excerpts are reprinted here.

The writer immigrated in the early 1880s to Boston, where he became well known as a Hebrew scribe and a skilled carver in stone and wood. He is reported to have engraved the ten Hebrew commandments on the head of a large common pin. A school that he opened in Boston employed Hebrew as the language of instruction.

Saklad was not enamored of lawyers and doctors—a good American tradition dating back to the colonial period: Lawyers and doctors destroy; they do not build!

Dear Children . . .

This little book is given to you by your ancestor to treasure all through the years of your lives. This little book, though not a Holy Torah, should be to you, my children, a precious treasure. These, then, are the thoughts, and these are the words of your grandfather:

> Beloved children, I plead with you with tears in my eyes.
> I charge you with an oath to keep this deep in your hearts:
> Love God with all your hearts, and you will be spared from evil.
> Be good Jews, and let all that is Jewish be close to your hearts.
> For the Jew is distinct among the nations wherever he may dwell upon this globe.

He is distinct by the Bris Milah, * and the Jewish woman is to observe *Chalah, Nidah, and Tvilah.***

The Jew must be of good conduct and, above all, must observe the Sabbath; do no manner of hard labor.

Because of the Sabbath you will find good luck and blessing in all your doings, and you will prosper all the other five days of the week.

Observance of the Sabbath is the greatest thing; for this you will merit health and well-being.

Should you, by chance, be employed in menial work, it matters not, for as long as the work is honest your soul will be clean and at peace.

Do not forever strive to be a doctor or a lawyer, for therein is trouble and travail everywhere.

Do not treat others with deception; and keep away from strife.

Do not speak evil of others; and always be fair.

Pray to God daily with new vigor and serve Him faithfully.

Honor your parents and obey them for they gave you life.

Respect others as you would have them respect you.

Beware of pride, but neither should you humble yourselves.

Help your brother with all your might, and the Father in Heaven will reward you for it.

Thank God morning and evening; and day by day be a support to the downtrodden everywhere.

Whatever you do, do honestly.

Beware of falsehood; and keep your conscience clear.

In your thoughts remember never to deceive.

In your actions always excel in good deeds.

Always exceed in charity.

Better than to read trite novels and romances, know well the story of your people.

Love the land of your forefathers, and come, like myself, to visit the Wailing Wall.

Dear children, pay heed to these words.

Keep them impressed in your hearts.

Children you are building a new world.

Build your world on firm foundations; and remember the teachings of our faith.

Remember the ways of your people, which I have taught you; and let them be unspoiled and whole.

These are the words of your father and grandfather. . . .

---

*The Jewish ceremony of circumcision.

**Religious laws dealing with the baking of bread and with menstruation.

43

Elias Greenebaum

Come Home in Due Time as a Young Man of Culture and Character

Grandpa Greenebaum Writes to Grandson John

1907–1909

Elias Greenebaum (1822–1913), a native of Eppelsheim, Germany, settled in Chicago in 1848. Although he was very much tempted to go to California during the days of the Gold Rush, he decided to remain in Chicago. After clerking in a dry goods store, he went to work in a bank; in 1877 he established a family bank, Greenebaum Sons. The Greenebaums, one of the most respected Jewish families in the city, were distinguished for their integrity, their devotion to civic advancement, and their religious liberalism. Elias became president of Chicago Sinai Congregation and the Hebrew Benevolent Society.

In 1907 and 1909, Elias, now a man in his eighties, wrote letters to his grandson, John; they reflect his views and his ideals.

Chicago, Sept. 17, 1907

Dear John:

Your resolution to go to college pleased me very much. I like to see in a young man, who has an eye for business, also first and foremost the ambition to acquire a good education, and furthermore to go away from home among strangers where he feels that he alone is responsible for his good behavior and the formation of a good character, and with reference to these I want to make few remarks. Scripture says: "Shun the evil and do good, seek peace and pursue it" [Psalm 34:14]. Lead a steady and regular life. Rise and retire at the proper time. Be moderate in eating and drinking. Beware of bad company. A young man is judged in accordance with his associations; use good judgment and reject bad influence. The way one sows, he reaps [Galatians 6:7]. The way one sows in youth—that is, the way he lives when young—thus the fruit will be in later years. I hope and trust you will come home in due time as a young man of culture and character in the acquiring of which I wish you God's blessing, adding my prayer for your welfare, your happiness, and success in all your undertakings.

Lovingly and paternally
Grandpa E. Greenebaum

Lake Forest, June 16, 1909

My dear John!

Accept mine and Grandma's best wishes to your birthday; we congratulate from the bottom of our hearts. May you celebrate many happy returns of the day up to high old age. Of the annual years I consider each decennium brings a decided change in life. I call from one to ten, childhood, from ten to twenty, boyhood. With twenty begins manhood, responsibility, application to duty combined with joy and pleasure. Happiness comes from within; it must be a self creation. Take matters in a contended and hopeful spirit.

With the beginning of the twentieth year I stop giving a small sum of money annually; it is done to learn and to show economy and saving. At twenty it is expected that the young man knows how to take care of money, and I prefer to give him a reasonable sum which he can invest and draw an annual interest. I enclose my check for Five hundred dollars and I know you will use it in the right way. With strong hopes and best wishes for your future welfare, adding my fatherly blessing, I remain with sincere affection

Your grandpa
Elias Greenebaum

44

Joseph B. Greenhut

Providence Was Guiding and Protecting Me

Captain Joseph B. Greenhut and His God

May 2, 1908

Joseph B. Greenhut (1843–1918), a native of Central Europe, came to the United States as a child of 9. He had little schooling. Leaving his Chicago home as a youngster, he made his way to Mobile, Alabama, went hungry for a few days, got a job as a tinner's apprentice, and learned the trade. When the Civil War broke out, he returned north to Chicago, volunteered immediately, and rose to the rank of captain. Decades later, he received a letter of commendation from Secretary of War Henry L. Stimson for his bravery at the battle of Gettysburg.

In the 1870s Greenhut left Chicago for Peoria, where he became a large-scale distiller and one of the town's important industrialists. Two decades later he moved east to New York City to become the owner and executive of a downtown department store, J. B. Greenhut Company.

The Captain was an autodidact; he wrote a good letter, spoke good English, and was an accomplished orator. In 1908, while on a visit to Peoria, he executed his will—apparently in a despondent mood—and accompanied it with a letter to his dear ones. In the letter he discussed in detail his relationship to God, who, he felt, had protected him for the last sixty-five years. He survived for over a decade more, enjoying his almost daily game of golf. He died in New York City on November 17, 1918.

To My Dear Wife, Children, and Grandchildren:

I have just executed my last will, and to the best of my judgement and belief

I have endeavored to treat you all fair and justly, in bequeathing to you all the material wealth of which I am possessed. I sincerely hope that what I leave to you will be fully appreciated as the offering from one who has worked hard all his life, and who has always striven to be a good provider for his family, and to secure a happy home for all those that belonged to him. I also trust and pray that all of you will solemnly resolve to perpetuate the close and dear affection for each other, which I have always tried to inculcate during my life time. My experience has taught me that there can be little happiness on this earth which does not emanate from, or include, the family circle.

Another subject near to my heart, and of which I desire to dwell upon at this time, and which I greatly desire to impress upon you all very solemnly, is the firm conviction, that I have felt since my childhood, of the existence of a kind providence and an almighty ruler, which we call God. You undoubtedly know that I never cared much for the ordinary ceremonies and formalities prescribed by our own, or any other creed or religion, as I have witnessed a great deal of sham and hypocrisy practiced by those who have been most loud and demonstrative in their religious professions. Therefore, I preferred to be devout in my own quiet and reclusive way, and I feel confident that my prayers have been effective in appealing to the Almighty God for his help, guidance, assistance, and protection during the many trials, dangers, and tribulations, through which I have passed. You will remember the many times in which I spoke of the conviction I felt that a kind providence was guiding and protecting me in all my affairs. I did not wish to appear too demonstrative in sharing my belief, for the reason that I feared I might be taken for a religious crank, in which event I felt my motives might be misconstrued and my influence lessened, while trying to inculcate a true reverence and devout belief in an almighty providence, in those nearest and dearest to me.

As a regular procedure I can say that I never arose in the morning, or retired for the night (and in addition as occasion offered itself during each day), without offering a prayer to the Almighty God, thanking him for all the goodness, kindness, blessing and protection which He had bestowed upon me and mine, and begging Him, for his further help, assistance, guidance, and protection in all my affairs and endeavors of every description which I named, including my business enterprises, and for the protection and health of myself and all my family. The response to my prayers did not always come direct and immediate, but sooner or later, in one form or another, I was assisted in attaining all, and I may say even more than I had ever hoped or prayed for. I also wish to say that I never neglected to plead in my daily prayers for the protection and rest of the souls of my beloved departed parents, child, sister and brother. It is my earnest wish and prayer that you all may be fully impressed with what I have herein imparted to you, as it will be the last communication from me on this earth, and I trust that you will all be guided by my good counsel for your welfare.

Wishing you all the blessings that can only come from the Almighty Father, and that you may all continue to be happy and prosperous, is the last wish with lots of love from

Yours affectionately,
J. B. Greenhut

Peoria, Ill., May 2d, 1908

45

Augusta Hammerslough Rosenwald

A Heart to Heart Talk

Augusta Rosenwald Writes a Farewell Letter to Her Family

1910–1918

In 1910, Danish-born Augusta Hammerslough Rosenwald wrote a letter—a testament, as it were—to her children. She was then 77 years of age. Augusta had a number of brothers, all aggressive businessmen. Her husband, Samuel Rosenwald, who was born in Germany, was a Springfield, Illinois, merchant who had started life in this country as a peddler. Julius, their son, became rich and famous as the head of Sears, Roebuck & Co. Mother Augusta was kind and unpretentious; her son Julius was equally unpretentious. (In 1918 she added a brief supplement to her "heart to heart" letter; both are included here.)

March 1910

My dearly beloved children:

I have tried so often to write a letter for you to read when once I have closed my eyes for the sleep eternal. It comes to me at wakeful nights and ever so many things as thoughts present themselves, what I would [want] to have you know or be. But to put them on paper is quite a different thing; they are sacred thoughts and hard to put on paper where they seem quite different. But as this is a heart to heart talk with those who are dearest to me on earth, it must be like a little testament.

First of all, nearest to my heart is, and with which you can revere my memory most, is to try and foster the love and affection for one another as tho I were among you. Try and not let trifles or differences of opinion mar the good feeling; bear with each other's shortcomings. God has not created us alike even to the children born of one mother. If there are differences, talk them over in good faith and they will not seem near so large or so bad. I am sure you have never hurt my feelings by word or deed and you would not my memory. Never was a mother blessed with kinder, better children, God be praised and thanked. I am sure the welfare of one of you will be that of the other. . . .

As to the last rites, I would wish absolutely no eulogy, only prayer by Dr. [Emil G.] Hirsch and Dr. [Joseph] Stolz as I love him [Stolz] as a sincere man and a good friend. Please omit flowers positively, only by those who are bound to me by love and affection, none from outsiders, as I do not like display; my good friends have always been kind and good to me. It needs no outlay or lavishness of money; better spend on the living needy. Should any one of you dear ones think fit to do anything for charity in our name do not forget to add your fathers. I of course do not expect you to wear deep mourning nor abstain from amusements. At the same time I should like you to allow enough respect not to rush in but wait a certain time. I am sure your feeling for me tells you that. As to the division of trinkets and little belongings, distribute it so that no feelings are hurt. . . .

I pray that you will live to see the joy on your children and grandchildren as I have been blessed to see them grow in loveliness and to inherit traits of character.

1918

You will be surprised when you find this continued in my old age—only to testify that nothing for which I have wished, prayed to God, has been unfulfilled. God bless you and give you as happy an old age as you have given your

Mother

46

Lev Levin

And God Knows If You Will Ever See Me Again

Lev Levin of Pinsk Writes a Departure Poem for a Son Going to America

March 22, 1914

When young Irving Levin—as he was later known—left Pinsk, White Russia, for America sometime before World War I, his father Lev gave him a departure letter written in Yiddish in rhyming couplets—doggerel, to be exact. The world of Lev Levin is reflected in these artless, sincere words; his thoughts are poignant and moving. Lev's is an important letter because it portrays the thinking, the ethos of a humble East European Jew, a father who is bidding farewell to a son as he leaves for the New World. Lev Levin lived in a world of poverty; his affluent grandson would live in a mansion-dotted metropolitan American suburb.

A goodbye letter of blessing written in Pinsk on the 22nd of March, 1914, given me by my parents [*the words of Lev's son*].

Be well my beloved child.
  May God bring you good fortune quickly.
I am saying goodbye to you.
  And God knows if you will ever see me again.
I sincerely hope
  That you will be fortunate in the place where you are going.
You know quite well my child;
  I am unhappy every second of the time.
I am sick and impoverished,
  And unhappy too.
My heart is as a stone; I cannot speak.
  I feel miserable because I am in pain.

I am oppressed on all sides.
    Obviously I would want to change my lot.
Everyone wants to better himself.
    Who knows whether you will ever come back.
It was very difficult for me to rear you.
    Now my child you are flying away.
Far, Far away.
    My child do not change your nature.
You are leaving your family behind,
    Like water that overflows.
There is no end to my pain.
    Everything was in order when you were here.
Now with whom can I speak?
    With whom can I pour out my heart?
I swallow my tears.
    God knows when we will be able to talk with one another.
I am miserably unhappy.
    I look at you and in a flash of a second you are gone.
I have pampered you and embraced you.
    I did all I could to help you.
All this when it was within my power to help you.
    Now I am completely helpless.
Now my son never forget me.
    If it will be well with you, we will not be unhappy.
You have good brothers in America and that's a lot.
    Maintain good relations with them, my child.
The best road is the most beautiful ornament.
    Live honestly; it's the best way to go.
Travel safe and sound, my beloved son.
    God bless you. Best of everything.
Travel safe and sound my beloved child.
    May God bring you speedily to your goal.
Send a note always to your parents,
    In order that you may relieve their anxiety.
Don't forget your parents.
    Don't change your kindly nature.
Your most beautiful adornment is your father and mother.
    Honesty is the best policy.
I kiss you with my whole heart.
    Pray God that we encounter no pain.
You know my circumstances.
    This is indeed unfortunate.
Travel safely. May God help us
    That we may see each other in good health. Amen.

Your father,
Lev Levin
Pinsk

47

Max Landsberg

Do Not Say Kaddish for Me

Max Landsberg, Radical Reform Rabbi, Confronts the Ultimate

January 16, 1918–March 3, 1922

Dr. Max Landsberg (1845–1927), a scholarly German rabbi, was invited in 1871 to serve Rochester's Congregation B'rith Kodesh. To his dying day, he remained a Classical Reformer—invincibly rationalist, radical, anti-Orthodox, anti-bar mitzvah, anti-Zionist. In his heyday he was probably Rochester's most distinguished Jew, respected even by Gentiles who were otherwise intolerant of Jews.

In 1918 and 1922—after his retirement—he wrote to his children venting his opinions on death, mourning, and the traditional prayer for those who had died. He also prescribed the type of funeral that he desired. These two letters are reprinted here. In still another note, not included here, he asked that his sermons be burned. Landsberg realized, sadly, that his German Classical Reform world was threatened; the future belonged to American Jews of East European stock.

Rochester, N.Y., January 16, 1918

Dear children,

To my letter written yesterday I wish to add a few parting words.

I hope that you will not feel distressed at my death. It is but natural for children to lose their father after he has lived more than seventy years. Besides my life has been one of uniform happiness. The only serious trouble in my whole life has been the loss of my dear wife, your good mother. For some time I thought that after that blow I could not continue to live. But your love and affection has made me more happy than I had supposed I could ever become again. However, in all those years I have always been ready for the end. Therefore I hope that you will not indulge in festations of mourning and not change the even tenor of your lives. Remember that I feel gratified if you do not interrupt your enjoyments on account of my death. *Do not say kaddish for me.* I have long been sorry for having included in that prayer, in my *Ritual [for American Worship]*, the allusion to the dead which the Reform books have adopted from the Portuguese [Sephardic] rituals, and for years have omitted it, whenever I officiated at services. The manner in which kaddish is regarded and practiced now is base superstition.

You have fulfilled all your duties to me while I was with you, and I trust you will continue to do so by leading a life which will be a blessing to yourself and others, and an honor to your name.

With the kindest wishes for your happiness I am your father

Max Landsberg

Rochester, N.Y., March 3, 1922

Dear [daughter] Grace,

My experiences since I wrote the above letters and my conversation with you during the last days induce me to add the following supplement: it is my wish that my remains shall not be taken to the Temple, and that no services shall be held there for me. As I have told you, dear Grace, I wish to have a private funeral at your house, where you and Harry have made me so comfortable during all these years. I wish that the whole funeral service consist in reading the ninety-first and the twenty-third Psalms.

My friends have been so much encroached upon by death, that there will be ample room in your house for those who still remain interested in me. It would please me if after my death you would have published in the daily papers the testimonial that was given to me by Congregation Berith Kodesh on my fiftyeth anniversary.

Again good bye.

Your loving father,
Max Landsberg

48

Herman Hecht

Be Honest & Upright to Your Self & Fellow Man

A Jewish New Year Letter to a Son

September 5, 1918

On the eve of the Jewish New Year, a German-born immigrant wrote a letter to his son, a letter of love, advice, and admonition. The father, Herman Hecht, a baker, lived in Bristol, Tennessee, whose Jewish community at the time numbered hardly more than fifty souls. It is interesting to note that Hecht was impelled to write to his boy because he himself, in turn, had once received a similar letter from his own father enjoining him to remember the parental teachings. Hecht's mastery of his new homeland's language is apparent despite the vagaries of his spelling and punctuation.

Sept/18

My Dear Boy Armand:

This morning I wrote you a short letter, because I had no time to write a long one, but now while I have lots of important work yet to do, & that is paying bills, yet I feel it is just as important to write you, for the fact that New Year is fast approaching & also that you are now practically starting out in life, to become a factor not only for your self but also for others.

To the New Year I wish you such wich only a good parent can wish a son who so far has held the utermost confidence of his parent. While you have had & possibly still have some minor faults wich are only due to your young years, but as a total your parents feel that they have an ideal son & our heart

& everything els is with you constandly, & may the Almighty keep you & watch over you for us.

Now my dear boy, I recall the first letter I have received from my dear father, *Selig* [of blessed memory], in wich he asked me not to forget the teachings of my parents & in this he said above all be honest & upright to your self & fellow man. This very advise I can [not] impress to strongly open you, for the temptations at times are great & trying, & it takes a strong character to allways withsdand it but those that withsdans it will have great satisfaction throut theire lifes.

Be kind to your fellow man & allways before acting aske your self how would I like this? By asking your self this question & with honesty of purpose you will always then treat your fellowman as he should be treated.

As to your education, I have spoken to your personally, never the less I shall put a few words in writing by saying that you know my pocket book is open for you to get all such education that you need & ought to have. I am ready to go to the full length but I will aske [you] to beware of temptations that might be put before you at times wich would mean neglect of your education. Remember you can not know too much & lost time can not be made up. In writing you all this I do not want you to misconstru the meaning of my advise for, as stated in the beginning of my letter, your parent have the utmost confidence in you. But no one knows better than I what temptations you likely have to content with. In advising you as I do I feel that it might take deep root in your heart & mind, so that no mather what comes before you that you allways have my advise in mind. That we miss you greatly goes without saying & when I notice your dear mother when she gets your letters how she tries to supress her feelings then I realize the more the sacrifice we are making for your future, but all is done willingly & with an abundance of love that you can only repay by doing the right thing at the right time, wich I am sure you will. In conclusion I will say do not be unmindful of your body & soul for only by doing this, you can acoplish the other duties as outlined above.

We received your letter & sorry that you have such a hart bed but no doubt by the time you get trough a days excersise you can sleep on wood. I am going to take this letter home to mother & will send it to morrow as mother wishes to write, so will close again sending my best wishes for the New Year and, for all time, a parent's love.

God bless you is the wish to your ever loving Dad,

Herman

49

Rachel Wolfe

The Right Road to Health, Love and Prosperity, and a Noble Life

The Widow Supports Twelve Children

December 27, 1919

Rachel Davis (Mrs. Max) Wolfe (b. ca. 1861), the author of this "farewell letter" to her children, was in many respects an unusual woman. Born in London, she married in New York City and finally settled in Ottawa, Canada, where she opened a shop selling furs and millinery. Widowed rather early, she was faced with the task of supporting twelve youngsters, which she did with gratifying results. Her children were an honor to her—all leaders in the Jewish and the larger Canadian communities. A daughter became a soloist with the New York Philharmonic Orchestra; a grandson became Canada's minister of defence.

She wrote her will after reading that of Liebman Adler, presented earlier in this book, and even borrowed a sentence from him.

Montreal, Canada
December 27, 1919, Midnight

My darling children:

Keep together in fraternal union. Let no sacrifice be too great to ensure your mutual helpfulness and the continuance of your brotherly feelings. Every act of love that you show unto one another will do my soul good. The example of eleven* children of one father and mother standing together in love and faithfulness, will be a more beautiful adornment to the memory of your dear parents than the most costly monument which you could erect and which I do not care for (although I do not wish to control your desires in that matter). The little property that I leave behind will be yours. I know that I can trust you. You will not show yourselves unfitted in carrying out my wishes as I have stated in my last will. The inheritance however which you possess, even now, is a good name and a training as good as I could give you. Only remain honest, true, industrious, and economical. Put your whole energy into the conducting of your chosen calling. Serve God and have Him always before your eyes. With your associates be amiable, courteous and modest and *all will be well with you.*

One more word, my darling children. Remain Jews and live as Jews to the best of your ability and in the manner of your times, not only for yourselves as individuals but also for the welfare of the community.

Now, my children, if you will remember my written request to you, and study [the] sam[e] whenever you might feel in doubt of the right path to follow, you will find it a standing light to guide you to the right road to health, love and prosperity, and a noble life.

From your loving Mother,
Rachel Wolfe

*One son had died by this time. Eleven out of twelve, however, was then a remarkable rate of survival.

50

Rose Haas Alschuler

Love Should Be the Motive Power of Action

An "I Believe" Avowal of Rose H. Alschuler of Chicago

ca. 1920

This statement, "I Believe—Today," is taken from Rose H. Alschuler's memoir, which she presented to her family on the occasion of her seventy-fifth birthday, December 17, 1962. The actual excerpt was written in about 1920.*

Rose Haas Alschuler was born in Chicago in 1887 to a cultured family, and her formative years included much travel across the United States and Europe. A graduate of Vassar College, Rose was still a young woman in her thirties when she penned these stirring lines, which reflect the essence of her thinking.

A niece of Hannah Greenebaum Solomon, the founder of the National Council of Jewish Women, Rose was very active in establishing nursery schools in the Chicago area. She was the mother of five children. Her husband, Alfred S. Alschuler, was a distinguished architect who trained in the atelier of Dankmar Adler. She became engaged to Alschuler in 1907 when he asked her whether she could live on $300 a month; she answered yes.

Mrs. Alschuler, influenced by Rabbi Emil G. Hirsch of Chicago's Reform Sinai Temple, helped establish North Shore Congregation Israel and its Sunday School. By the 1930s she had become interested in Jewish Palestine, and by the 1950s she was actively identified with a number of Israel's cultural institutions.

---

*This is from *Oral History Interview with Rose Haas Alschuler*, recorded with Mary Lynn McCree, 1973, and edited by Richard H. Alschuler (Chicago: Published by the Alschuler family, 1985).

Life is a mirage and life is an effort – and the fullness of life for every individual depends on the strength and beauty of his vision and the strength and beauty of his effort.

And I would have my child know that one lives by truth – but that truth is only relative. That in this great world so full of positive impressions, sensations, and experiences, there is only one unchanging truth, and that is the spirituality of the world. This spirituality is evidenced in power – human and superhuman, in the creative powers of nature, and the creative powers of man.

I would tell my child and live for him an inner freedom – a freedom from fear, a freedom from the outlived traditions of the past, and from the futile allegiances of the present – a freedom which should enable him to think thru every experience, to act and to react freely, and to realize daily living with all the capacity of a free spirit.

I would tell him that life must be lived constructively, that love should be the motive power of action – I would have him know that hatred, envy, malice, evil in any form is a boomerang and consumes its begetter.

I would have him think that every human being has unrealized and almost unlimited possibilities which it is his joyous responsibility to fulfill. But I would have him keep his sense of personal accomplishment balanced by realizing that any individual accomplishment is infinitely small, if one thinks in terms of the cosmos – of what is being done, what has been done and what remains to be done.

And in time I hope he shall come to know that a talent for living consists in a capacity for adjustment, that happiness and fulfillment consist in realizing life to the fullest at every moment and in losing one's self thru giving one's love and one's power to the sum of human welfare.

Can we teach those things – appreciation of truth and beauty – understanding of inner freedom – the joys of world love and service? Probably not! One can only sense them and perhaps impart them thru the quality of one's own being.

51

Alfred Segal

To Regard with Respect the Essential Dignity of My Fellowman

Alfred Segal, Popular Cincinnati Columnist, Writes a Propaganda Ethical Will

1927

Alfred Segal (1883–1968), a native of Lithuania, was a widely read columnist for the Cincinnati Post. *As "Cincinnatus," he helped sponsor the city charter movement, which drove a political gang out of power and gave his beloved city good government. Segal was a co-author of Boris Bogen's* Born a Jew* *and wrote regularly for the national Seven Arts Feature Syndicate, which distributed articles of Jewish interest.*

In 1927 Segal wrote a will that he published under the name "I. M. Goodman." It was a propaganda piece, for he sought to encourage people to give charity to Jewish and non-Jewish causes. Note his sympathy for the city's African-Americans. The three years that he had spent at the Hebrew Union College in Cincinnati helped to make him an idealist, an ardent Jew with a strong interest in ethics and Jewish history. This will reflected his convictions.

In the Name of the Benevolent Father of All, Amen: I, I. M. Goodman of the City of Cincinnati, County of Hamilton, and State of Ohio, being of sound and disposing mind and memory, do make publish and declare this my last will and testament, hereby revoking and making null and void all other last wills and testament by me made heretofore.

*New York: The Macmillan Company, 1930.

First—My will is that all my just debts and funeral expenses shall be paid out of my estate, as soon after my decease as shall be found convenient.

Second—I give, devise and bequeath $25,000 to be divided in sums of $5,000 each and given to each of these institutions: Jewish Hospital of Cincinnati, Jewish Orphans' Home of Cleveland, the Orthodox Orphans' Home of Cincinnati, the Jewish Home for the Aged and Infirm, and the Orthodox Jewish Home for the Aged.

Third—Believing, as I do, that charity must be as broad as mankind, I give, and bequeath $15,000 to be divided in sums of $3,000 each to each of these institutions: The Colored Orphan Asylum, the Children's Home of Cincinnati, the Home for Incurables, the Colored Home for the Aged, and the Altenheim.

Fourth—The entire residue of my estate shall be invested in bonds yielding a fair return, and income thereon applied to the support of such charity, social service and educational enterprises, as may from time to time make its needs known to the public and which my executor, hereinafter named, shall deem worthy.

Fifth—During my lifetime I have devoted myself to my sons, giving them such educations as would fit [them] for worthy places in the work of the world. They possess, therefore, ample equipment for the business of making a living which they are doing now, and even making a success which they are now attaining. They need, in consequence, no financial aid from me.

Sixth—To my five sons I give, and bequeath that which surpasses all the material wealth I have gathered, namely, the inheritance of our faith which came to me thru a vast line of devoted ancestors. There were times in their long and majestic history when they could have purchased their lives with their faith; but they chose to die rather than yield their ideal, and gave up their ghosts crying joyously, "Hear, O Israel, the Lord our God the Lord is One." Such is the precious inheritance I bequeath to my sons. It is a way of life, leading him who follows it to lofty spiritual eminences from which he may look down upon the little foothills of business and social success, and look up and capture the image of God in his heart.

It is that which made noblemen of our forefathers, sustaining them in martyrdom, and giving life to the Jew in all the generations, despite the many deaths that were decreed against him. For Judaism is a substance of character and by character alone peoples and institutions can continue to live. I have tried myself to be faithful to this inheritance and have found it to be good for man in all the walks of his life. It has pointed out to me the things that are worth pursuing and the things that are not, so that long ago I came to contentment which is the foundation of happiness. It taught me to regard with respect the essential dignity of my fellowman and to deal with him in justice and kindness. It gave the love of peace to my heart and imbued me with a sense of kinship to all mankind. This ennobling faith I bequeath to my sons, knowing it is more precious than money and that without it money is an evil in the pocket of the Jew. And I charge them to teach it diligently unto their children.

In testimony whereof, I have set my hand to this, my last will and testament . . . in the year one thousand nine hundred and twenty-seven.

I. M. Goodman

52

Simon Glazer

Fear My Mother! The Very Idea Seems Repulsive

Rabbi Simon Glazer Comments on Leviticus, Chapter 19

1928

Rabbi Simon Glazer (1878–1938) came to the United States in 1897 soon after he was ordained in his native Lithuania. He was a very ambitious and a very able man. By 1904, less than a decade after landing on American shores, he had already published his English-language history of The Jews of Iowa,* *one of many books and articles he would write in English, Yiddish, and Hebrew. Glazer was the author of a general history of the Jews, and also published a translation of Maimonides' famous code. After serving congregations in Canada and in several American cities, he finally settled in New York City in 1923. There he became a leader in local and national Orthodox rabbinical circles and was an active Zionist propagandist. He knew that Orthodoxy had to come to terms with the secular American milieu, which is why he wrote English handbooks intended to tie the new American generation to traditionalism. He was well aware of what he had to do if East European Jews were to survive religiously in the modern Anglo-Saxon world. He was no rock-ribbed conservative; one of his synagogues was called a temple, and his son, B. Babel Glazer, became a notable Reform rabbi.*

This remarkable Orthodox rabbi wrote several manuals in English; among them was the Bar-Mitzvah Pulpit: Sermonettes for Bar-Mitzvah Boys and Others,** *in which the following address appeared. He wrote this book to help Orthodox teachers prepare American lads for their bar mitzvah, and to provide examples of suitable speeches for the occasion.*

---

*Des Moines, IA: Koch Brothers Printing Co., 1904.
**New York: The Star Hebrew Book Co., 1928.

My Dear Parents, Ladies and Gentlemen: In the Sidrah of this Sabbath we read: "And the Lord spoke unto Moses saying: Speak unto all the congregation of the children of Israel and say unto them: Ye shall be holy; for I the Lord your God am holy. Ye shall fear every man his mother and his father, and ye shall keep My Sabbaths; I am the Lord your God."

God is holy, and He charges us to be holy. He gave to us the same title as His own.

The Torah here charges: Every man shall fear his mother and his father. The ancient sages of Israel, in commenting on the precedence given here to the mother said: "It is known to the Holy One, blessed is He! that the son fears the father more than the mother; the verse, therefore, mentioned the mother first, to emphasize that a mother should not be considered slightly by a son."

There is a kind of fear which is derived from reverence, and there is a kind of fear which is derived from contempt. One fears his enemy. He has no use for his enemy. But his enemy is liable to injure him. He fears to be injured, to suffer pain, to sustain a loss. One fears his most honored friend, his teacher, his parent; none of these will do him harm, but he fears to harm them, to misbehave in their presence, to have them think ill of him.

We are commanded to fear God. That fear is derived from reverence. When we think how our being is of such small account in comparison with all that which God created, we are seized by a wave of awe. When we realize that our lives are in the keeping of God, we fear to offend Him. When we think of all the goodness He bestows upon us, how merciful His dealings are with us, how He provides for all that live upon earth, we are overtaken by an awe which leaves us but little else to think about.

We are commanded to honor our fathers and our mothers, and we are also commanded to fear our mothers and our fathers. The kind of fear one experiences when in the presence of one's father is not a fear of a physical nature. A father will not harm his son, even though the son might be deserving of a severe punishment. A father may correct his son, even by not sparing the rod; but he does it for the son's good; to teach him to know better. But for the world and all that it possesses, I can not imagine of being afraid of my mother. I know I love her. I love her with such love that I can not imagine her to inspire fear in me. I know that in returning home from a day of mischief, as I often did, only kisses awaited me, in addition to plenty of good things to eat. Fear my mother! The very idea seems repulsive to me. My whole being adores her with such love that I can express it only when returning her embrace, or only when I miss her.

And, yet, our Torah teaches me to fear my mother, and that fear is placed in the Torah ahead of the fear I certainly retain for my father.

But our Torah is true. And, as a bar-mitzvah, I am in duty bound to observe this commandment.

And I will observe it; and for my mother's sake, perhaps, with more zeal than any other commandment in our Torah.

I will always fear to offend my mother. By not fearing to offend her, I will injure her. And the fear that I feel, lest my mother be hurt, is the strongest fear I am capable of feeling.

I will always fear to do wrong, lest by doing it my mother's heart will break. The fear I feel lest my mother's heart break, is so strong that its influence is of sufficient strength to keep me out of mischief.

I will always keep away from bad company, lest my mother be ashamed. The fear I feel, lest my mother suffer shame, is so strong in me that its effect will prevent me from falling in with any but the friends my mother may approve of.

In honoring my mother, in revering her, in fearing her, I have but one distinct feeling for her—love!

I do understand why our Torah gave precedence to mother when the subject is fear.

To my father I owe the reverence, which is second only to the reverence I owe to God. God gave me my soul; and my father developed it. The love I owe my father is second only to the love I owe to God. God provides for all living; and my father provided for me, from that which God gave, and thereby I was enabled to grow up. The fear I owe to my father is second only to the fear I owe God. God is my father in Heaven; my father is my father upon earth.

And loving, fearing, and honoring as I do the Almighty God of us all, I approach His Throne of mercy in supplication now, when I have reached a state of life which makes me an independent being. May He shield me against all evil. May He bless my father and my mother. May He bless you all, Amen.

53

Alfred M. Cohen

My Hope Is that You Will Prove Worthy of Your Heroic Past

Alfred M. Cohen, B'nai B'rith Leader, Congratulates a Confirmand

May 15, 1928

Alfred M. Cohen (1859–1949), the writer of the following congratulatory note, was one of Cincinnati's distinguished Jews. In 1876, when only 17, he had organized a Young Men's Hebrew Association, which in those days functioned as a literary society. Later, in 1890, he helped establish a national association of such cultural and social groups. After becoming a lawyer, Cohen, a Democrat, went into local and state politics and served as a member of the Ohio State Senate. This Jewish communal worker was president of Congregation B'nai Israel, the Board of Governors of the Hebrew Union College, and the international B'nai B'rith. In the 1920s, as head of B'nai B'rith, he helped develop the national Hillel Foundations, which minister to Jewish university students.

In 1928 Cohen wrote to Seymour Zipper, a confirmand in Akron, Ohio. It is a sententious note: Cohen, a moralistic Victorian, was expected to pontificate, and he was only too happy to do so. Young Seymour was flattered to hear from the great man. And what happened to Seymour? He grew up in Akron, became a jeweler, and worked on a national scale to control the ravages of cerebral palsy. He loved to help disabled children and would dress up as Santa Claus at Christmas and distribute gifts. A World War II veteran, Seymour Zipper died in 1979.

Cincinnati, Ohio
May 15, 1928

My dear S[e]ymour:

Through your Confirmation you are passing from boyhood to manhood and I heartily congratulate you upon the important event.

If you will observe the lessons of our faith taught you by your dear Rabbi, your life will be happy and useful. Those self-same lessons so fortified our fathers as to make them invincible in spite of all who rose up against them.

My hope is that you will prove worthy of your heroic past, for your own sake as well as that of your coreligionists. Always remember that the weal or woe of all Israel is in the hands of every individual Israelite. If this admonition be ever before you, you cannot fail to realize the fondest expectations of all who are dear to you.

With every good wish,

Sincerely yours,
Alfred M. Cohen
President

S[e]ymour Zipper
988 Delia Ave.
Akron, Ohio

54

Leo Jung

God Wants the Jew, and Especially the Jewish Boy, to Be Jolly

Rabbi Leo Jung Addresses a Bar Mitzvah Lad

1929

Rabbi Leo Jung of New York City wrote the following letter to a bar mitzvah youngster. Jung believed that a good Jew is a happy Jew. He said that to be happy, one must perform the "good deeds," the mitzvot enjoined by Jewish law; one must remain within the ambit of ritual, custom, and practice that has endured for centuries. He was a native of Austria (b. 1892) who came to the United States in 1920 and soon distinguished himself in the circles of the middle-of-the-road Orthodox. Embracing the modern world, he became a leader in the American Jewish Joint Distribution Committee, the National Jewish Welfare Board, and the Union of Orthodox Jewish Congregations of America. Jung was a prolific writer on Jewish topics.

My dear boy:

There are some Jews who do not realize that to be a good Jew one must be happy. They think that, to be a good Jew, one must be sad or melancholy. But our sages tell us that the Shechinah—the divine presence—does not abide with him who is unhappy or with him who is in pain; that God wants the Jew, and especially the Jewish boy, to be jolly, and full of the strength of happiness, all his life.

The phrase which I should like you to remember is, "Simcha shel Mitzvah." That means "joy of the Mitzvah."

A Jew ought to be happy when he fulfills a Mitzvah. Every Mitzvah that you fulfill makes you a finer boy; every Mitzvah that you fulfill makes your father stronger and happier; for there is nothing that makes Jewish parents happier and stronger than good Jewish children. There is nothing which makes them sadder than children who are disloyal to our Holy Faith.

The Hebrew word for "children" is "bonim," which [also] means "builders."

Don't you see, my dear boy, that the children build up what their parents have started to build. Every child adds something to what his father has done. Nobody will build a house if he is not happy in building it; nobody will build a house well, if he does not do his work with joy. God does not want us to think of Mitzvoth as burdens. They are not meant to be burdens to us; they are meant to be pleasures. A Jewish boy is happy when he fulfills a Mitzvah—happy for himself, happy for his parents.

I want to tell you a story that will make clear to you how children are their parents' builders. There was once a father who climbed a mountain with his boy. The boy enjoyed it at the beginning. But, as they climbed higher and higher, the boy became tired and, perhaps, a little unwilling to go on. Then his father said to him: "My son, if you will climb to the top with me, I will make you bigger than myself. You will be higher than I am."

The boy wondered how that could be possible; but he trusted his father. He knew that he could rely on his father's truthfulness even though he could not understand, just then. So they climbed higher and higher; and the boy felt increasingly tired. And the father again spoke: "My boy, we will soon reach the top. When we do, you will not only be bigger than I am; you will see farther than I do." And the boy, happy in so much encouragement, made another effort. At last they reached the mountain peak and the boy looked questioningly at his father. The father answered the boy by lifting him upon his shoulder. And then the boy understood what his father meant.

The same is true of the Bar Mitzvah boy; the same is true of every Jewish boy. If he climbs with his father, if he struggles with him in his labors for God, then whatever the father has done helps the boy to become a finer man. . . . Whatever the father has done is like a foundation upon which the boy can build. And so, he can stand upon his father's shoulder and look toward the promised land of his own. Amen.

55

Kalman Whiteman

We Keep the Torah and the Torah Keeps Us

Kalman Whiteman Writes a Yiddish Bar Mitzvah Speech

1929

In 1929, Kalman Whiteman wrote a bar mitzvah book, which included talks in Yiddish and Hebrew. There is an address for every pentateuchal and prophetical portion read weekly in the synagogue. Whiteman (1885–1946), a native of the Ukraine, came to the United States in 1906 and soon distinguished himself here as a skillful pedagogue in both the Yiddish and Hebrew fields. Ideologically, he aligned himself early with the Zionist-Socialists and the Territorialists; later, he espoused the ideals of the Orthodox among the Zionists, the Mizrachi. Whiteman, a pillar of the Hebrew-speaking movement in the United States, was one of the founders of the Histadrut Ivrith of America, which emphasized the importance of Hebrew in Jewish life and culture. The following is one of Whiteman's suggesteed addresses for confirmands.

Ye Shall Be Holy (Leviticus, Chapters 19–20)
The Weekly Portion

We have read verses in today's biblical section which expressed wonderful thoughts. Let's just mention a few. . . . Be holy because I your God am holy. . . . when you harvest your crops don't cut the growth that is in the corner of the field; whatever falls down from what you glean don't pick up . . . don't rob or steal from your fellowman . . . don't withhold the wages of the hired man until the next morning . . . don't do anything wrong in a case in court . . . judge your friend justly . . . don't bear a grudge and don't treasure any feeling of revenge in your heart . . . love your neighbor as yourself . . . treat the stranger in your midst as one of your own citizens.

These are the laws of our Torah. And from now on and in the future I take upon myself the responsibility to observe them.

Will I be able to do so? I don't know.

But deep in my heart lies the desire to implement them. My whole being seeks to be good and to befriend my neighbor. This is my heartfelt request of the Lord—blessed be He. May He help me to accomplish what I set out to do, in order that I may be a true son of our people and a follower of the Torah.

The Haftarah (the prophetic reading, Amos 9:7–15) According to the Ashkenazic Ritual

We read the following verses in today's prophetic section. . . this means: The eyes of God are fixed on this sinful kingdom. I will wipe them off the earth. But, says the Lord, I will not destroy the House of Judah. I will warn and I will shake up the House of Israel among the nations as one shakes with a sieve, but not a shred will fall to the earth. These verses express a sad and a good prophecy. God will destroy the Jewish kingdom but not the Jewish people. God will scatter the Jewish people among all the nations but they will not be lost. The evil prophecy and the good assurance have come to pass. We lost our state but we have remained a people. Through what power? What has protected us from destruction?

Our Torah! We keep the Torah and the Torah keeps us alive. I have not learned much of our Torah but I do know how divine it is and how strong it is in its might to watch over and protect us. How great is my good fortune today at this my bar mitzvah, when I tie myself to my people and our Torah.

56

Leon Dalsimer

Cling to the Sunnier Side of Doubt

Leon Dalsimer Addresses His Family

ca. 1929

Leon Dalsimer (1844–1930) was a native of Louisiana. His parents had emigrated from France and landed in New Orleans, where he was born. Dalsimer went to Princeton at a time when relatively few young men went to university. He married a Baltimore girl and settled in Philadelphia, where he became a successful shoe merchant and realtor and a highly respected member of Congregation Keneseth Israel. His rabbi, publishing Dalsimer's final message to his dear ones, said that the deceased congregant was "one of the loveliest souls it has been our pleasure to meet along life's way." Dalsimer was a man of culture. His Princeton background is reflected in this ethical will, which was written in the form of a letter to his family.

My dear Wife and dear Children:

I am making a few requests and adding a few additional lines, which I hope may be of some comfort for you.

Please do not have a funeral sermon preached over my remains; comforting prayers only, short but impressive. No one can inform you better than you know if I have merited your love and appreciation.

Exposing one's physical remains for public view does not appeal to me as proper, but I leave the decision to your judgment. You can dispose of my physical remains in whatever manner you prefer. I do not object to cremation, as cremation seems preferable to decay.

My dear Ones, you should derive much comfort from the thought that for many years we were permitted to live together happily, and enjoy comparative good health. We have been blessed in very many ways. There comes a summons now for one of us to be laid at rest. Our Heavenly Father, the Source of our blessings, has called. "He hath given, He hath taken, His will be done!" In due time each one will receive his call to enter the future spiritual life, where I trust we all may meet again, somehow, somewhere. As the sun rises after its setting, Spiritual life after this earthly existence is a reasonable hope, and should be cherished for the consolation it affords. The Spirit returns to the Parent-Spirit. To conceive an existence for the human spirit elsewhere is not unthinkable even though it cannot be explained. Many conditions in life, our motives, our emotions, are without proof. Time and space are inexplicable, yet they exist. Love, affection, sympathy, and the other beautiful attributes of the heart and soul, are the real things in life. You cannot see them, nor explain them, yet you know they exist.

We understand better now, through added experience and knowledge, things that we heretofore could not readily grasp, and when the human mind has developed so as to reach and to understand a higher scientific and spiritual standard, we will see and know and realize better the spiritual mysteries of today. While there is no direct, absolute proof for continuous life, we all recognize the invisible and mysterious Influence of the Unseen, Guiding-Spirit. In Him we should put our trust and hope for future existence. Cling to the sunnier side of doubt. It is the healthiest atmosphere for your permanent happiness.

In resignation and faith you will find consolation and strength. A mystic tie binds us together forever. Let us then commune in spirit with each other, with the confident hope to meet again somehow in the Spirit-world, where the pain of parting is unknown. They never die who live in the hearts of those who love them.

And ever near us, though unseen
  The dear immortal spirits tread—
For all the boundless universe
  Is Life! there is no death!

57

David Klibanoff

That My Children May Always Live in Peace

The "Ten Commandments" of David Klibanoff

February 18, 1931

On February 18, 1931, David Klibanoff of Providence, Rhode Island, wrote a Yiddish ethical will. In a beautiful script, in terse and simple Yiddish, he made his last requests of his dear ones. This will, in its cogency and directness, is truly classical. Each line of the document is numbered; there are ten lines. Obviously, these are Klibanoff's "Ten Commandments."

A Plea to God

1. That I may die before any member of my family.
2. That I may not become a burden to my family or the community.
3. That I may die a natural death (not by accident or violence).
4. That I may not die in debt (knowingly).
5. That my children may always live in peace.

A Plea to the Inmates of My House

6. That all the children should observe the commandment: honor thy mother.
7. That they should say the prayer for the dead on every anniversary of my death (if impossible they should give alms).

8. That no words of praise should be uttered of me (because I did not earn them).
9. That there be no mourning of me (because the loss is not great).
10. That all my tangible goods shall be at the disposal of my wife Zelda.

Signed—David, the son of Abraham, Klibanoff
2nd day of Adar 5691—Providence, 1931

58

Hyman Moses Hillson

Pleas Avied [Avoid] All the Uncanny Custums that I Allways Disliked

An Orthodox Jew with Views of His Own

November 22, 1932

Hyman Moses Hillson was an East European Jew who came to Boston in the late nineteenth century. He settled in nearby Somerville and was one of the founders of the first Orthodox synagogue in that suburb. As this letter to his family indicates, he knew exactly what he wanted. These instructions were written shortly before his death; they are reproduced here in his own highly individual style and his own spelling of the language of his adopted country.

Somervill, Mass., November 22, 1932

Please take notice that it is my desire and wish that my funeral be as simple as possible. My body to be embalmed and kept at least three days unless I die of a contagies disease. A plain or staind wood coffin without any trimmings except a plate with name and dates of birth and death: Hyman Moses Hillson. . . February 23, 1853. . . English and Hebrew date of death.

Please avied all the uncanny custums that I allways disliked such as the *keriah* or tearing the cloth, a pillow with [Palestinian] earth, and such other things and custums which are not nice and not Jewish at all. I do not wish any of the societies that I belong to [to] take part in the services. I do not want my children to wear mourning after me, but it is my wish and my prayer that my children and my grandchildren to lead a good law abiding and *observent* Jewish life, to *remember* the *Sabath* day and to keep it holy and observe all other Jewish holy days. Keep and observe *kashruth* to the best of their ability and try their outmost to bring up thire children and grand children to lead the same kind of a life.

"Fear God and keep his commandments for this is the whole dudty of man" [Ecclesiastes 12:13].

This letter may be read by some one at the funeral.

Hyman Moses Hillson

59

Israel Davidson

Do Not Waste Any of Your Eloquence on My Accomplishments

Professor Israel Davidson Writes His Own Eulogy

ca. 1939

Israel Davidson (1870–1939) was an American scholar who wrote and edited a number of important Jewish literary works. His most notable publication was the multi-volume Ozar Ha-Shirah we-ha-Piyyut (Thesaurus of Mediaeval Hebrew Poetry),* *a catalogue of over 35,000 Jewish religious and secular poems. It is a truly indispensable volume for all who work in the field of medieval and early modern Hebrew literature.*

Lithuanian-born Davidson came to the United States in 1888, at the age of 18, after studying in East European talmudic academies. For him America was no immediate land of opportunity, for he peddled in the streets and taught Hebrew until 1921, when he finally secured his Ph.D. in Semitic languages at Columbia University. A modest appointment to the Jewish Theological Seminary, and other assorted jobs, made it possible for him to engage seriously in scientific work.

Some time before his death, he wrote a few parting words to be read at his funeral. If nothing else, the statement is certainly an honest avowal.

You who have gathered here to take leave of my earthly remains, do not mourn. Death only robs life of its sting. To live and witness our own follies and those of others is the bitterest cup which fate holds to the lip of man. What a relief it is to shake the mortal coil, to be rid of envy, jealousy, hatred,

*New York: Jewish Theological Seminary, 1924–1933.

greed, vanity, lust, all the plagues that mortify the flesh. Here I am with you, but no desires gnaw at my heart, and nothing you may have against me affects me. To those who will study my books a hundred years hence I will be as much alive then as I was to those who studied them yesterday. So please do not mourn.

Also do not waste any of your eloquence on my accomplishments. I would rather tell you some of the weak points in my armor—a sort of Vidui [confession]—with the object of showing that I too was made up of a dual personality, or perhaps a treble personality, i.e., good, bad and indifferent. But I fear such a Vidui would turn out rather a long recital, and if I made you listen to it, I would be committing a greater sin now than I ever committed in my lifetime. So let us pass both praise and blame, the dust return to dust and let the spirit go on living, free of all mortal entanglements which we erroneously call life.

Glorified be the spirit—the pure spirit.

60

Palmyre Levy Weill

There Are Certain Standards that Never Change

Palmyre Levy Weill Instructs Her Two Daughters

August 31, 1942

During World War II, Palmyre Levy (Mrs. Samuel) Weill of Oxnard, California, addressed her daughters in an ethical letter. The note is brief, but the advice is sound. If the letter truly reflects the woman, she was indeed an admirable human being. Her father was Achille Levy, one of the founders of a local bank.

Go through life shedding all the kindness and happiness you can; it will repay you in mental satisfaction alone. We were put on earth to be helpful to others and there are always many who need help, in various ways, who have no one to turn to, those who are worthy and yet have had the misfortune to be left alone.

Be careful in choosing your friends and associates, rather brains and breeding, than riches. Be kind and courteous to all, but judge those carefully whom you want as intimates.

Above all I want you to have faith and strength. Many hard problems will come up in your life and the faith you have will give you strength to carry on, when you most need it. Each day brings changes and one is never sure of anything, not even ourselves. But there are certain standards that never change, and it will be well to remember them.

Never forget your prayer of thankfulness for all your blessings and for

America. We are going through a terrific struggle with the world so torn with war and strife and injustice, it makes us wonder how it could ever happen.

Life is sweet and we have so much to be thankful for, but we often take too much for granted. Think over each day and resolve to make each tomorrow a little better.

61

Solomon Henry Blank

Evidently It Was Not Intended that I Should Be a Rich Man

Sol Blank Makes a Few Requests of His Children

November 27, 1942

Solomon Henry Blank—Sol to everybody—was born in Germany in 1866. His father had eked out a modest living as a teacher and Hebrew scribe. At the age of 15, Sol left home to make his fortune in the land of unlimited opportunity. He went to work for Bloomingdale's Department Store and wept because he had to work on the Sabbath. He learned his trade as a clothier in several small towns before he finally settled in Mt. Carmel, Illinois. Sol threw himself wholeheartedly into the life of the general community and belonged to almost every organization: the Odd Fellows, the Knights of Pythias, the Improved Order of Red Men, the Modern Woodmen of America, the Rotary. It was his boast that he held ten civic offices in town, all without compensation, and that he had been treasurer of the Salvation Army for almost twenty-five years. No one in Mt. Carmel was more respected. His integrity and honesty were beyond cavil. Those who did not love the genial, kindly, red-cheeked little cherub did, at least, respect him. This was one Jew the towns-people and farmers trusted and whose business they patronized. Sol never became rich, but he and his wife—the former Birdie Haas—reared a family of three children. Their two boys became college teachers, one at Harvard, the other at the Hebrew Union College.

The following requests "To Our Children" were written in 1942, after Sol had recovered from a heart attack.

18th of Kislev, 5703, according to the shorter (Hebrew) reckoning, Nov 27, 1942

By the grace of the Allmighty, now having passed the seventy-sixth milestone of my earthly career—born on April 10, 1866, 25th Nisan, in Lendershausen, Bavaria, Germany—and like all human beings not knowing its end, I want to write here a few requests, just as my good father *selig* [of blessed memory], Seligman Blank did, about the time he reached his three score and ten.

At this writing I hav'nt a copy of his last will, but as it had left a deep and lasting impression on my mind on account of its remarks and requests, I shall attempt to follow in his footsteps and state here some of my wishes and requests to my good children.

He used the words—part of the Yom Kippur prayers—*hatati, aviti, u-fashati*, "I have sinned, I have transgressed, and I have done evil." I also acknowledge these sins only in a much larger measure. I wish I had lived like him as a *zadik* and *chosid*, a religious and pure-in-heart man. He practiced the saying, *talmud torah keneged kulom*, "the study of the Torah is above everything" [Talmud Yerushalmi, Peah 1:1]. And, believing this, it has pleased us very much to see our son Sheldon enter the rabbinate and practicing this saying. For the sins I have committed against our Heavenly Father, I ask His forgiveness, and for the sins against my family and the people at large, I ask their forgiveness. The Lord saw fit to preserve me as the last survivor of my generation of the Blank family of Lendershausen, Germany. It is my wish and hope that I may have the health and strength required to do good deeds to my fellowmen during the time yet allotted to me.

The Lord blessed me with an exceptionally good wife, an *eshet hayil* [a woman of valor] who bore me three good and kind children. Long may they live, and may the reward held out in the fifth commandment be their heritage. No doubt my good wife will outlive me, and I am sure that the love and all that goes with it will be showered on her by you our good children. I doubt if ever a mother had greater love for her children than she has. I trust that I have appreciated all she has done for me during the past forty-eight years of our married life.

There has been an understanding between us two that when we have passed out that our bodies be cremated. However, I do not insist on this if such procedure should be against the will of the majority of our children. I desire a funeral without any unnecessary expense and without show. Just as my father, *selig*, expressed it: "Forgive me, my good children for not leaving any wealth." It is true that I cannot say as he did *verschwendet habe ich nichts* ("I have not wasted anything"), but I will say that I tried to be economical. Evidently it was not intended that I should be a rich man. Please attend to paying off any debts of mine that you know of.

If convenient say kaddish, or have it said in the first year and on jahrzeit.

May the good Lord watch over you and shower his richest blessings on you, is the wish of

Your loving father,
Sol H. Blank
Shelomoh ben ha-Rab Yizhak Blank (My *Jewish name)*

62

Jacob Philip Rudin

All I Could Think of Was a Hot Pastrami Sandwich

A World War II Chaplain Writes Home to His Congregants

March 1943

During World War II, Rabbi Jacob Philip Rudin (1902–1982) served in the Pacific theater as a United States Navy chaplain. He regularly published an Open Letter in his Great Neck, Long Island, Temple Beth-El bulletin, directed primarily toward parents with sons overseas. This letter enabled the rabbi to keep in touch with his congregants. They loved to hear from him, and he loved them. Among a host of good rabbis he was outstanding; he was sensitive, imaginative, compassionate, and beloved by his congregants. Wherever he went he evoked admiration and respect.

The Open Letter for March 1943 dealt with a Jewish Marine on Guadalcanal, lying in a fox-hole, under fire, slavering at the thought of a pastrami sandwich. What is there ethical in a slice of bread and a piece of highly seasoned smoked beef? More than meets the eye or the palate, the rabbi believed.

Dear Friends,

Everything that happens in war isn't grim and tragic. Amusing incidents occur, too. I want to tell you one which falls, I think, in that category. It was related to me by a Jewish Marine from Brooklyn. I am certain, however, that you would have discovered that fact for yourselves, without my telling you.

This happened on Guadalcanal, during the time when the fighting was heaviest and hardest. But I'll let the Marine talk for himself; although these, of course, are not his exact words.

"I was in a fox-hole not far from Henderson Field," he said. "The Japs were letting us have it with all the stuff they could throw at us. It was really a hot spot. Their big guns were banging away; planes were coming over and dropping their loads; bombs and shells were crashing all around us. The noise was indescribable and I never knew whether that particular breath I drew was going to be my last one.

"But honest, Chaplain,—and you will think I was crazy—all I could think of in the midst of that confusion and thunder, all I could think of was a hot pastrami sandwich. If I only had a hot pastrami sandwich! And right there in that fox-hole on Guadalcanal, I vowed that if I ever came away from the Solomons alive, the very first thing I was going to do when I hit the good old U.S.A. was to buy myself the biggest hot pastrami sandwich in the country."

Well, the Marine was wounded in a subsequent engagement and he was shipped back to the States to a Naval Hospital here on the Pacific coast, not very far from San Francisco.

"The big day came, Chaplain," the Marine continued, "and I was well enough to go on liberty. I went straight to the nearby town looking for my hot pastrami sandwich. Not a delicatessen in the place! So I went into a store and I asked where there was a good delicatessen, with real rye bread and real pastrami. The Jewish storekeeper told me that the closest one was in San Francisco and he gave me the address.

"It was too late to go that day; but I knew just where I would head on my next free day, you can be sure of that. So when I got my next liberty, I boarded the bus and was soon en route for San Francisco. All through the trip, I rehearsed how I would go into the shop; how I would look around and ask for the sandwich; how the fellow behind the counter would answer. In my imagination, I could see him cut two big slices of rye bread. I could smell the hot pastrami as he took it from the steamer and cut off thick and tasty pieces—not too fat and not too lean—just right, the way I like it. The only thing I couldn't make up my mind about was whether or not to put mustard on it. I finally decided that I would put some on one half of the sandwich and eat the other half plain.

"At last I arrived in San Francisco. I got my bearings and was soon walking down the street where the store was. I could see the sign, 'Delicatessen,' sticking out from the side of the building. I was there!

"I came to the door and turned the knob. It didn't budge. I tried again. No use. The door was locked. Then my eye caught sight of the neatly typed card in the corner of the door frame:

> In order to cooperate with the Government in conserving meat, I am observing meatless Tuesdays. Therefore, my store will be closed all day today.

But the story does have a happy ending.

The Marine went on: "That soured me. I decided to wait until I could get a couple of days leave so that I could go down to Los Angeles. Which I did. There I found the delicatessen store I had been waiting for all these months. I went in and I ordered a hot pastrami sandwich that thick." He held his hands about four inches apart.

"And, Chaplain," he concluded, "do you know, it tasted so good that I didn't even know I was chewing."

Hot pastramily yours,
Jacob Philip Rudin

63

Sidney Rabinowitz

I Wanted to Do Something to Help Make the World Better

Death at Hill 609, Tunisia

April 26, 1943

Sidney Robins (né Rabinowitz) was working in the advertising department of R. H. Macy's store when he joined the United States Army during World War II. On April 26, 1943, in Tunisia, knowing he was going to the front, he wrote a letter to his dear ones. It was to be sent to them only if he died in action. Three days later, at Hill 609, he was mortally wounded. As he lay dying, he plucked his "last letter" from his pocket; it was found tightly clutched in his hand when his body was recovered. He was 21 years of age. What a pity!

April 26, 1943

Dear Pa and Adele:

This is my last letter to you. I am keeping it in my pocket, and if I should be killed, I hope somebody will mail it to you.

Ever since I arrived in North Africa, I have been moving closer to the front. I finally got here yesterday, Easter Sunday.

We have just been told that we are moving up to the front lines in a few hours. Tonight or tomorrow morning I will be attacking the Germans. In case something happens to me, I want you both to know how I feel now.

I'm not scared or frightened. I feel tense, but I suppose that is to be expected. If I get shot, I would rather be killed than horribly wounded.

I'm only worried about how sad you would be if I get killed. But I hope you will also be proud that your son gave his life for the greatest cause in the world—that men might be free.

Pa, if I caused you heartaches and disappointments, I'm sorry. You'll never know how much I have always loved you, and how much more I love you now. Please take care of your health, for my sake.

Adele, whatever good qualities I may have, I owe to you. You were always kind and helpful, and you understood me better than anyone else did. I'm proud to call you "Mother." I leave you all my love.

To both of you, I want to say that you were the best parents in the world and I love you both. I hope God will take good care of you.

There is so much I wanted to say to you when I see you again; about how I was going to take care of you in the future and how I would make you proud of me.

Well, you will have something to be proud of anyway.

Do you remember, before I became a soldier, how I used to say that I wanted to do something to help make the world better?

Now I have the chance. If I die, at least I will know that I died to make the world a better place to live in.

I'll die, not as a hero, but as an ordinary young man who did all he could to help overcome the forces of evil.

I don't have time to write a letter to anyone else. So please give my love to Midge and Ben, Ralph and his family, Willie and the Rosenbergs, and all our friends and relatives. But most of all, give my love to Bobby and Larry. Please don't let them forget their uncle. I've always been so proud of them and I like to feel that they were proud of me, too. I hope they grow up in a peaceful world and become fine men.

God bless you both. I'll always love you,

Your devoted son,
Sidney

64

Samuel Furash

Your Life Will Be Full of Love

Corporal Samuel Furash Sends a Love Letter to His Infant Daughter

February 3, 1944

On February 3, 1944, Corporal Samuel Furash sent a letter to his baby daughter, who was not yet a year old. This young noncom, born in 1922 in Washington, D.C., was stationed in England; World War II was raging. Furash, a graduate of a Jewish high school, had already spent some time at a teachers' college. He was a political radical who hoped that his daughter would grow up to help build a world where all men and women would be free. He wrote movingly and eloquently. For many of us today, it is a sad letter; we no longer cup our ear to hear the clop-clop *of the Messiah on his white steed rushing to greet us and to usher in a new heaven and a new earth.*

Somewhere in England
February 3, 1944

My dearest Toby:

Probably by the time you receive this, you will have reached your first birthday; and by the time you will be able to read and understand it, we will be together as father and daughter, living through the days being missed now. Then again, there is always the possibility that never shall we know the relationship which is so deserving of us, but that possibility is quite remote. However, whatever the future holds in store for us, now is the time for us to get acquainted. As difficult as it may be, your mother's words to me through letters are descriptive enough to offer a realization of your habits, characteristics, personality, and other traits of you in different stages of your young life, [but] the scene still remains incomplete, of course, because we are still strangers to each other. However, Toby darling, I'm speaking to you now, because the words I say are my sincere beliefs and always will be, and some day you, too, shall share these thoughts with your mother and me.

You were born into a world which was experiencing the second stage of the "dark ages," a world filled with turmoil, suffering and grief, and a civilization on the verge of destruction and total chaos. By this statement you might easily assume that the responsibility for all this lies upon the shoulders of all mankind; and you would be right! I do not mean by this, that man is evil; to the contrary, man is good, *but* he has been lax and smug and because of this has allowed his basic principle of life, freedom, to be snatched from his hands by the long, murderous talons of fascistic tyranny through the rule of a small group of individuals. At this moment, this group of men have not succeeded in their attempts in this nation and a few others, but even though the people of these nations are in an all-out war against fascists and the principles of fascism, these men are still in important positions in our own set-up of government. And that is where you come in Toby, dear. You see, though we are fighting a war now, which we will undoubtedly win, the victory alone will not bring about the complete and happy change in our way of life. No! The struggle will then only begin and you and your generation will be the spearhead and main body of our fighting forces. We have begun the drive; you will finish it! Our victory will destroy tyranny; yours will establish freedom, freedom in every sense of the word; and that job constitutes the renovation of our whole system of society. Your mother and I are the fighters of the present; *you* are the builders of the future.

You are lucky, Toby, because your life will be full of love. It can be no other way; you see, you were born out of love. Never has there been a more perfect relationship than your mother's and mine, for when we are together, we are united as one individual, laughing as one, crying as one, thinking as one. We are melody, harmony and rhythm, together with courage, forming the most stirring symphony of love. Your mother is the "zenith" of kindness and understanding, and you originated within her, and will learn from her now; you will be the same. You are under the watchful and loving eyes of four grandparents who cherish you as their own child; and you have a father, who as yet has offered you nothing materially, only a little help in the assurance of your free future.

You shall benefit by your parents' tutelage, and soon will be aiding us in the education of your younger brothers and sisters, for there will be more, and we shall be more than a family for we have a foundation which is stronger than the very earth that holds us, the belief in truth, righteousness, and the right of all men to live and work happily in a society of social and economic equality, and to receive all the fruits of his labors. You shall believe as strongly as we, and shall fight to achieve such a glorious goal.

The things I am trying to say are difficult, but you will understand later, for you will read the works of the great poets and authors, listen to the music of great composers, and their words and melodies shall fill your heart and mind with the understanding and spirit to carry on in the battle for freedom.

Though my body be miles away, my heart is with you and I remain forever, your father, whose heart is filled with love for you and your mother. You are the nearest stars in my heaven and each night I sing out my love and best wishes.

Cpl. Samuel Furash

65

Harold Katz

I Asked for a Combat Assignment

Corporal Harold Katz Died for a Principle

1945

On March 30, 1945, Corporal Harold Katz, a youngster from the Bronx, was cited for bravery in action. After two of his comrades had been wounded in an attack on the German town of Attweilmann, this medical technician exposed himself to enemy fire, gave first aid to his comrades, and was himself seriously wounded. Although unable to move his legs, he pushed the other wounded soldiers to safety. Later, he was killed in action. A letter found on his person was sent to his mother. This is what he wrote.

Dear Mom,

I realize that this is a war and that men will be killed winning it, and since I am included in these I know there is a possibility of my not coming back.

If you receive this letter it will be because that possibility has come true. I am writing this letter now, while I have the chance, in the hope that it will ease the weight of the sad news, in that it will make you better understand my viewpoint on the matter.

Mom, I want you to know that I asked for a combat assignment. I did so for several reasons. One is that I had certain ideals within my own mind, for which I had often argued verbally. I didn't feel right to sit safe, far behind the lines, while men were risking their lives for principles which I would fight for only with my lips. I felt that I also must be willing to risk my life in the fight for the freedom of speech and thought I was using and hoped to use in the future.

Another reason. . . is the fact that I am Jewish. I felt again, it wasn't right for me to be safe behind the lines, while others were risking their lives, with one of their goals the principle of no race prejudice.

I knew this meant fighting for me and my family because if Hitler won, my family—you, Rolly and Pop—would certainly suffer more than the families of other soldiers who died in the fight.

I felt that I must risk my life, on that point, so that I could earn the right for my family to live in peace and free from race prejudice. I didn't think it right to stand by and let others fight for things which would benefit me. I asked for combat for the above reasons. Those are the feelings I had inside me, Mom, and I could not push them aside. I felt if I did not face them, I was not a man of true good character.

I hope you realize exactly what I am trying to tell you, Mom. I want you very much to be more proud than sorry. I don't want you to think of it as losing a son for no good reason, but rather as sacrificing a son so that all of mankind could live in a peaceful and free world.

66

Harris Pearlstone

Anti-Semitism Has Made Deep Inroads in America

Harris Pearlstone's Last Will

May 1, 1946

Harris Pearlstone (1870–1947), a native of Lomza, Poland, came to America in the early twentieth century with his wife and their six sons. After they settled in Canada, his wife bore him a seventh child, a girl. Pearlstone, a man of some Hebraic learning, made his living as a Hebrew teacher. Like his professional confreres, he barely managed to survive. Hebrew teaching was the first and last resort of the unskilled. Pearlstone was an unhappy man when he sat down to write his will—in Yiddish, of course. Old, wracked with pain, he was conscious that, for him, the New World had never been "a land of unlimited opportunity." (Did he ever stop to think that, had he remained in Lomza, he might well have ended in Auschwitz or Treblinka, murdered by the Germans?) Free America had left its impress on him; this Orthodox Jew made no religious demands on his children; he realized that this was a new, a different world. His will, poignant in its realism, underscores the problems that plagued him.

Last Will and Testament

My Dear Children and Grandchildren:

I feel that I shall not be with you much longer. I am growing weaker from day to day. Soon I shall go to join your mother and your brother Itzchak. Therefore, dear children, I beg of you not to grieve too deeply nor to mourn too much for me. No man is immortal. I am no longer a young man: last Chanukah I became seventy-five years old—a few years more or less do not make much difference—especially in the miserable circumstances in which I am spending my last years. I did not experience any great happiness in my younger days either—my life was a constant struggle and I cannot remember one single happy year—but they were golden years in comparison with those of my later days. The Almighty has seen fit to burden me with a very bitter old age, filled with sickness and pain, shunned by friends and acquaintances, isolated from the whole world. I was even denied the pleasure of playing and conversing with my dear grandchildren. I was a severed, useless limb in the body of humanity. Believe me, to forego such an existence is no great calamity and it does not merit an extra tear.

Dear Children, I have caused you too much trouble in my later years: I should like, therefore, to free you from trouble, as much as possible, after my death. I realize that it is very difficult, almost impossible, to attend kaddish prayers three times daily for a period of eleven months. I know, also, that you do not believe in this ritual; I myself have but little faith in the need or efficacy. Therefore, I absolve you from the obligation of saying kaddish the whole year and from observing my jahrzeiten. I forbid you to hire anyone to say kaddish for me. In the first place, it would be meaningless and, secondly, I want to spare your pride. I beg of you only that you all get together at the time of my jahrzeit and that each one of you contribute, in my name, to some worthy cause or institution which will appeal to you, each according to his means and goodwill. This would be more pleasing to God, to me, and to all thinking men than all the prayers you could say.

Now I wish to deal with a delicate problem, one which was a source of much pain and sorrow both to me and to your mother, namely, the Jewish education of your children and grandchildren. Do not think for one minute that this thought represents a "fixed idea" on the part of an old fogey. Study my words well and you will see that these are the words of a practical father who seeks, above all, the happiness and well-being of his children and grandchildren.

I did not give you as good a Jewish education as I could have wished for. This was due to my poverty and economic distress, my running around all day to give lessons so as to earn enough to buy bread for my family. The result was that I saw you only from one Shabbas to another. I had to devote my whole energy to the task of making a living, so much so that I had very little energy left to struggle with you. The gulf between me and you was too great, and I found it impossible to bridge it with my feeble strength. I was deeply rooted in Lomza, while you, on the other hand, threw yourselves with all the heat and energy of your young blood into the American way of life, and looked upon each Jewish teacher as superfluous. All my efforts were of no avail.

With you, however, the situation is altogether different. No gulf exists between you and your children. You speak the same language and received the same education. Also the burden of making a living does not fall as heavily upon you as upon your father. You understand your children and your children understand you. You are in a position to exercise the greatest influence over them. You, my children, have at least spent your younger years in a Jewish home where the Shabbas, Yom Tov, and many other Jewish customs were observed. Some recollections of these customs must, of necessity, linger in your minds. Your children, however, were taught none of these things and are consequently growing up like wild grass, neither Jews nor Christians. When they grow up and come to their true understanding they will offer you no thanks for this neglect. To all intents and purposes, there has developed among American youth a great tendency to revert back, back to Jewishness, back to nationalism, even back to religion. All this deals with moral issues. Now let me comment on the practical side of the problem.

Anti-Semitism has made deep inroads in America and all indications point to its spread and growing powers. It cannot be otherwise. Wherever Jews live in compact masses, anti-Semitism will rear its head. You are all familiar with discrimination against and insults to Jews. All anti-Semitism bills will burst like air bubbles when they come to contact with hard, practical, real life. No legislation can force a man to love another where no love exists. The native American, even the best of them, merely *tolerates* the Jew, but, so far from recognizing him as an equal, not to say loving him, he will soon find an excuse to employ the Christian and not the Jew, as long as he has no need for Jewish talent and abilities. I sincerely hope I am wrong, but the truth is that your children and grandchildren will inherit insults and discriminations on account of their race.

Then they will approach you with the inevitable question: "In what way are we . . . Jewish . . . ? What . . . do we know of Jewishness . . . ?" How will you face this critical problem? On the other hand a shining perspective is opening for Jews in their own land, Eretz Israel [the Land of Israel]. I shall not live to see its fruition, but you, and especially your children, will be fortunate enough to see the day. And on that day all idealistic Jewish youth will gather in strength to spurn the so-called American freedom with its prejudices and discriminations and will emigrate to the Promised Land where they will be able to walk with uplifted head and will devote their talents and capacities to the building of a country which will serve as a model for humanity. Well, if your children and grandchildren are to be numbered among this sensitive youth, they will certainly need a Jewish education. And even if they should bow their heads and endure recrimination and insult, they at least ought to know why they suffer and that it is worth while to suffer. It is immaterial to me in which language they are educated; in Hebrew (which would be the best), in Jewish [Yiddish] or in English. Let them be well versed in Jewish history. Give them the privilege of marvelling at the colossal panorama of events which the Jewish genius has produced, wherever they happened to be, for the enhancement of the culture and civilization of the whole world.

Give them to understand how the Jew was repaid by the Christian world with stones, pogroms, ghettos, and inquisitions—all in the name of a God of love. Your children will then know that truth and righteousness lie with them and that for the truth it sometimes pays to suffer.

I am bequeathing you no great inheritance, so that I can dispose with the services of a lawyer and you, on your part, will be spared the necessity of quarreling among yourselves. In fact the money is not actually mine, but yours. True, I managed to salvage $900 from the house; the rest represents hardearned savings. As you know, I lived very economically, but if you, my dear children, had not come to my help in my later years, there would not have been a cent left of this money. The only inheritance I can really call mine is my good name. I beg of you, therefore, to hold our family name dear and sacred. Lead an honorable, respectable life. Let no blemish sully our name. You have lived in a friendly and brotherly way during my lifetime and I beg of you to carry on the same relationship after I am gone. . . .

All the things that I brought into Esther's [his daughter's] house after my wife's death shall belong to her. She may do whatever she wants with them. These I leave her as a mark of thankfulness for her faithful and loyal service to me in my latter years. I do not mean to disparage the loyal and model treatment of my other children. I know well enough that you all treated me with the greatest devotion and God will certainly repay you for it. But Esther has endured more than all of you on my account. She was on her feet day and night, always ready to listen to the complaints and to tolerate the whims of her old, sick father. Her husband also, has always shown me the love and respect of a devoted son and for this I give him my thankfulness and good wishes. May God repay him. . . .

And now, good-bye, my children and grandchildren. I wish you all a successful, happy life. May you grow old pleasantly and honorably with your families and derive pleasure and honor from your children and grandchildren. May the memory of your father's honor which you treasured so highly sustain you to a good, happy, healthy old age. Good-bye Masha, Yitshak, all my relatives. I wish you all a healthy, happy life, much pleasure from your children and a good, healthy old age. Good-bye.

Written in sound mind May 1, 1946.

Yeshayahu Tsvi son of Yitshak Abraham Perlshtein [the original name]

67

David Eli Lilienthal

All Men Are the Children of God

David E. Lilienthal Defines Democracy

February 4, 1947

David Eli Lilienthal (b. 1899), a lawyer, was one of America's most distinguished public servants. From 1933 to 1946, he served on the board of the Tennessee Valley Authority; in 1946, he was made the head of the Atomic Energy Commission. Before he was confirmed as AEC chairman, Lilienthal had to appear before the Senate Section of the Joint Congressional Committee on Atomic Energy. Senator Kenneth D. McKellar, a friend of the private utility corporations, set out to smear him, by innuendo, as a "Communist" and the son of an immigrant. Lilienthal's rejoinder to this attack, his apologia pro vita sua, *is reprinted here.*

At the age of 18, Lilienthal had won an oratorical contest at his university. In that address, "The Mission of the Jew," Lilienthal cried out: "I am a Jew!" It was the task of his martyred people, he said, to preach the unity of God and the brotherhood of all mankind. However, in his later years, when he was a national figure, he edged away from Jewry and moved toward marginality. He was in no sense an ardent Jew.

Credo of an American : A Statement by David E. Lilienthal before the Congressional Committee on Atomic Energy

This I do carry in my head. I will do my best to make it clear. My convictions are not so much concerned with what I am against as what I am for; and that excludes a lot of things automatically.

Traditionally, democracy has been an affirmative doctrine rather than merely a negative one. I believe—and I do so conceive the Constitution of the United States to rest upon, as does religion—the fundamental proposition of the integrity of the individual; and that all Government and all private institutions must be designed to promote and to protect and defend the integrity and the dignity of the individual; and that is the essential meaning of the Constitution and the Bill of Rights, as it is essentially the meaning of religion.

Any form of government, therefore, and any other institutions which make means rather than ends, which exalt the State or any other institutions above the importance of men, which place arbitrary power over men as a fundamental tenet of government or any other institutions, are contrary to that conception, and therefore I am deeply opposed to them.

The communistic philosophy, as well as the communistic form of government, fall within this category, for their fundamental tenet is quite to the contrary. The fundamental tenet of communism is that the State is an end in itself, and that therefore the powers which the State exercises over the individual are without any ethical standard to limit them. That I deeply disbelieve.

It is very easy simply to say one is not a Communist. And of course, if my record requires me to state that very affirmatively, then it is a great disappointment to me. It is very easy to talk about being against communism. It is equally important to believe those things which provide a satisfying and effective alternative. Democracy is that satisfying affirmative alternative.

Its hope in the world is that it is an affirmative belief, rather than being simply a belief against something else and nothing more.

One of the tenets of democracy that grow out of this central core of a belief that the individual comes first, that all men are the children of God and their personalities are therefore sacred, carries with it a great belief in civil liberties and their protection, and a repugnance to anyone who would steal from a human being that which is most precious to him—his good name; either by impugning things to him by innuendo or by insinuations.

And it is especially an unhappy circumstance that occasionally that is done in the name of democracy. This, I think, can tear our country apart and destroy it if we carry it further.

I deeply believe in the capacity of democracy to surmount any trials that may lie ahead, provided only we practice it in our daily lives. And among the things we must practice is that while we seek fervently to ferret out the subversive and anti-democratic forces in the country, we do not at the same time, by hysteria, by resort to innuendo and smears and other unfortunate tactics, besmirch the very cause that we believe in, and cause a separation among our people, cause one group and one individual to hate another based on mere attacks, mere unsubstantiated attacks upon their loyalty.

I want also to add that part of my conviction is based on my training as an

Anglo-American common lawyer. It is the very basis and the great heritage of the English people to this country, which we have maintained, that the strictest rules of creditability of witnesses be maintained and hearsay and gossip shall be excluded in courts of justice. And that, too, is an essential of our democracy.

And, whether by administrative agencies acting arbitrarily against business organizations, or whether by investigating activities of the legislative branches, whenever those principles of the protection of an individual and his good name against besmirchment by gossip, hearsay and the statements of witnesses who are not subject to cross-examination are not maintained, then, too, we have failed in carrying forward our ideals in respect to democracy. That I deeply believe.

68

Samuel Rosinger

There Is So Much Goodness, Kindness, and Sweetness

Rabbi Samuel Rosinger of Texas Rehearses His Guiding Principles

1950s

Rabbi Samuel Rosinger (1877–1965) of Beaumont, Texas, served his congregation for forty-seven years. His favorite biblical verse was "Speak O Lord, for Thy servant heareth" (1 Samuel 3:9). A truly pious man, he believed that it was not for mortals to question God. Essentially, he was a Jew who accepted the faith and the traditions of his ancestors.

Rosinger, born in a Hungarian village, studied in Budapest, Switzerland, Berlin, and New York, where he was ordained at the Jewish Theological Seminary, the hearth of Conservative Judaism. After a brief stay in Toledo, he answered the advertisement of the Beaumont Jews for a rabbi who was a "good mixer." He knew they were not looking for a bartender. But when they chose him over many other candidates it was because he wrote a calligraphic hand! He became one of the city's leading citizens; he was certainly its outstanding Jew.

The following statement—an excerpt, to be sure—was originally written at the request of the Director of the American Jewish Archives.

Ever since I have been mature enough to think of the problems of human existence, I have trained myself to look at the positive side of life. I know that all is not well with the world, that evil is rampant abroad, that injustice wrings bitter tears from the victims of our imperfect social system, that life has its shady and seamy sides, and that sorrow, suffering, and misery sound very discordant notes in the symphony of the universe. Yet, withal, there is so much goodness, kindness, and sweetness, and such an abundance of beauty, grace, virtue, and wisdom in the ordinary course of life, that a person whose mind is not morbid will turn his face as the sunflower toward the source of light, which renders these divine blessings visible, and not in the direction of darkness, where the pall of gloom hangs over all.

I believe that the Almighty has placed us in this world not to censure, not to cavil and criticize, but to construct and correct, to build and improve, so as to make this sphere a better and fitter place to live in. Hence, I have adopted for my motto the maxim of our sages: "Judge every man in the scale of merit" [Abot 1:6]. Instead of searching for the flaws and foibles, let us try to find the good and noble qualities in our fellowmen. When viewing a landscape, let us not fix our gaze on the few ugly spots which detract from its beauty, but feed our eyes on those sights which fill us with delight and rapture. . . .

Let the pseudoscientist and the half-baked thinker presume a godless world. My horse sense tells me that if a claptrap of a shack is not the work of chance, but of a builder, how much more does our marvelous universe presuppose an Architect of supreme wisdom and intelligence? "The heavens declare the glory of God, and the firmament showeth forth His handiwork" [Psalms 19:1]. There is a deeper truth in this scriptural statement than in all the labored speculations of philosophy. One glimpse of the majestic sky lends me surer guidance than all the fine theories which scientists have spun on the looms of their brains.

True science, gaining an ever-increasing knowledge of the universe, discerns a directing intelligence behind it. The time will come when science will discover not only manifestations of intelligence, but also revelations of benevolence in the world. The universe is governed not only by law but also by love, and behind the cosmic forces which keep the universe in balance, there is a compassionate heart that beats with tender love for the humblest creature that breathes on earth. In the midst of all the doubts and uncertainties of life, in the flood of all the confusing and conflicting theories evolved by scientists, in all the flux of this ever-changing world, cling to the Rock of Ages, and you will find safety, security, and stability. . . .

It is not for man to question the dispensations of Providence. Our implicit faith in divine justice must admit of no doubt, no matter how strongly assailed we are by the sordid realities of life. We must reconcile all discrepancy between facts and faith by asking in the words of Abraham, the father of faith, the question that has only one answer: "Shall the Judge of all the earth not exercise justice?" [Genesis 18:25].

It is in such a reverential and submissive spirit that we should seek to find a meaning and a purpose in every misfortune that befalls us. We cannot pierce the veil. We cannot comprehend the divine plan. Yet this much we know, the innocent do not suffer in vain. Divine truth grows out of the soil drenched with martyrs' blood. The tears of the righteous quicken the earth more than the dew of heaven. Out of the broken and contrite heart flow the healing waters of love, charity, kindness, and helpfulness. The scalpel of the surgeon hurts, yet heals. The storm destroys yet cleanses the atmosphere. Pain is not a measure of punishment, but a purification. Cast in the crucible of suffering, we emerge free from the dross of selfishness. Adversity is the balance in which God weighs His children. The man and woman of character and faith and worth will not to be found wanting. . . .

69

Leonard N. R. Simons

Love, Respect, and *Generosity* Are the Three Most Important Words in the Dictionary

Leonard N. R. Simons Reveals His Personal Creed

ca. 1951

Leonard N. R. Simons (b. 1904) made a living as an advertising executive, but his real job was helping others. He once wrote: "There's a big difference between sticking your nose in other people's business and putting your heart in other people's problems." There is a consensus: No other individual in Detroit has been more active as a humanitarian than Leonard Simons. In every field—in welfare, interfaith relations, culture, social advancement—he has reached out to advise, to aid, to comfort.

He wrote the following statement in or about the year 1951. These are not mere words; they reflect not only the intent but also the deeds of a dedicated human being.

I believe with all my heart that man was put on this earth to serve mankind. The satisfaction I get whenever I have the opportunity to accomplish something worthwhile for someone, or some group, is proof to me that life's biggest thrills are secured from deeds of kindness and good will.

For me to earn the warm thanks, expressed in a sincere handshake, for something which I have done, is reward beyond measure.

When I was a boy, I lived with my grandparents. Here were two people who had very little of the material things, yet I never heard them complain. The affection and respect they had for each other and for those with whom they came in contact, made an indelible impression upon me.

In the tradition of my religion, when a boy reaches thirteen he becomes of age—a man. My grandfather, at the time, gave me these words of wisdom:

"Love, respect, and generosity are the three most important words in the dictionary. If you have certain talents that permit you, some day, to make a lot of money, then remember this, my boy, 'A shroud has no pockets.' "

My grandparents' philosophy of life has been the inspiration for my own.

Twenty-three years ago I became a partner in an advertising agency. I determined then that I would set aside a part of my time to the job of helping—without payment or fee—organizations and people who had need for the type of assistance which I was particularly qualified to give.

Since that time I have lived by that plan, and while our list of business clients is far from the most impressive one in our profession, our list of charitable, civic and national organizations which we have assisted, represents an effort on my part to really place service to my fellow men on as high and universal a plane as I can attain.

That list gives me the most satisfaction when I take inventory of my assets.

I am indeed fortunate because I lead a full and happy life. I believe that by trying to live usefully I have become a better man myself, and in so doing have earned the respect of my neighbors and the love of my family. What more could anyone ask?

I believe that death is not final . . . if, by virtue of what I have been able to contribute to the happiness of others, I continue to live in the memory of the many people with whom I have been associated.

It is my belief that the money I earn is only as good as the good it can do during my lifetime. Beyond what I need for my family's security, the rest belongs to the service of my fellow men.

I believe that I should try to help, in my own small way, to create a better world in which to live and in which to raise a family by continuing to extend a friendly hand to those who need my help. I try to judge men by the goodness in their hearts. I have found peace of mind in trying to do the things that I hope will find favor in the eyes of God.

Years ago I read a statement of Charles Schwab, former president of the United States Steel Corp., and it strengthened my own philosophy of life. He said:

> Most of my troubles have been due to my being good to people. If young folks want to avoid trouble, they should be hard-boiled and say "No" to everybody. They will walk through life unmolested. But they will do without friends and won't have much fun.

I believe he is right and that my own true worth—my real wealth—is the large number of friends I have.

If I reach a ripe old age, I believe I shall be able to draw on a rich storehouse of memories.

70

Louis J. Sigel

Demand the Freedom to Be Yourself

Papa and Mama Sigel Talk to Their Newborn Daughter

November 4, 1955

When Judy Lee Sigel was born in 1955, her father, Rabbi Louis J. Sigel of Temple Emeth in Teaneck, New Jersey, prayerfully addressed her as part of the ceremony in which he named and blessed her. Rabbi Sigel, a 1951 graduate of the Hebrew Union College, is a well-known Reform Jewish spiritual leader and the author of Judaism Without Illusions**. The address to the baby, written by both of her parents in the form of a letter, follows here.*

Dear Judy,

Your mother and I have written this letter to you more or less as a guide for ourselves in helping you to grow. You don't know us yet, and we hardly know you. But, we do have an advantage over you. We have a fair idea of what, with God's help, you may become; of what kind of person, given a fair and normal amount of health and love, you may grow up to be. It is the idea of this very miracle which still overwhelms us. The miracle that someday you will become a feeling, thinking, complete organism thrills every fiber of our beings.

First of all, we'd like to tell you that you are wanted. We consider your arrival in this world truly a blessed event. It is an event which blesses us because it fills our lives with growth and with warmth and with love. It is an

*Teaneck, New Jersey: Temple Emeth, 1976.

event which blesses you because you are now part of the life of this world. Already, you are an important part of its dreams and its hopes.

It's such a wonderful feeling to feel that you belong to this world, that it's a friendly world, that the sun shines for you, and that the birds sing for you and that the ability to love exists just for you. Of course, Judy, you must remember that almost everybody else feels exactly that way, and so you must try never to keep other people from enjoying the world.

Do you know that you've come to us at a time when there are more humans on earth than at any other time in history? It's also a time when there are more of the world's goods available for more people than at any other time before. Life has become longer and healthier. Life has become much more pleasurable and leisurely than ever before. We hope that you will learn to use these resources wisely and carefully. Try to learn not to gorge yourself upon them. Leave a little for tomorrow. However, let no one deprive you of them, as you would not deprive anyone else of them. Let no one ever tell you that you don't deserve the blessings of this world, that you're too wicked to be even privileged to earn the right to them. You're not wicked, Judy. You're not evil. The very fact that soon, very soon, you will have feelings of wanting to be good, of wanting to be better than you were yesterday, shows us that God and not wickedness is in you, shows us that good, and not evil is in you. Just think of it, Judy; this world has been constantly becoming a better place because of men and women who were all at one time as small and helpless as you are now, but who found out that the world wanted and needed them—that God, Himself, needed them as His partners—to make this world a better place in which to live. Yes, Judy, we want you and we love you and we shall always be proud of you because you are Judy.

What a wonderful thing it is—just to be Judy! To grow up and try to be nothing other than the best of yourself, the best of Judy! You may learn from others—nay, you *must* learn from them—not for the purpose of being what you cannot be, only for the purpose of becoming the best that's in you to be.

Judy, you are part of an ancient people whose members always tried to be themselves. Centuries of living had taught them that to try to escape from yourself is the greatest sin, and that the greatest virtue is to *demand* the freedom to be yourself, to demand it not only from men but from God Himself. Of all the stories on this subject in our great literature, your mother and I like this one the best of all. Rabbi Zusya once said: "When I pass from this world and stand before God's judgment, God will *not* ask me: 'Zusya, why, in your lifetime, were you not Moses; why were you not Isaiah; why were you not Jeremiah?' No, God will ask me: 'Why were you not Zusya?' " So, little Judy, learn not to escape from yourself, from your people, from the great heritage which is now yours. Seek the freedom to do this. Seek the peace to do this in quiet and in confidence. Your mother and I know that, within this natural instinct of yours to be yourself, you will someday try to break away from us, you will try to rebel against what you will consider a little too much parental control. But Judy, that pain will vanish for us, for we know that this, too, is part of you trying to be yourself.

In your struggle to be yourself, Judy, try to keep before you always the image of many people who are trying desperately to be themselves. Deprive them not of that opportunity. You would do this at the risk of losing your own identity, at the risk of losing the feeling of being in harmony with this world, of being in harmony with God. It's as true today as when Rabbi Hillel uttered it: "If you're not for yourself, then who will be for you." But, Judy, if you are only for yourself alone, then what really are you!

Simply, these are the things that Mother and I have been trying to say in this letter, a letter which you probably won't read until you're much older. We hope that, by then, you will be well on the road to loving this world and being loved in return, to being aware of yourself and your friends as children of God, and to realizing that this is exactly what God wants from you. We pray in words which all Jewish parents have used for centuries for their newborn children . . . : "May you grow in such a way as to enter into knowledge, into the maturity of personality through marriage, and into a life of good deeds." Amen.

71

Samuel Wolk

Man: "A Little Lower than the Angels"

Rabbi Samuel Wolk Writes a Will: The Will Is the Man

March 14, 1956

Rabbi Samuel Wolk (1899–1957), a native of Baltimore, was rabbi of Temple Beth Emeth in Albany, New York. When in 1953 he was awarded an honorary Doctor of Divinity degree, the president of the Hebrew Union College read this citation:

> Rabbi Samuel Wolk, a man of integrity and humility, of deep sense of duty, exalted ideas, and broad vision, beloved for his sympathetic personality and all-embracing humanity, social and communal worker of lofty aspiration and manifold achievement, devoted leader of his people, faithful servant of God, embodiment of all that is truest and finest in Judaism, and loyal son of a proud alma mater.

This tribute was no exaggeration. Samuel Wolk was one of God's gentlemen. His nobility is reflected in the following document, the brief will that he wrote a year before he died.

I, Samuel Wolk, of the City and County of Albany, State of New York, make this my last will and testament:

All worldly goods that I own, after the payments of my just debts, I give, devise and bequeath to my wife Mary C. Wolk, absolutely, to be used or disposed of by her in whatever way she may see fit, and I name her executrix of this my will.

Should it be our fate to die jointly, I bequeath these possessions to our son

Daniel. In that case, I name him, together with Robert C. Poskanzer, as executors.

These worldly goods are of small material value. I am in possession of a far richer store. It is a way of life transmitted to me, through thousands of years, by prophet, sage and martyr of my people. It embodies a counsel for life which if taken diligently to heart and practiced by all men, would lead to larger understanding, less bloodshed, and more brotherhood. It is a counsel which thinks of man as "as little lower than the angels" rather than as kin to beasts. That counsel I gladly bequeath to all mankind, without regard to family ties or color or creed. It is a rich heritage which, without distinction, I will to friend and foe alike.

In witness whereof, I have hereunto set my hand and seal this 14th day of March, in the year one thousand nine hundred and fifty-six.

Samuel Wolk

72

Rockdale Temple Confirmation Class

I. To All Young People I Bequeath Tolerance

II. Many Jewish People Place Too Much Value on Money

Teenagers Write Their "Testaments"

1958

At the conclusion of the academic year 1957–1958, the Reverend Dr. Victor E. Reichert of the Rockdale Avenue Temple in Cincinnati executed a pedagogical tour de force. He asked the boys and girls in his confirmation class to write ethical wills, as if they were parents instructing their children on how to conduct themselves as they faced the challenge of the world about them. Older readers of these wills who grew up in the decades before radio and television cannot help but be impressed by the maturity, the intelligence, the literary skills of these youngsters. In a foreword to these published documents, Dr. Reichert wrote:

> These testaments speak eloquently of the ethical idealism and religious faith of the coming generation. In a day when there is so much pessimistic talk about juvenile delinquency and the waywardness of our youth, it is refreshing to behold here a group of young men and women on the threshold of maturity who already display keen insight into the mystery of life, and high resolve to add to the richness of the human adventure. . . . Call them not children for they are the builders of tomorrow.

Two of the wills are reprinted here. The names of the two testators—probably a girl and a boy in their middle teens—are not known.

I

I wear lipstick, heels, and chemise dresses, but I am still a child. I go to formals, read historical novels and current affairs, but the thought of snow and water pistols still produces a happy, impish feeling. I know that my heart is divided into many rooms; the first contains goodness; the second, selfishness, thoughtlessness; the third, sadness. And as the delicate lilac absorbs from its growing place the tiny drops of dew and gives forth fragrance, so does my heart admit and release those qualities of goodness, thoughtlessness and sadness. This has been my year of learning. Through happy and disappointing experiences, I think that I have become a little more tolerant and understanding of people. I mention these facts about myself because I wonder if I am mature enough to make an ethical will.

The dictionary defines ethical as "relating to moral action, motive or character." I bequeath the qualities of character or motive which I think help produce moral action. The first is sympathy and understanding for the feelings of others. Although parents seem to perceive their child's dreams and emotions, they say to a friend, "How lucky she is, not having anything to worry about. Little does my child know of the harsh world." How little do the parents remember the agitation and uncertainty of childhood, unless they can relive their own, the little things. . . the broken doll, the yearning for a sled, the feeling of a left out child.

To all young people I bequeath a sense of justice. To see another viewpoint than your own is the hardest work in the world. To be fair in your dealings with others, you must be honest with yourself. When I argue with my best friend, I try to remember that she thinks she is right, too. This is very difficult. Not so hard is seeing injustice when it doesn't concern you. When I see a little child overpowered by a bigger one, I grow angry. When I see someone persecuted who cannot help himself, I do not like it. I try to help. Trying to make fair the unjust is one quality I believe makes a better person.

To all young people I bequeath tolerance. If a child goes to a foreign school and dresses oddly and speaks with an accent, I think she should not be laughed at. Even if a child is American, but behaves differently from his schoolmates, I don't think he should be ridiculed. A little kindness will help the one who receives and the one who gives.

To all young people, I bequeath a love of learning. Learn, always learn, for learning is life. Learning blooms at sunrise and fades away at dusk. Learning is like sewing. One takes one stitch, then another. It is not always easy. Sometimes the light grows dim, but the finished dress makes the struggle worthwhile.

To all young people, I bequeath high standards, the strength to do what is right, because it is right.

II

My own life is guided by the goals which I have set for myself. Inspired by

God and by the love and encouragement from my friends, I shall unceasingly strive to make these aspirations my way of living.

Though my parents' worth and values have affected my way of thinking to a great extent, I feel that every individual must find for himself his place in the plan of the universe. The guidance which I receive in my home will undoubtedly have a long-lasting influence on my character, but equally significant are those experiences with people of all races, religions and social positions, with poverty, with success—with everything and everyone connected with my life. Thus, as I mature, my experiences, as well as the guidance of my parents, may serve as a lasting influence on my relations with God and with my fellow man.

To my unborn children I promise my love and guidance; more specifically, I shall try to make them so secure in my love for them that, no matter what problems they are forced to face, no matter how difficult their trials and tribulations, no matter what their misfortunes, their faith in God and in themselves will never shatter.

My life, as I see it now, is a coalition of two entirely different types of goals. One type is self-improvement. This goal of mine is not so much concerned with "How to get popular in ten easy lessons" as it is with the development of my character. I want to be a person unselfish in my desires, a person who has the courage of his convictions (as long as they harm no one but himself), and an individual capable of loving his neighbor as himself. At this period of my life, though I have little trouble with racial or religious prejudice against others, I do find it difficult to like certain types of people, namely the materialist, the social-climber and the snob. However, when I keep in mind the idealistic commandment, to love my neighbor, I find that I have a greater interest in understanding people and in discovering just why they act as they do.

So to my unborn sons and daughters I offer this advice: Try to understand all people, their beliefs and their actions. I hope that, through your home environment and by means of your own experiences with people, you will be broadminded enough to gain an appreciation of those who think or look slightly different from yourself.

The second type of goal concerns my fellow man. My main career interest is social work; I like to be with poor people, and I feel that there is a great deal which I can do to better their understanding of life and to help them bear their poverty more easily. Equally important in my mind is the brotherhood of the human race. Until the day I die, I will always be trying to convince my friends not only that Negroes are equal, but also that many are wonderful, sincere people, worth getting to know. Always, also, will I remain loyal to the Jewish people, for I feel a special closeness to the group as a whole, even though I think many Jewish people place too much value on money.

My children of tomorrow, to whom I leave this will, I pray that, through the guidance of your parents, you will be able to live satisfying and meaningful lives.

73

Irving Leibowitz

Treat Your Sister Like a Little Lady

A Father Advises His Son

May 2, 1958

On May 2, 1958, Irving Leibowitz wrote a bar mitzvah letter to his son Alan. Leibo—as the writer was known—was a Conservative Jew, a World War II veteran, and a major in the U.S. Marine Corps Reserve. Professionally, he was a journalist, an assistant editor of The Indianapolis Times, *and the author of a column entitled "Hoosier Headlines." His letter reflects the sturdy ethical interests of a committed Jew and an ardent acculturated American.*

Dear Alan:

You are on the threshold of manhood. Tomorrow, as is customary in the Jewish faith, you will be confirmed. We call it "Bar Mitzvah."

As a young man, now, you have certain rights and obligations.

You ask: "What can I do? Where can I go?"

I shall tell you. Go home. Study your lessons. Mow the lawn. Wash the car. Get a job. Read a book. Help your mother.

Get it out of your head that the world, and your parents in particular, owe you entertainment, recreational facilities, and a handsome living.

This is a time for you to grow up. Quit being a crybaby. Develop a backbone, not a wishbone. Treat your sister like a little lady.

Do not expect your parents or teachers or friends or relatives to make excuses for you, to protect you, to deny themselves needed comforts for your every whim and fancy.

Do not misunderstand. Your mother and I are proud of you.

We realize that a boy of your age is slow to take a bath, slow to study lessons, slow to come home on time, slow to help around the house, slow to feed Champ, and fast to run out of the house (and bang the door) to play basketball and baseball.

As a good Jew, you must remember your heritage . . . that you come from religious people who pioneered in liberty, learning, and law.

As a good American, you must remember, too, that you were born and brought up in this great nation that has made freedom for everyone a daily, living thing.

You must be prepared to live and give your energy and talents so that no one will be at war or in poverty, or sick or lonely again.

You must be prepared to fight, and die, if necessary, to protect this country that welcomes the oppressed of the world so that your own children may continue to live in freedom.

May God grant you the courage and wisdom and faith to be a man.

74

Chaim Yaakov Bloom

Educate Your Children at a Yeshivah

Chaim Yaakov Bloom Prescribes His Postmortem Ritual

October 15, 1958

Chaim Yaakov Bloom's final injunctions to his children were addressed to his son Ezekiel. Written in Yiddish, these injunctions were ritually prescriptive, not overtly ethical. The father, a professional circumciser (mohel) *in Brooklyn, outlined no moral program; he took it for granted that his son would live Jewishly and ethically. Bloom's prime concern was that his children be meticulous in their observance of Jewish ritual and that they educate their sons in a Jewish academy. The father was convinced that ritual practices and Hebrew schooling were the best guarantee for their survival as Jews. There is no mention of a kosher kitchen; it may well be that adherence to the dietary laws was the practice in the homes of his children.*

"B'ezrat Hashem" [With the help of God]
1st day of Heshvan, 1958

To my son Ezekiel, may he live long.

When you will read this *shrift* [writing], I will no longer be with you. Therefore you shall know that this is my last will and testament which I write while I am of sound mind and clear understanding. After a long deliberation, I decided that the time has come (feeling that my heart gets weaker from day to day, and since your mother, of blessed memory, my devoted companion, is not with us, to whom I would give all these instructions), therefore I write to you and beg of you that you fulfill my last testament as follows:

1. That when you and your brothers and sisters will stand by my open casket and after your final respects to your father, the casket shall not be closed until your brothers Isaac and Mordecai make peace between them and live in peace for ever after. This will give consolation to my soul, which was denied to me during my lifetime.

2. You shall observe a full shivah in my last *home* and have services for Shachrit, Minchah and Maariv [morning, afternoon and evening].

3. Each of you shall conduct services according to your ages, and read from my Sefer.

4. The entire eleven months of mourning you will use your tallith and tefillin and recite kaddish at a regular service.

5. Before the Jahrzeit of your dear mother, of blessed memory, and my own Jahrzeit, you and your brothers and sisters shall assemble at our Resting Place and recite the proper parts of Psalms and *el mole rachamim* and light a Jahrzeit candle which shall burn the whole day. In other years if you will find it inconvenient to light a Jahrzeit candle, then at least do it once a year in the month of Elul.

6. Each holiday when yizkor is recited, attempt to do it in a place of worship (yizkor in private is not proper).

7. After services, you shall all go home and eat a meal together at the home of one of you; each year at the home of a different member of the family, and at this time you will reflect on the memories of your dear parents who did so much for you, and review the contents of the two books of our memories. These books will always be with your brother Isaac.

8. At each Jahrzeit of your mother and mine, each of you shall donate $10.00 to the yeshiva which Rabbi Rabinowitz will designate. Your sister Mary will attend to that.

9. From the ceremonial objects [I own] I give you the silver Chanukah lamp that burns with oil; also a kiddush cup. The succah [the Tabernacles hut] is a present for my dear grandchildren. Take the succah with you, after the period of shivah, at my expense.

10. Educate your children at a yeshivah so they will be assured of the knowledge of how to be a Jew and why.

11. Hoping that you will honor my will and fulfill my last desires, I wish you and your wife Marlyn a lot of *nachas* from your children, my dear grandchildren, Gitel Rena, Abraham Zev, and Tamara. This is the wish of your father, who is going to meet your mother, of blessed memory.

Chaim Yaakov Bloom

75

Harry Levinson

What Shall I Do to Protect You, My Son?

Harry Levinson Speaks of Anti-Semitism to His Young Son

July 1959

Dr. Harry Levinson of the Menninger Foundation in Topeka, Kansas, wrote a letter to his 22-month-old son. The writer has been praised by his fellow Jews and others for his work in the field of mental health, and for his reforms in the Kansas State Hospital system.

Dear Marc,

From the moment you pulled the covers from me this morning and said, "Daddy, get up," until you kissed me goodnight, this was a wonderful day. We had fun together all day long. Never in your twenty-two months had you been so busy so long.

Now the evening is quiet. There is time to reflect on the day, and to relive its pleasures.

But reflection, as you will learn all too soon, is not confined to pleasure. As I look forward to your joys, I see also your sorrows. The time is not far distant when, still a child and still without understanding, you will come home with pain in your heart and tears in your eyes. You will ask me, as I asked my father and he asked his father before him, "Daddy, why did Johnny call me a dirty Jew? Why did he say I killed Christ? Daddy, what does kike mean? Daddy, who is Christ? Daddy . . . but why . . . ?" And you will expect your daddy to lift this pain from your heart and keep it from ever searing you again. You will not know that your pain is thousands of years old, nor will it make any difference. For you will have touched the hot fire of hate and the burn will not hurt any less because others have been burned before.

What shall I do to protect you, my son? For this affliction there is no miracle Salk vaccine, no surgery, no medicine. My only alternative is to give you strength to withstand the disease of hate.

First, I will teach you that you *are* a Jew, for to know who you are and where you belong in this vast scheme of living will be the cornerstone of your strength. I will teach you that being a Jew is a way of life. Once having started out on that way, there is no turning back. I will warn you that sometimes, perhaps, doubt will come upon you in moments of pain and you may want to take another path. I will tell you that in despair others have tried to do so. But no matter how hard they tried to flee, whether by change of name or change of God, they could not escape from themselves. Even if they could, they could not escape from others, in whose eyes they would always be Jews.

Second I will teach you what it means *to be* a Jew. You will find that some Jews believe all the answers have been found, and that one need only obey the rules which are written. But you will also find that our tradition is based not on laws alone, but on the constant adaptation and re-adaptation of basic precepts to the needs of each generation. And you will find, too, that those written rules which detail man's obligation to man are not meant to be strait jackets, but avenues to richer living. Nowhere in the sacred writings of men is the individual human being regarded with such high esteem as in the sacred writings of the Jews. To love your neighbor as yourself—and note that it does not say "Jewish neighbor"—is an ancient Jewish heritage.

You will discern something of the meaning of being Jewish in the tradition that each man, regardless of his imperfections, is of equal dignity in the eyes of God. Among Jews there are no ecclesiastical attorneys, no humans deified to perfection, none who exclusively know the only path to man's ultimate goals.

You will find something of the meaning of being Jewish in those moments of pause we call Holy Days. You will observe that we do not in revelry abandon the old year as "good riddance." Rather we examine ourselves, as we have lived that year, to learn how we can live better the next year. You will note that even our most sacred rituals do not free us from our obligations to our fellowmen, for the way of the Jew is to *do* unto others in justice and mercy—not just talk about it. And we are ever mindful of and grateful for the fruits of the earth and the blessings of life.

You will hear much of religious freedom in this, the land of the free. And so you will observe with pride and a deep sense of satisfaction your forefathers' contributions to that freedom. Passover, Chanukah, Purim—what magnificent traditions of freedom have we given to the world—gifts purchased dearly with millions upon millions of Jewish lives.

You will find something of the meaning of being Jewish in the *symbols* of the Jew—the Torah, Sabbath candles, menorah, matzo, and all the others. Each summarizes an experience of living, and it is in these experiences that you are rooted. They give your life meaning—but only if you *know* what they mean.

Third, I will tell you something of the history of the Jews. There is a wonderful story behind being Jewish, so old we don't know when it really began. We are few in number; never have we been powerful. But we have been great in achievement and even greater in endurance. Again and again we have been devastated, only to rise once more. We are scattered, but united. We are independent and individual, but we are one. We are of many nations, but a single faith. We are persecuted, yet free. We are humble, but not without pride. This is our history. . . .

Each of us needs to feel that he is a person who belongs somewhere and to someone, that he "fits," though he may forever be independent. It is out of such belongingness that we derive our feelings of security, familiarity, and comfort. Out of what the sociologist calls the "in-group" we derive traditions and values, a point of view and a way of life. Therefore, if you are familiar with the traditions and customs of your group, you will always be "among friends," for you will have a way of relating to life. If you know the values your group has developed over thousands of years, you need never be insecure about what you believe or why you believe it.

My son, all this is a ponderous way of saying that the strength in living lies in knowing what one is living *for*. It is not enough for Jews to be against something, to be united in defense, for when there is no longer a cause for defense, then the union crumbles. But when you are "for," my son, you will be strong.

76

Herbert H. Lehman

I Am a Jew Both by Birth and by Conviction

Senator Lehman Discusses the "Jewish Problem"

November 1960

Young Steven Schlussel, a pupil of the religious school of Temple Beth-El of Great Neck, Long Island, addressed a number of questions to New York's former senator, Herbert H. Lehman (1878–1963). Lehman's answers are reprinted here. In the 1940s, as Director General of the United Nations Relief and Rehabilitation Administration, he had presided over the feeding of millions throughout Europe. By 1960 Lehman had long been recognized as one of America's most notable citizens and a distinguished Jew. This former banker had served four terms as governor of the state of New York and nine years in the United States Senate. As a Jewish communal leader, he had worked hard to help his co-religionists in Eastern Europe, the land of Israel, and New York's immigrant ghetto. Lehman, a highly respected liberal and worker for social causes, was a member of Temple Emanu-El in New York City.

Dear Steven:

I have just received your letter of November 16th, and even though my desk is piled high with work, I hasten to answer it, since I believe the questions you ask are of importance.

1. I believe that all religions play a useful and very necessary part in people's lives, and I respect all religions that teach belief and faith in God. I

am a Jew both by birth and by conviction. It satisfies my spiritual needs and I have strong faith in its teachings.

2. I do not believe that being a Jew has either helped or harmed me in my public life. I believe that generally speaking the American people choose their public officials by their impression of the man or woman, and although of course bias and prejudice still exist to some degree in this country, in my opinion it is far less than it was 30 or 40 years ago.

3. Yes; I have found prejudice, both as a youngster and as an adult, but I believe to a very great extent these can be overcome by an individual or group by showing that they are not justified. As I have said, there is no doubt that social prejudice still exists, but I do not believe that it greatly handicaps a person in taking an active part in the worthwhile things of life. Whether a boy or a man may join a particular fraternity or club is of no great importance. The important thing is to demonstrate that you are a good citizen, willing to bear your share of the responsibilities of citizenship as well as its blessings.

4. You ask whether I have a comment to make to my fellow Jews who may want some day to become publicly known and feel that Judaism may hold them back because of either discrimination or prejudice. My answer is that I think any man who is seeking public office and allows his ambition to affect his religious affiliation is not worthy of the confidence of his fellow citizens. I know of very few instances in which a man was looked down upon because he was a Jew. On the other hand, I know of many instances where a man who sought to hide his religion lost the respect of his fellow citizens.

I am glad you asked me these questions. Apparently you are a very young boy and have your whole life before you. Mine is rapidly coming to a close. My advice in a word, is: Never be ashamed of being a Jew. Never try to hide it. Never try to compromise with your convictions because they may not agree with those of the group in which you find yourself.

Thank you for your letter. I hope that what I have said may give you something to think about now and in later years.

With kindest regards and warm wishes,

Herbert H. Lehman

77

Jane Meinrath Bloch

And When There Are No More Tomorrows

Jane M. Bloch of Cincinnati Writes to Her Son Peter

May 4, 1963

Jane Meinrath Bloch was born on February 28, 1926, and died on September 7, 1967. A native of Kansas City, Missouri, she attended Westport High School in that city and graduated from Vassar College in 1945. She moved to Cincinnati, Ohio, with her mother in the early 1940s.

The following excerpts are from Jane Bloch's typescript account of her experiences while living in an "iron lung." She was placed on this life-support machine in 1949, when she contracted polio, and she remained on it for nearly eighteen years. In simple but poignant prose, she tells her son—and now the world—how she was able to cope with the knowledge that she would never again be able to live outside of the iron lung. In spite of this, Jane Bloch never despaired. During those eighteen years she learned to read Russian, studied Plato, and constructed a philosophy of life that is both instructional and ennobling. This remarkable document, written in 1963, is the testimony of a remarkable woman.

May 4, 1963

My dear Peter:

I have wanted to write you a special letter for a very long time.

I have wanted to tell you about all the things that have happened these past fourteen years—starting from the hot August days in 1949 when the hospital ward was filled—sometimes with death or physical destruction, or sometimes miraculously with returned health. These were the days of the polio epidemic.

I want to take you with me through those dim summer days and then through the many that followed in increasingly shining succession. . . .

We have not spoken together, you and I, much about God. Because I have felt so deeply, I have remained silent—too silent. And if you have felt, because my life has had little formal religion, that I have removed myself from deep belief, you would have been given reason to have concluded this.

I can only tell you that I have felt very close to God. In the very early days of my sickness, half-destroyed and understanding little, I began a prayer, and each night the same simple words returned again and again to me: "Grant me the strength, the courage, and the wisdom." There was no ending to the prayer, just those words, and the feeling that some spirit far greater than mine would hear me, and help me. And in my room over the years, this belief has grown stronger.

Although I know that there are disbelievers, I doubt that there are many men among us who in time of darkening trouble do not feel the need to turn to an unknown, but omniscient presence.

And in my room, thinking and believing, I have been restored. I share with you your deep feeling, and in a larger sense, like that calendar of time which I once feared, I am no longer torn when I acknowledge the force of my feelings. I have learned what I might not have learned had the hand of destiny not guided me into this very different life. Or was it, perhaps, the hand of God?

And so, Peter, dear, the chapters come to an end, but the story continues. There are just a few things left to be said.

When the time comes, as it inevitably must, that you and I will again be separated, I shall meet this with the greatest possible freedom of spirit, because I know, despite our closeness and great affection, you will be equally prepared for any separation. You are young, and independent, and strong, and you will find temporary sadnesses breached for you by your own freedom of spirit. You will always go ahead, even while welcoming the memories of what I hope is perhaps a uniquely experienced and enriched past.

I know now the hurdles of the years that you have passed, and so I know too the hurdles you will pass in the future, and by this knowledge I am freed.

And so, we will continue to enjoy our tomorrows, you, and your father and I, each of us prepared in our own way for the future, and each of us supported by the bonds of our united pasts.

I have chosen to end my writing on an especially sun-warmed, summer day. The leaves are moving slowly in the beautiful tree outside my window, and the golden morning light throws shifting patterns into my silent room.

There will be many happy, sundrenched days ahead, and I will see you tomorrow and each sun-filled tomorrow thereafter.

And when there are no more tomorrows, we will have shared a splendid bond. And so as I began, with love, I end for now.

78

Sherman G. Finesilver

We Are United by Beliefs, Adversity, History

Be a Proud Jew, Judge Finesilver Tells His Son Steve

October 11, 1969

Annette and Judge Sherman G. Finesilver of Denver wrote a pamphlet on the occasion of the bar mitzvah of their son Steve. In this twenty-three page brochure, they listed hundreds of American Jews, men and women, who had made names for themselves in the arts and sciences. Their accomplishments are briefly recounted. It is obvious that the parents wanted Steve to pattern himself on those notables, although they were careful to point out that even the humblest laborer may well achieve spiritual greatness. Following is a letter that introduced this pamphlet.

Dear Son:

On this occasion, I am giving to you the greatest gift within my capacity to give if only you have the wisdom to recognize its value. I give you this booklet on the lives of great Jewish men and women.

The poet Alexander Pope had enlightening and inspiring thoughts concerning greatness:

> Lives of great men all remind us,
> We can make our lives sublime,
> And in parting leave behind us
> Footprints in the sands of time.

I give you these living legends of greatness because these are not only great human beings but they are great Jews. There are several reasons for my belief that a study of these great people can bring you the richest fulfillment of your life.

First, I believe *you will never discern your future until you first comprehend your heritage.* You do not live in an obscure vacuum. You live in the context of the continuing drama of Jewish history. The tribulations and victories of your ancestors should and will influence your thoughts and convictions about your world today. Your knowledge of the adversity endured and overcome by your predecessors in history confers upon you a confidence in your place and role in the world.

Second, because *we cannot fulfill ourselves until we recognize the qualities of greatness in others.* When you were a baby and toddler you were, like all children, a great imitator. You copied and imitated everything you observed "big people" doing. To you that was fun. But our Creator made it fun for children as a means of helping them to learn. That is the same method I hope you will employ as to great lives. Imitate them. Do not be content merely to recognize greatness in others; take the further step and imitate it. For in the imitation of greatness is greatness itself.

I would add one cautionary note, however. Do not confuse notoriety and fame with greatness. Many of the titled in today's world obtained their fame and fortunes outside their own merit. Many are morally neutral or worse. Although they are loosely referred to by undiscerning masses as "great" simply because of their titles, theirs is a counterfeit greatness and not to be copied. On the other hand, I have met great people in the most obscure roles in life. For, you see, *greatness is a measure of one's spirit not a result of one's faith in human affairs.* Nobody, least of all mere humans, confers greatness upon another, for it is not a prize but an achievement. And greatness can crown the head of a janitor just as readily as it can come to the President of our country or someone of great rank.

Not only are these men in this booklet great men, but they are Jewish. I wonder if you have ever asked yourself, "Who are the Jews?" Many answers could be forwarded to that question. But I believe ultimately, we are a people united by three circumstances.

First, *we are united by beliefs.* It was our people who first understood that God was not many beings but only one. Our greatest gift to the human race, and our greatest uniting factor, is monotheism—the insistence that there is but One God. That concept flew in the faces of our pagan neighbors at history's dawn. For men had conceived of "gods" as various inanimate objects or personalities acting in arbitrary and frail ways. We professed a singular, ultimate God who was Just. We have many times fought for and reconfirmed that belief.

Second, *we are united by adversity.* Our greatest asset as a people is not uninterrupted military strength, for we have often been conquered. Our ultimate weapon is rather our ability to come back from defeat, to overcome adversity, to insist that to lose is not always to be defeated. And that no man or people are ultimately and finally subjugated until they consent to be. We have felt the chains of slavery but never the pangs of defeat. My generation has observed the greatest atrocities ever against our people. Even now our co-religionists in Israel are very alert, forced to keep constant watch against neighbors who with unreasoning passion seek their destruction.

Finally, *we are united by history*. Someone has said that it is only in the most recent times that a lonely sentry on the hillside has been superseded by the scanning radar. There is a danger to you in the very affluence of your society and the very security as Americans. The danger is that we will forget that most of human history has been lived not among the present luxuries but amid the despair of poverty, disease, ignorance, and prejudice. In our fashionable homes which are superior to those inhabited by most kings of history, we may forget that our forefathers lived for generations in tents. Not until King Solomon did our ancestors even have a permanent place of worship made of wood.

Thus, as we enjoy our present estate in life, we must not forget the price at which it was bought by our ancestors. We must revere history, for in it we find the cohesive force which unites all Judaism.

We are united. More loosely at times but fervently when necessary. In these pages I believe you will find the highest benefit if you discern the thread of unity and oneness which is the heritage of all Jews.

So, my son, cling to Judaism and handle our heritage with loving care and sincere respect.

You are part of this great heritage that has enriched all mankind. May you lengthen and strengthen the pride of accomplishment that has been the hallmark of our people from time immemorial.

With love,
Your Dad

79

David de Sola Pool

Life Has Been Inexpressibly Sweet to Me

The Spiritual Testament of Rabbi David de Sola Pool

ca. 1970

Rabbi David de Sola Pool (1885–1970) was one of America's best-known Jewish leaders. There was hardly a national Orthodox organization in which he did not play an important role. In addition, he was the spiritual head of American Sephardic and Levantine Jewry because he was the rabbi of the Spanish–Portuguese Shearith Israel of New York City, the oldest Jewish congregation in North America. Shortly before his death, Rabbi Pool formulated the "Affirmation of Life" partially printed here.

Whensoever death shall come, it will find me unafraid. I pray that it may find me ready. I have ever tried so to live that I might be prepared to meet my God. I love life and the exquisite gifts of work, of play, of joy, . . . of light, of laughter, and most of all, of love that it has brought me. I am, and have always been, deeply grateful for the abundance of life with which I have been blessed. Life has been inexpressibly sweet to me. Yet, come death when it may, I yield up life as gladly, as gratefully, as I have accepted its gift for the while . . . it would be selfish to ask for more. All my life long I have been blessed with the gifts of love, far, far beyond my deserving, I have tried, haltingly, inadequately but sincerely . . . to repay through service some of the debt I owe to life for its profuse bounty towards me. I gave three years (the happiest of my life because the richest in service) to the Holy Land. I have tried at all times, and for all who called upon me, rich as well as poor, gentile as well as Jew, to give service through such poor gifts as my physical strength, my mental power and my spiritual resources enabled me to offer. I have tried so to do. More than that I cannot say, for I know that often, pitifully often, I have failed through weakness and inadequacy—physical, mental, and spiritual. Yet the stimulus and the joy of trying have been mine.

From anyone towards whom I have failed in human kindness I ask forgiveness. I do not feel, and I never have felt, any unkindness or malice in my heart towards anyone. Where I have failed, it has been through my insufficiency, never through ill will.

But I would not leave with you who care to hear, and even perchance to cherish, a message from me, any emphasis on failure. Though in tangible achievement I have not done what perhaps I dreamed of doing and what the world may rightly have expected me to achieve; the very living of my life has been supremely successful. There has been no day in which my heart has not leaped with gratitude to God for the joy of life and its fulfillment in the perfect love that has been given to me both as a child and in every moment of my sacred married life. There has yet never dawned the day when I have not been able to give thanks unto God for His goodness, and the day of death shall be but one more such day.

Therefore I would not have my death darken the life of anyone. Life to me has always been joy with humor and laughter and happiness. I would have it so, and I have tried to make it so for all others with whom my lot has been cast. I have tried to comfort others in their sorrow and to show them the sunshine of life's path. So if any would remember me, let my name be mentioned with a smile, with brightness, with humor, with happy memory, with wholesome gladness. Paint not my memory with tears or regrets, but let my spirit live among you after death as it has on earth, with joyousness. I would have the children of the religious school of my congregation gladdened on the Sunday nearest its anniversary or, should that be in the summer, then I would have some other children's lives made sweeter on that day, and at all times I would have my wife and children and those who have been the sweetest blessings in my life recall me with a smile as they think how much of heartwarming love they gave to me.

I can never even begin to express my thanks to all whose goodness, whose forbearance and whose friendships have made my life so wondrous an adventure. May God bless you all for the blessings you have given to me. I have had all and more than man could dare ask for—a life that has known no want, a life of wide and varied interests, with music, travel, humor, work, opportunities of spiritual service. But most of all I have had friendship and kindness from everyone, and a perfect, exquisite love from my life's partner.

> Many waters cannot quench love
> Rivers cannot drown it. . . . [Song of Songs 8:7]

To all I would sum up what I have tried to be in the deep wisdom of the ancient words: "The end of it, when all has been heard, is to revere God and keep His commandments, for this is the whole of man" [Ecclesiastes 12:13].

So,

I rest my spirit in His hand,
Asleep, awake by Him I'm stayed.
God with me still, in life, in death,
I face my future unafraid.

80

Jerrold Franklin

The Thirteen-Year-Olds of My Generation Are More Sophisticated

Jerrold Franklin of Brooklyn Is No Child

1971

The bar mitzvah speech reprinted here was delivered in 1971 by 13-year-old Jerrold Franklin at Temple Beth Emeth in Brooklyn, New York. One is quick to suspect that a very sagacious modern person wrote this talk, that Jerrold was not the author. On the other hand, it is by no means improbable that Jerrold himself was the author. Let us not be hypercritical. There seems to be ample evidence that, in times past, many Russian-born youngsters, child prodigies of only 10 or 12 years old, knew whole tractates of the Talmud and Mishnah by heart and apparently understood them. There can be no question about Jerrold's high intelligence, perceptiveness, and idealism.

My father tells me that when he was bar mitzvah—about a hundred years ago—every bar mitzvah speech contained the expression, "Today I am a man." The boys of his generation must have been good actors. I could never say a line like that with a straight face.

No—I can't honestly say that "Today I am a man"—but I can say that the thirteen-year-olds of my generation are more sophisticated and more aware of the problems in the world around us than my father's contemporaries ever were. These problems are far more serious, too, and call for far more thought and effort on our part—the drug problem, schools crises, race problems, and environmental destruction.

The society in which we live has even lessened the importance of religion, and many bar mitzvah boys, unfortunately, consider this occasion as a money-making proposition, rather than as a time to think of the future.

I have often said to my parents that politicians have made a mess of the world, and that perhaps we young people should take over and use our fresh ideas to make things right. I hope that, when we are men, we can work together to do what previous generations have failed to do—make the world safe for people.

How do we go about this? What is it that Jews consider most important for their children? It must be education, since such a large percentage of young Jews go to college—a much larger percentage than would be expected for such a small minority of the American population. Why do Jews emphasize education so strongly? Not only because it is something no one can ever take from you, but because it is preparation for the future. The more training you have, the more likely it is that you can help to make changes in the world. It is a hard fight, and a long way to go, but it is worth the effort.

My father tells me also that part of his bar mitzvah speech was the expression of gratitude to his parents for all their help, and the promise to be a good Jew. I do want to thank my parents for their love and support in all things always, but I don't know if I can make the same promise. I can only say that with their help I will do my best. I pray that with my parents' love, and God's guidance, I will grow up to be a decent human being and a worthy Jew. . . .

81

Rabbi ______________

I Will Not and Cannot Sell My Conscience

A Jewish Professor in a Christian College Refuses to Convert in Order to Advance Himself

1973

When, in 1973, the vice-president of a Catholic college resigned, the position was offered to a Jewish professor of religious studies, who was also a rabbi. The offer was conditioned on his conversion to Catholicism. The rabbi—whose name is not known—responded to this offer with the following letter.

[Dear Mr. President:]

I hardly deserve the honor which you have accorded me inviting me to become your Vice President after Dr. Abbot shall have resigned from that office. I cannot imagine that there is anyone, no matter how modest he may be, who would be unappreciative of the honor which you want to confer upon me and I am truly touched by your offer.

But you, in your great earnestness and in your sincerity, are asking a great price for the proffered honor. You want that I should abandon my Judaism, become a convert and henceforth be a Catholic. This shows me how deeply in love you are with your own religion, which has certainly rendered great services for civilization, and for humanity.

But permit me to ask you why you are not willing to allow me, a son of an ancient people with a rich spiritual heritage, the similar right to love my own ancestral faith even as you love yours. You are a very dedicated Christian and therefore you are a fortunate man indeed. But please explain to me why you have not striven with greater zeal to impart some of your deep love for your faith into those other Christians who have in our generation burnt to cinders millions of my people for the only reason that they did not belong to your faith.

You want that after my persecuted people had gone through the hell of the Holocaust, that I, who am a member of this incinerated and gassed human family, should make a courteous bow to the Christian church and say: "As an expression of gratitude to you of the Christian faith for the ashes of my six million brothers and sisters, I am now prepared to become henceforth your committed servant."

It seems fitting in your eyes, that after my persecuted people had for two millennia prayed for its Jewish homeland in Palestine, and after that fought sacrificially to be able to live in that historic land, that I should spit in the face of my heroic brothers and sisters and say to them: I mock your struggles and your sacrifices! And all that you have achieved in finding a haven and a home for our persecuted people in the Holy Land, is less important in my eyes than the little Golden Cross which a Christian Priest wants to put upon my breast. No, my worthy Father Quigley! I will not and cannot sell my conscience for a title and for a job. It is apparent to me that you do not truly understand the Jew and that you do not sense his Jewish pride and his Jewish stubbornness.

Dear Father Quigley, there is one thing that I have learned from you. It is not nice to imitate, in monkey-fashion, the faith of another man. My frequent discussions and lectures concerning the Prince of Peace have apparently misled you into thinking that I have an inclination toward the Christian religion and therefore you felt free to try to convert me to your faith. But the lesson you have taught me, not to ape another man's religion, I have learned well. And for this reason the time has come for me to seek another job where I can continue, undisturbed, to express myself in total loyalty to my own faith and to leave Christianity to those to whom it belongs, namely the Christians.

Your Jewish friend,
Rabbi _______________

82

Author Unknown

We've Had Our Share of Arguments

A Father and Son at Odds

March–April 1973

The culture that fascinated adolescents in the 1960s and 1970s was a real youth movement, the rejection by a new generation of much that was dear to their fathers and mothers. The amenities, the hopes, the traditional ideals of the parents were flouted by a new breed of young men and women. Fathers and mothers were shocked and dismayed; their children had set a dangerous course of their own. For many parents, the world they loved was about to founder on the rocks of indifference, irresponsibility, and contempt for time-honored values.

The following letter appeared in Brotherhood *magazine, the official publication of the National Federation of Temple Brotherhoods. Whether the anguished cry of a parent or the work of an office editor, it reflects the problems that wracked families in the last third of the twentieth century.*

Dear Son:

I wish I could put on paper the thoughts that are in my heart. Somehow or other, the words come out very stilted on paper and are not exactly what I'm trying to say. But this letter is long overdue and I shall do my best.

Son, we've been through a lot together . . . your early years to age eleven . . . your later teens through high school . . . Israel, college, and now you're living away from home in college and just about out of your teens to early manhood. You'll be twenty next month, just in case you've forgotten!

Through all this, I have tried to be mostly myself and have hoped that by my action, as much as by my words, I have tried to show you a good way of life . . . a set of values, right from wrong, from which you could pattern your life. Somewhere along the line, I feel I've missed the boat. We've had our share of arguments and differences of opinion. Perhaps that is normal. I've stuck to my guns only because I love you. If I didn't care, why bother?

I'm sure we both have the same ideals. I'm sentimental, altruistic, and idealistic like you. I believe in most of what you do. I know it's common today to write off anyone over thirty. . . including your parents. In that you're wrong. I want the same changes you do. We just differ greatly in how to go about it.

Son, I don't like your dress. I don't like your hair-style and beard. I've tried to tolerate it and understand. You can accomplish all your goals just as well with a neat appearance without lowering your beliefs one iota. I appreciate your honesty in telling me you've smoked marijuana and have tried LSD. Honestly, son, this scares the hell out of me! I believe in your basic goodness and integrity, but I worry nevertheless.

There are many wrongs and ills in the world. It's been that way since Adam ate the forbidden apple. I've lived through Hitlers, Mussolinis, Stalins, and God knows how evil our world was then. We have another set of evils today. And you know what? There'll always be crusades to make this world better. Read your history. I guess it's just the nature of the human animal. It is easy to find fault with what is happening, but what we must be able to do is show a better way, and then do our darndest to make the better way work.

It hurts me that you have pushed religion aside as another example of the established order that has allowed our world to be what it is today. Read your Jewish history and what Judaism has always stood for. Look at the work being done today through the Jewish channels . . . in the cause of peace and the dignity of man. Who has been more in the forefront than the Jew in trying to make this a better world for all to live in? Look at the attempts at ecumenism today. Look at the work the Jewish Chautauqua Society is doing. Gosh, son, there's fifty lifetimes of work ahead for all of us, and another fifty after that! I'd like nothing better than to see you involved in this.

Son, perhaps much of what I have written is repetitious to you. You've always accused me of repeating myself again and again. Perhaps so. I do know that this is the first time I've put these thoughts on paper. Do me a favor. Please don't throw this letter away after you've read it once. These are my honest feelings, right from the heart.

So son, let's try something. You have a good talent in writing. Please write me a letter of your thoughts. Who knows . . . maybe we can get our thoughts over to each other better on paper.

I love you, son. I can only pray that you will have a rich, full, long and rewarding life.

Dad

83

Emanuel Rackman

Do Not Deny or Conceal Your Jewish Identity

Rabbi Emanuel Rackman's Son Goes to College

1974

When Emanuel Rackman's son went off to college, his father, one of the country's outstanding Orthodox rabbis, gave him "food for the road." He wrote him the letter excerpted here, a contemporary variation of the earlier "departure letter" that European parents and elders gave emigrants leaving for the New World.

Although Rabbi Rackman's son was not leaving for a distant, strange continent, he was sailing into a world of confrontations where the danger of foundering spiritually was real and ever present. This eminent clergyman spoke with clarity and certainty to his son. There was no mistaking his message: Be a Jew!

Dear Son,

You may recall that when you began to study Torah more than a decade ago, your mother and I made a party in honor of the event. Jews were wont to do this in years gone by. Now you leave us to become a student at the university. And again we rejoice that you have attained a milestone, one which will help you deepen your learning, broaden your vision, acquire new skills, and cultivate new friendships. But this time we are also filled with misgivings—with anxiety. How will your new career effect your loyalty to our people and our heritage? Will your separation from family change your values-system? Will you exercise your new freedom to reject your past or will you exercise it to make that past more poignantly your own? . . .

Do not deny or conceal your Jewish identity and do not hesitate to be different. Yet, you may ask, why should one maintain a stance which makes one overtly conspicuous? Is it not more normal to adjust and acculturate and don the coloration of one's environment? No, my son, it will be to your advantage even as a student to cherish the value of individuality, of personal uniqueness. You must not lose your identity in a pool of sameness with other human beings. Respect all mankind because of that which all men have in common—the inviolable endowment of personality—but be firm in the knowledge that you are what you are and must give expression in the classroom and in the dormitory, in social and intellectual circles, to your own feelings, views, interpretations, and your own mode of living. . . .

The Jew, with a strong sense of Jewish identity, who does not hesitate to lead his own distinctive Jewish life, and seeks to master much of human wisdom with a Jewish stance, can champion his people's cause as well as humanity's. He learns how to maintain a proper balance between particularity and universalism, which was the special gift of the Biblical prophets and their descendants. The university should not make you exclusively the universalist. Your vision will then be blocked by the forest and you will fail to seek the health of the individual trees. . . .

It is only with a sense of uniqueness that an individual can live meaningfully and creatively as a person and that applies to a people as well. The greatest contributions to human progress have been made by men who opted to be different, who challenged the majority or dissented from the general consensus. The very existence of the Jewish people was and continues to be such a challenge and dissent. And because of it we enriched civilization in a measure totally disproportionate to the smallness of our number. . . .

You know that I am not a Freudian but who will gainsay that the sexual drive is strong and perhaps in this connection you will find at the university the greatest personal challenge to the values and mores we have sought to transmit at home. What can I now add to that which your mother and I have said before?

Neither your mother nor I, nor anyone else for that matter, should invade your right of privacy. Thus what you will do is a matter of conscience between you and the girls you will meet. Except for truly heinous and criminal behavior, you are accountable only to God and your own psyche for that which you will do. But not to your psyche alone. One overriding consideration must be what you will do to the psyche of the girls with whom you will establish relationships—social and sexual.

If you were a girl I would perhaps impart even stronger words of caution. But society being what it is, and especially men being what they are, women bear the greater burden in the consequences of sexual promiscuity. Yet men ought to act with a sense of responsibility. Nothing in our tradition is as important as respect for one's fellow-man. The use or exploitation of another human being exclusively for one's pleasure without regard to the evil done to that person—I refer to the long-range evil even if there is immediate gratification in the "now and here"—is the cardinal sin of Judaism. It is abuse of another's divine image. . . .

The sum total of all that I have written is that I want you to perform the Mitzvah of Kiddush Hashem—sanctifying God's name in everything that you do. The essence of that Mitzvah is not martyrdom, although it sometimes calls for that. However, our sages define it differently. "So act," they enjoin us, "that all who behold you will say, 'Blessed is that man's God.' "

It is thus that I pray you will act. And you and we shall rejoice.

Love,
Dad

84

Jacob J. Weinstein

I Know I Cannot Impose My Values and Judgments on You

Rabbi Weinstein Offers Advice in Troublous Times

ca. 1974

Some time before his death, Rabbi Jacob (Jack) Joseph Weinstein (1902–1974) wrote an ethical will intended primarily for his wife and his four children. Weinstein, a former president of the Central Conference of American Rabbis, was a courageous warrior in the battle for social justice. He was particularly devoted to the Labor Zionists both in Israel and in the United States. His eloquence, his natural gifts, and his personality brought him recognition in high places.

It was a custom in ancient times for the father to leave an ethical will together with the legal testament. I hesitate to follow in this fine tradition for fear of imposing my will on yours. The state of the world which I leave you hardly testifies to the wisdom of my generation, or those immediately before. I would be remiss, however, if I did not warn your generation that, in your anger and frustration, you fail to distinguish between the conventions that enshrine the past because it is the past and the traditions which have in them the seed of a more meaningful future. There is no single, simple, or automatic way in which one can learn the art of this discretion—but I sincerely believe that the history and teachings of Judaism contain implicit and explicit guidelines for achieving a viable synthesis between the tried values of the past and the liberating needs of the present and the future. This belief and the understandable, though inarticulate, loyalty to the choices of a lifetime compel me to urge you to consider well the rock whence you were digged.

[Because of] the attrition of the tradition in my lifetime . . . there is a real danger that it will disappear in your children's lives. I would consider this an affront to principle of continuity and a loss of a fine family resource. I know I cannot impose my values and judgments on you, but I can and do request that you not let this heritage go by default—but that you study it, participate in it, and make your decision on the basis of knowledge as well as sentiment. You will find that it may be a very real help in holding you together as a family. One of the most painful experiences I have had as a rabbi has been to witness the weakening of family ties—brothers and sisters who come together at funerals and weddings as strangers asking querulously of each other: "Why have we not heard from you? Why do we have to wait for a funeral to bring us together?" As love becomes more ambient, less focused, more dependent on necessity and convenience, it will need the more elemental instinctive support of family affection, of common womb genesis. So hold fast to the family affection you have so far maintained and try to pass it on to your children.

85

Arthur F. Burns

Economic Improvement Is Not the Only or the Main Purpose of Life

Arthur F. Burns Congratulates a Bar Mitzvah Lad

May 4, 1976

Arthur Frank Burns (1904–1987) came to this country from Galicia as a 6-year-old. He worked his way through college and ultimately received his doctoral degree from Columbia University in the 1930s. A decade later, he had already become a respected economist; he had taught at Rutgers University and at Columbia. Burns was an economic counselor to President Eisenhower in the 1950s and to President Nixon in the 1960s and 1970s. In 1970 he was appointed chairman of the Board of Governors of the Federal Reserve System, one of the most influential positions in the United States government. It was during his tenure in that position—in which he worked to fight inflation and to maintain fiscal stability—that he wrote the following letter. In 1981, President Reagan appointed him ambassador to West Germany. By that time, he had received some forty honorary degrees.

This letter is a congratulatory note—accompanied by a gift, of course—to a bar mitzvah boy, Elliot Nathan Stone. It is a friendly, personal letter reflecting the man himself—kindly and unpretentious. He identified with his fellow Jews.

May 4, 1976

Dear Elliot:

I'm a friend of your father's. Therefore I am also your friend. Your father may have told you that I'm the Nation's "money man." It gives me pleasure to send you the enclosed coin set to help you celebrate your BAR MITZVAH.

I wish I could be with you and your parents when you are called to read the TORAH. But I must go off to Europe and discuss a few problems with my European counterparts. Our purpose, I should tell you, is not to make money for ourselves, but to help the great mass of people in our several countries to improve their economic conditions.

But economic improvement is not the only or the main purpose of life. That is especially true of the Jewish people. God gave us the TORAH so that we may lead righteous lives, love our neighbors, and help the needy. Your BAR MITZVAH symbolizes the privilege of living by the noble teachings of the TORAH. To the extent that you do so, you will enjoy God's blessing and bring honor to your parents.

With every good wish,

Your friend,
Arthur F. Burns

Enclosure

86

Art Buchwald

So Let the Tall Ships Sail and the Fireworks Explode

Art Buchwald Writes to His Pop

July 4, 1976

Art Buchwald, the columnist, was born in Mt. Vernon, New York, in 1925. While still a teenager he joined the Marines. Later, he wrote for the Paris edition of the Herald Tribune *and finally became an American columnist. Buchwald has been awarded a Pulitzer Prize for his commentaries; he has written, all told, over twenty books. By the 1980s his humorous columns were appearing in about 600 newspapers, many of them published in foreign lands. His humor is friendly, intimate, and effective. He wants a better and kinder world. Buchwald writes with a universal message; no one can fail to understand this sentence: "It isn't too farfetched to assume that in a couple of years the entire Communist Party will be made up of FBI informers."*

Buchwald sets out to make people laugh . . . and think. But there is nothing funny about the following column, "Letter to Pop"; it is a tribute to the young argonauts who left European evil and poverty behind them and set out for a free and challenging America. This same letter could have been written by the children of millions of American immigrants.

July Fourth

Dear Pop:

It's been four years since you passed away at the age of seventy-nine. On this Bicentennial holiday, with all the hoopla and overkill, I am not taking the 200th anniversary of the country lightly, mainly because I know you wouldn't.

First, I would like to thank you for leaving your home in Galicia which you once explained was part of [Austrian] Poland, in 1910, when you were seventeen years old. I know it wasn't an easy trip for you. You had to cross Europe all by yourself, and then you had to find a ship in Rotterdam that would take you to New York City.

I've tried to imagine what it was like for a seventeen-year-old boy to arrive at Ellis Island without being able to speak a word of English. There were thousands like you, and fortunately there were people who came before you to help you through the maze of paper work and bewildering ways of New York.

You wound up on the Lower East Side with so many of your fellow immigrants. They offered you a chance to go to night school, but you said you would learn English by reading every New York City newspaper every day. You kept reading them for sixty-two years and you seemed to know more about the country and the world than any of your children who had been "educated" in American schools.

I know you started out working in a raincoat factory fourteen or fifteen hours a day, and when World War I came you worked even longer. They wouldn't let you serve in the Army because [as an immigrant from Hapsburg territory] you were considered an "enemy alien."

Then you went into the curtain and drapery business—The Aetna Curtain Co. The business consisted of you, a man named Sammy who helped you hang the drapes, and a seamstress. "Gimbel's we're not," you used to tell me, much to my chagrin. But you did save enough money to bring your two sisters and a brother to America. And you did manage to get out of the Lower East Side.

"Making it in America in those days," you once told me, "was moving to the Bronx."

You even got as far as Mt. Vernon, when business was good, before the depression. Then during the depression it was back to the Bronx.

The thing I shall always remember is how you felt about the United States. You kept telling me there was no better place to live than America. And I could never appreciate this unless I was a Jew who had lived in Europe.

You were like so many foreign-born Americans—Jewish, Russian, Italian, Irish, German, Scandinavian and Greek—who considered this country the only land where your children would have a chance to become what they wanted to be.

You told me, "Everyone has dreams for their children, but here it's possible to make them come true."

Well, Pop,I just wanted you to know, as far as your children are concerned, you made the right decision when you left Poland. There are four of us, [who are like] all first-generation Americans whose mothers and fathers arrived here in more or less the same way.

I don't know if all those great men in 1776 had you immigrants in mind when they signed the Declaration of Independence and formed a new country, but even if they didn't they made it possible for you and millions like you to come to a free land.

So let the tall ships sail and the fireworks explode. We're probably overdoing it, but if you were here I'm sure you would say, "It's probably a good thing people remember what a great place this country is, even if it's going to cost the city a lot of money."

87

Frances Katz Green

Dying Is a Part of Living

The Last Letter of Frances K. Green

February 1977

Frances Katz Green died on March 4, 1977. The wife of Alan S. Green, rabbi of Temple Emanu-El of Cleveland, she was a cherished mother and a tower of strength in the congregation that her husband had built with her aid. Mrs. Green was a leader in the sisterhood. She wrote the first curriculum for the new congregational school, and when a wing was built to make provision for the school's many new pupils, the admiring members of the synagogue called it the Rabbi Alan S. Green and Frances Green Religious School. She lived to see, on videotape, the dedication of this new religious school building; it was dedicated two months before her death.

Stricken with a dread disease, she never lost hope: she was a woman of great courage and great faith, one destined to influence profoundly those who were privileged to know her.

The following letter, to her synagogue's Sisterhood Board, was written in longhand on the evening before she entered the hospital for the last time.

Dear Friends of the Sisterhood Board:

How can I describe to you what a wonderful weekend of love and devotion all of you made possible for Rabbi Green and me February 4–6, 1977. We are still floating on cloud nine and still receiving letters on how deeply the events touched the lives of our members and members of the community.

Altho I knew that I would not be able to participate in any events outside of our home, I had prayed for only one thing, that I would be able to be part of the beautiful Shabbat dinner we had before the services.

The good Lord was so good to me. I was able to get dressed and sit at the table with all of my dear ones. Your delicious basket of fruit had arrived earlier in the day and we were able to enjoy it for dessert.

This has been a very trying time for all of my family, and I have had some very rough days and some better ones. I would like to take this opportunity to try to help some of you face up to terminal illness.

You know there are really two different people involved. One is Frances Green with a sick body. There is nothing I can do about that but have faith in my doctors and the new medical miracles and techniques. But the real Frances Green is the person I have always been—with plans, drives, projects, so much to do and plan. And this is the Frances Green that needs your prayers and concern. Nothing is so important as the hope one gains from the knowledge that her friends are pulling and praying for her. A little note, a telephone call, a card, etc., all lift her spirits and give her courage.

I do so believe in the power of prayer. It revitalizes one. Now of course one cannot always answer the phone but I always know someone called and is helping. So never hesitate, wondering, "What shall I say, what can I say." Just say what's in your heart. "We're pulling for you."

You know, dear friends, dying is a part of living. And I have been such a lucky blessed person. I have had such a wonderful, wonderful life, a devoted husband of almost forty-three years, two beautiful, successful sons with their lovely wives, three grandchildren, talented, loving and the source of so much joy; and the feeling that in my own way I have made some contribution to my community, my temple, and my family. I have no regrets, just thankfulness for all my blessings.

And lots of hope. Who knows, I may yet lick this crazy disease and have some very happy times with my "founding rabbi" and all of you.

God bless you all,
Frances

88

Bertram Wallace Korn

No One Is Immune to Despair, Fear, Retreat from Reality

Reaching Out to Friends After a Long Stay in a Hospital

March 15, 1978

Released after a long stay in a Philadelphia hospital, Rabbi Bertram Wallace Korn (1918–1979) wrote the members of his congregation a letter. In many respects it was a love letter, for he poured out his heart, grateful to a host of men and women who had rallied to help him when he was stricken. It is an exceptionally beautiful message, but then Korn was one of America's most distinguished clergymen—a magnificent orator, a scholarly historian, a devoted minister. His books on the Jewish experience during the Civil War and on early New Orleans Jewry are definitive studies; his chaplaincy work with servicemen during and after World War II culminated in his appointment as a rear admiral in the Naval Reserve. Korn's admirers and fellow historians elected him president of the American Jewish Historical Society. Less than two years after he wrote the following letter, he died in New Orleans while listening to a concert of the classical music he loved. His death at the relatively early age of 61 was inexpressibly sad. American Jewry could ill afford to lose a man of his ability and intellect.

It is simply not possible to thank each person individually for loving thoughts and offers to help and expressions of care and concern. There is not sufficient time to write to each of you who have cheered me on. And I cannot pretend to be able to remember who sent me a get-well card, who called the office to inquire of my progress, and who offered to help to reorient my life. But it all means more than it is possible to put into words, a warm, supportive feeling that life and health matter, that personal affection counts for a great deal, that the struggle to cope with physical disability is not a lonely one.

No one is immune to despair, fear, retreat from reality. They say that physicians make the worst patients, but they were the best "rabbis" for this patient. They were gentle and communicative and kind and consoling. They didn't "baby" the patient, but they helped him over some very rough spots. Hospitals are said to be depersonalized factories where no one is valuable and everyone is a victim. Not so, at least for this patient. Nurses and other personnel demonstrated exquisite tenderness and concern; they understood how difficult it was for the rabbi to be the object of ministry rather than the subject, they encouraged the patient to understand that what he felt was typical and characteristic, not a loss of wisdom or perception.

To one who has often had his mind on centuries past, occasionally on eternity, to one who attempts to trace the progress of humanity and our people through the ages, it is a challenge to live one day at a time, to do what one can and not feel inadequate in the face of all that cannot be done in one day or planned for many. To accept the limitations of a medical condition which must take insistent priority over all else, when one had been accustomed to functioning over a period of many months at a time and sometimes years, is a psychological as well as physical shock. The hardest thing for the patient to learn is to be patient! . . .

Where is God in all this? I do not hold to the theology which ascribes direct responsibility to God for illness. I do not believe that prayer would have helped me to avoid this affliction. I do believe that when all else fails within, when blackness and bleakness overwhelm you with despair, God gives you a little push upwards, imperceptibly, gently, with a reservoir of remaining strength which you did not believe you possessed, and in the form of a host of helpers who take you by the hand and lead you when you are utterly helpless. To trust in the good-will of others, to accept reality and be willing to take each hour as it comes, to be confident of the wisdom and dedication of physicians and nurses, is a way of being religious too.

I have crossed a great divide between what I was before and what I will be in the years to come. I can no longer hope to be able to do all the things that I once took in stride. But always, in all ways, I will hope to be able to respond to the most urgent needs, to perceive the places where help is most immediately required, to set a tone and goals and standards for the achievement of a vast variety of programs for the edification and ennoblement of our people and the community.

I have always felt that my life was filled with blessings extraordinary, with rewards and satisfactions I did not deserve, and with opportunities and honors I could never have earned. I still feel that way.

God bless you all.

89

Samuel Levenson

Everything I Own I Owe to America

Sam Levenson Offers Some Four-Letter Words for All Occasions

ca. 1980

Samuel (Sam) Levenson (1912–1980) was among America's best-known humorists. A native of Brooklyn, he taught Spanish in high school for many years before he convinced himself that, as an entertainer, he could make thousands smile and laugh. His humor was folksy, gentle, kind; it was Jewish, ethnic, Yiddish, universal. His tender nostalgic touch made the whole world his kin.

Levenson died on August 27, 1980. The ethical will he addressed to his grandchildren was written some time earlier. Perhaps it is somewhat contrived—Sam was a master showman—but it is desperately sincere.

Samuel Levenson's Ethical Will and Testament
To His Grandchildren

I leave you my unpaid debts. They are my greatest assets. Everything I own, I owe:

1. To America I owe a debt for the opportunity it gave me to be free and to be me.
2. To my parents I owe America. They gave it to me and I leave it to you. Take good care of it.
3. To the biblical tradition I owe the belief that man does not live by bread alone, nor does he live alone at all. This is also the democratic tradition. Preserve it.

4. To the six million of my people and to the thirty million other humans who died [in World War II] because of man's inhumanity to man, I owe a vow that it must never happen again.
5. I leave you not everything I never had, but everything I had in my lifetime: a good family, respect for learning, compassion for my fellow man and some four-letter words for all occasions: words like help, give, care, feel, and love.

Love, my dear grandchildren, is easier to recommend than to define. I can tell you only that, like those who came before you, you will surely know when love ain't, you will also know when mercy ain't and brotherhood ain't.

The millennium will come when all the "ain'ts" shall have become "ises" and all the "ises" shall be for all, even for those you don't like.

Finally, I leave you the years I should like to have lived so that I might possibly see whether your generation will bring more love and peace to the world than ours did. I not only hope you will, I pray that you will.

Grandpa Sam Levenson

90

Frank J. Riesenburger

It Was Meant to Happen to You and Every Other Jew

A Father Imagines the Holocaust in America

1980s

In the 1980s, Franklin J. Riesenburger, an attorney in Vineland, New Jersey, addressed a letter to his young son telling him how things might have turned out if the Germans had murdered his grandparents in the Holocaust. Franklin Riesenburger was the son of refugees who had managed to escape to the United States.

My dear Ron, you were born in 1975, but you began living in 1933. Your great-grandfather, Joseph Riesenburger, your great-grandmother, Lina Riesenburger, your great-uncle, Isidore Riesenburger, your great-aunt, Paula Riesenburger; they all died. So did six million more Jews, and in their stilled hearts their dreams of children and children's children. The most innocent of all, the unborn. They were never to be, only blackness forever in eternity. So decreed Hitler and Nazi Germany. So also decreed the German people and the world by the sound of silence none dared disturb. You were never to be. You see, my boy, as much as anyone from the concentration camps, as much as your grandfather and your grandmother, as much as your father and your mother, you in every sense of the word are also a Holocaust survivor. To know who you are, and where you are going, to know a purpose and value in life, you must begin with and know from where you come. My boy, you have come from the ashes of almost the total annihilation of a people. You come from what was started in 1933. You must go back. You began living then.

Alas, but a child you are! How best to relate this? Imagine! Imagine your world turned round. Your father came home one day crushed that his practice was taken away. Your friends, Luke, Todd, and Timmy, refused to even speak to you. The police, who you had known as friends, forced you from your room and home. One night you were told that Judge Brotman was no longer to be found. The next morning, Dr. Packman disappeared. Suddenly, a mass of troops assembled all of the Jews of Vineland at the train tracks. Your friends, your family; the mayor tried but couldn't stop it. You were all packed, standing, in freight cars. You remember the moment well. It was the last time you saw your parents. Later, you cherished meeting by chance your old friends Danny and Lisa from the old neighboring town, Bridgetown. The bonds that you formed were everlasting, creating new families where there had been none. Somehow you survived. Imagine no more, this happened to your grandfather and millions more. It was meant to happen to you and every other Jew. You were never to be.

Oh, what a cherished being you are! You have life. You also have a past that teaches life. Look at that past, your past, and you will know, you will know what freedom means. You will know what you mean to your family and your people. You will know the consequence of standing silent in the face of injustice. People talking without speaking. People listening without hearing. You will know what equal opportunity and treatment under the law means to you. Look at that past and you will know that the Holocaust teaches far more than "never again"; it also teaches you every day to think about and embrace and cherish life, your freedoms, and moral values. It directs the course of your life.

91

Author Unknown

To My Wife—Your Love Has Been to Me Beyond Measure

A Perfect Ethical Will

ca. 1983

This will was published anonymously. In many respects it is a remarkable instrument—remarkable because it appears to be the perfect ethical will: it embraces all hopes, all aspirations. Moreover, the writer has been singularly fortunate. The author of this farewell note to his family is the model husband; his family shines resplendently; they are completely beyond reproach. A famous Jewish historian, a hypercritic, once remarked: "The fact that something may be true is no reason why it is not true." Nevertheless, one suspects that this letter is too good to be authentic; it may have been concocted in an editorial workshop.

Dearest . . .

Weep not and dry your tears. At least on my behalf. The years that God has allotted to me have been good, and I have no *tayneh* [grievance] to our Maker. Death is the final state of all human beings, and a few years more or less do not matter. I have drunk fully of the cup of life, and a few remaining drops left unsipped need cause no grief or regrets. If there is one thing I do ask, it is that I may be permitted to see all my children happily married—if not, I'll be watching from somewhere anyway. Marriage is the fulfillment of life, and I have been blessed with a jewel of a wife and four wonderful children whose love has sustained me during those times that try a man's soul and has nourished me during times of *simchah* [joy].

To my wife—your love has been to me beyond measure. Remember what has been and weep not. Time is a wondrous healer even as you and I have forgotten not our son nor our parents. You are too much a woman to live alone, and the children will mature and go their own way. Look for a man you can respect and love and know that I want only that you be happy.

To my children—in material things I have seen to it that you will not want. These are the least important things, although the lawyer has prepared a megillah [a long document] to safeguard them. Remember to be Jews, and the rest will follow as day follows night. Our religion is not ritual but a way of life. To us, as Jews, life is its own raison d'être, its own self-justification; we await neither heaven nor hell. Ritual is only a tool to remind us who we are and of the divine commandments. Jews do not lie, steal, nor bear false witness—*past nisht*, as our parents used to say—such things are simply unbecoming for a Jew. Take care of one another, and in honouring your mother, honour yourselves. I know the love she has lavished on you without thought of self. Marry within your faith. Not to please me but so that you may be happy. Not because Gentiles are inferior—they are not—but because marriage is complex enough without the complicating variables of different viewpoints. You are the bearers of a proud tradition of four thousand years. Do not let the torch drop in your generation.

Turn not away anyone who comes to you for help. We Jews have seen more suffering than any other people. That which you give away, whether of money or of yourselves, is your only permanent possession.

Money is only a tool and not an end in itself. Your grandfather taught me that man should earn his money until the age of forty, he should enjoy it between forty and fifty, and later he should give it away. A man who dies rich is a failure as a human being. I say this because I know that your abilities will make you materially wealthy. But my real desire is that you be rich in heart and soul.

To all of you—let your word be your bond. Those mistakes that I regret most keenly are the times when my human weaknesses let me forget this. Unfortunately, it is always difficult to learn from the experiences of others, particularly parents. But if there is one thing I beg you to take to heart, it is this . . .

Say kaddish after me but not for me. Kaddish is the unique Jewish link that binds the generations of Israel. The grave hears not the kaddish, but the speaker does, and the words will echo in your heart. The only immortality I seek is that my children and my children's children be good Jews, and thereby good people.

God bless you all and keep you.

GLOSSARY

Hazan, Hazzan (plural, **Hazzanim**): The cantor-reader of the synagogue service; sometimes refers to the rabbi.

Jahrzeit, Jahrzit, Yahrzeit : Anniversary of a death.

Kaddish : Prayer recited by mourners.

Kashruth : The Jewish dietary laws.

Mitzvah (plural, **Mitzvot**): A commandment. Hence, a good deed, religious duty. An honorary function in religious service performed in the synagogue.

Nachas: Joy.

Sefer : Book.

Sefer Torah : The Book of Law. The parchment scroll of the five books of Moses.

Shabbat, Shabbas, Shabbos : Sabbath.

Shivah : The first seven days of mourning.

Takhlis : Goal, success, result.

Tallith, Talet, Tallis : Prayer shawl.

Tefillin, Tephillin : Small Hebrew parchments in a leather case attached to a man's head and arm in prayer.

Torah : Teaching. The five books of Moses. The total Jewish lore.

Tzitzith : The fringes on the tallith worn by a Jewish man during prayer.

Yeshivah, Yeshiva, Yeshiba : House of higher Jewish learning.

Yiddishkeit: Jewishness.

Yizkor : Memorial service for the dead.

Yomtov, Yom Tov, Yomtob : A religious festival.

Most of these definitions have been adapted from David and Tamar de Sola Pool, *An Old Faith in the New World* (New York: Columbia University Press, 1955), pp. 539–545.

SOURCES OF DOCUMENTS

1. *American Jewish Historical Quarterly* 55:326–328.
2. Leo Hershkowitz and Isidore S. Meyer (eds.), *The Lee Max Friedman Collection of American Jewish Colonial Correspondence: Letters of the Franks Family, 1733–1748* (Waltham, Mass., 1968), pp. 7–8, 57–58, 66, 116–119, 137; Jacob Rader Marcus, *Early American Jewry: The Jews of New York, New England, and Canada, 1649–1794* (Philadelphia, 1961), vol. 1, pp. 58–59, 68–69.
3. Jacob R. Marcus, *The American Jewish Woman: A Documentary History* (New York, 1981), pp. 47ff.
4. Sidney M. Fish, *Aaron Levy: Founder of Aaronsburg* (New York, 1951), p. 56.
5. Jacob R. Marcus, *American Jewry. Documents. Eighteenth Century* (Cincinnati, 1959), pp. 77–78.
6. Morris U. Schappes, *A Documentary History of the Jews in the United States, 1654–1875* (New York, 1950), pp. 92–96.
7. Sheftall Papers, Keith Read Manuscript Collection, University of Georgia Library; *American Jewish Historical Quarterly* 54:275–277.
8. Morris U. Schappes, *A Documentary History of the Jews in the United States, 1654–1875* (New York, 1950), pp. 122–125; Joseph L. Blau and Salo W. Baron (eds.), *The Jews of the United States, 1790–1840: A Documentary History* (New York, 1963), vol. 1, pp. 28–32.
9. Jacob R. Marcus, *Memoirs of American Jews, 1775–1865* (Philadelphia, 1955), vol. 1, pp. 27ff.; *American Jewish Archives* 6:13.
10. Grace Nathan Papers, American Jewish Historical Society Library, Waltham, Mass.

11. Jacob R. Marcus, *The American Jewish Woman: A Documentary History* (New York, 1981), pp. 133–134.
12. Henry Aaron Alexander, *Notes on the Alexander Family of South Carolina and Georgia and Connections* (Atlanta, 1954), p. 47.
13. Probate Court, Charleston, S. C., Will Book, 41 (1834–1839), pp. 819–820.
14. A copy and a translation of the original German letter and roster of Lazarus Kohn are in the American Jewish Archives, the gift of Abe Nebel of Cleveland.
15. Mendes Cohen Collection, Maryland Historical Society, Baltimore; Jacob R. Marcus, *The American Jewish Woman: A Documentary History* (New York, 1981), pp. 146–147.
16. *American Jewish Archives* 15:17–20.
17. Isaac Leeser, *Discourses on the Jewish Religion* (Philadelphia, 1868), vol. 10, pp. 249–252.
18. *The Occident and American Jewish Advocate* 9:470ff.; *American Jewish Archives* 18:155ff.
19. Copy in American Jewish Archives.
20. Fred H. Roth Papers, American Jewish Archives.
21. *American Jewish Archives* 6:6ff.
22. Copy in American Jewish Archives.
23. Courtesy of the New York Historical Society, New York City.
24. *Miscellanies, The Jewish Historical Society of England* (London, 1948), vol. 5, pp. 193ff.
25. Sophie Lilienthal, *The Lilienthal Family Record* (San Francisco, 1930), pp. 60–61, 72–73.
26. *Beaumont Enterprise*, January 13, 1946.
27. *Confirmationsrede, gehalten von David Appel, in Philadelphia an seinem Barmizwahfeste, am 3. Maerz 1866* (16. Adar 5626, Sabbath Ki-Thissa [Exodus 30: 11ff.])) (Baltimore, 1866). The translation is the work of Aaron Levine of Cincinnati.
28. Copy in American Jewish Archives. The English translation—a rather free one—was made by Samuel Leve, April 8, 1934.
29. Louis Heilbrun, *Religious Teachings: Morals and Maxims* (Washington, D.C., 1877), pp. 9–14.
30. Copy in American Jewish Archives.
31. *Western States Jewish Historical Quarterly* 12:341–344.
32. Jacob R. Marcus, *The American Jewish Woman: A Documentary History* (New York, 1981), pp. 335–336.
33. Copy in American Jewish Archives.
34. *A Memior of Julius Ochs: An Autobiography* (Chattanooga?), pp. 52–56.
35. M. Katz (ed.), *Shriften* (London, 1909), p. 232.
36. Copy in American Jewish Archives; *Western States Jewish Historical Quarterly* 3:193ff.

37. B. Felsenthal and Herman Eliassof, *History of Kehillath Anshe Maarabh, Congregation of the Men of the West* (Chicago, 1897), Appendix, iv–ix.
38. *Publications of the American Jewish Historical Society* 23:116. The translation of the will into English was made by Aaron Levine.
39. The Louchheim Papers, American Jewish Archives.
40. *Jewish Currents*, July–August 1981, pp. 26ff.
41. Transcription of the August 30, 1895, record in the Marcus Collections.
42. *The Boston Jewish Advocate*, January 27, 1955. Tercentenary issue, 16A, 36A.
43. Copies in American Jewish Archives. Gift of John Greenebaum, Chicago.
44. Copy in American Jewish Archives.
45. Copy in Marcus Collections.
46. Copy of original Yiddish letter in American Jewish Archives. It was transliterated by Professor Herbert Paper of Cincinnati.
47. Original letters in American Jewish Archives.
48. *Journal of the Southern Jewish Historical Society* 1:17–18.
49. Marcus Collections. I wish to express my thanks to the Rev. Dr. W. Gunther Plaut of Toronto, who sent me this will together with a biography of the Wolfe family.
50. *American Jewish Archives* 31:46–47.
51. Marcus Collections.
52. Simon Glazer, *The Bar-Mitzvah Pulpit: Sermonettes for Bar-Mitzvah Boys and Others* (New York, 1928), pp. 123–126.
53. Copy in American Jewish Archives.
54. Leo Jung, *Toward Sinai! Sermons and Addresses* (New York, 1929), pp. 289–291.
55. Kalman Whiteman, *Bar Mitzvah* (New York, 1929), pp. 67–68.
56. *The Temple Bulletin of the Reform Congregation Keneseth Israel* (Philadelphia, 1929).
57. *Rhode Island Jewish Historical Notes* 2:92–93, 111.
58. Copy in American Jewish Archives. Courtesy Barbara Hillson Abramowitz, Washington, D.C.
59. Copy in American Jewish Archives.
60. *Western States Jewish Historical Society Quarterly* 1:181.
61. Sol Blank Papers, American Jewish Archives.
62. *Bulletin of Temple Beth-El*, Great Neck, Long Island, March 1943.
63. Isaac E. Rontch (ed.), *Jewish Youth at War: Letters from American Soldiers* (New York, 1945), pp. 153–155.
64. Isaac E. Rontch (ed.), *Jewish Youth at War: Letters from American Soldiers* (New York, 1945), pp. 58–60.
65. I. Kaufman, *American Jews in World War II* (New York, 1947), vol. 1, pp. 185–187.

66. I wish to thank my colleague, the Rev. Dr. W. Gunther Plaut of Toronto, for making this ethical will available to me. Mr. Lawrence Tapper of the National Archives of Canada and Dr. Stephen Speisman of Toronto Jewish Archives were most helpful to Dr. Plaut in his search for data on the Pearlstone family.
67. "Credo of an American," a statement by David E. Lilienthal before the Congressional Committee on Atomic Energy. Distributed by Community Relations Service, New York City.
68. Stanley F. Chyet (ed.), *Lives and Voices* (Philadelphia, 1972), pp. 149ff.
69. Leonard N. Simons, *Simons Says: Faith, Fun, and Foible* (Birmingham, Mich., 1984), pp. 15–17.
70. Louis J. Sigel, *Judaism Without Illusions* (Teaneck, N.J., 1976), pp. 1–3.
71. Copy in American Jewish Archives.
72. Victor E. Reichert (ed.), *My Ethical Will: Teenagers' Testaments* (Cincinnati, 1958), pp. 7–8, 22–23.
73. *The Indianapolis Times*, May 2, 1958.
74. American Jewish Archives, courtesy of Rabbis Leon Kronish and Herbert Bloom.
75. *National Jewish Monthly*, July 1, 1959, pp. 6ff.
76. *Bulletin of Temple Emanu-El*, New York, February 1961.
77. *To Peter on His 15th Birthday, July 24, 1963* (Cincinnati, 1963); *American Jewish Archives* 31:80ff.
78. Annette and Sherman G. Finesilver, *Pride of Accomplishment . . . Written . . . on the Occasion of the Bar Mitzvah of Their Son, Steve, October 11, 1969* (Denver, 1969), pp. 1–2.
79. Copy in Marcus Collections.
80. *Temple Beth Emeth Bulletin*, Brooklyn, New York, 1971 (?). Printed in part in the *Las Vegas Israelite*, August 20, 1971, p. 4.
81. *Detroit Jewish News*, March 30, 1973, Editorial page.
82. *The Har Sinai Brotherhood Bugle*, Baltimore, reprinted in *Brotherhood* – The Jewish Chautauqua magazine–6(3): March–April 1973, pp. 27–28.
83. *The View from the Pulpit*, Winter 1974, pp. 5ff.
84. *Reform Judaism*, February 1976, p. 3.
85. Copy in American Jewish Archives.
86. *Jewish Digest*, September 1976, pp. 75–76. My thanks to Mr. Art Buchwald, Washington, D.C., for permission to publish this letter.
87. *Bulletin of Temple Emanu El*, Cleveland, April 1977.
88. *Reform Congregation Keneseth Israel Bulletin*, Philadelphia, March 15, 1978, pp. 1–2.
89. Copy in American Jewish Archives.
90. Copy in American Jewish Archives.
91. *The Temple Bulletin*, Rodef Shalom Congregation, Pittsburgh, March 2, 1983.

INDEX

L

M

O

P

R

W